Americans and the Wars of the Twentieth Century

American History in Depth

General Editor: A. J. Badger
Advisory Editor: Howell Harris

The New Deal
A. J. Badger

The American Revolution (2nd edn)
Collin Bonwick

American Foreign Policy: Carter to Clinton
John Dumbrell

Colonial America: From Jamestown to Yorktown
Mary K. Geiter and W. A. Speck

McCarthy's Americans
M. J. Heale

Women in the United States, 1830–1945
S. J. Kleinberg

The American Civil War
Adam I. P. Smith

Americans and the Wars of the Twentieth Century
Jenel Virden

Americans and the Wars of the Twentieth Century

Jenel Virden

palgrave
macmillan

© Jenel Virden 2008

All rights reserved. No reproduction, copy or transmission of this
publication may be made without written permission.

No paragraph of this publication may be reproduced, copied or transmitted
save with written permission or in accordance with the provisions of the
Copyright, Designs and Patents Act 1988, or under the terms of any licence
permitting limited copying issued by the Copyright Licensing Agency, 90
Tottenham Court Road, London W1T 4LP.

Any person who does any unauthorised act in relation to this publication
may be liable to criminal prosecution and civil claims for damages.

The author has asserted her right to be identified as
the author of this work in accordance with the Copyright,
Designs and Patents Act 1988.

First published in 2008 by
PALGRAVE MACMILLAN
Houndmills, Basingstoke, Hampshire RG21 6XS and
175 Fifth Avenue, New York, N.Y. 10010
Companies and representatives throughout the world.

PALGRAVE MACMILLAN is the global academic imprint of the Palgrave
Macmillan division of St. Martin's Press, LLC and of Palgrave Macmillan Ltd.
Macmillan® is a registered trademark in the United States, United Kingdom
and other countries. Palgrave is a registered trademark in the European
Union and other countries.

ISBN-13: 978–0–333–72660–0 hardback
ISBN-10: 0–333–72660–X hardback
ISBN-13: 978–0–333–72661–7 paperback
ISBN-10: 0–333–72661–8 paperback

This book is printed on paper suitable for recycling and made from fully
managed and sustained forest sources. Logging, pulping and manufacturing
processes are expected to conform to the environmental regulations of
the country of origin.

A catalogue record for this book is available from the British Library.

A catalog record for this book is available from the Library of Congress.

10 9 8 7 6 5 4 3 2 1
17 16 15 14 13 12 11 10 09 08

Printed and bound in China

To

Otis Pease
Professor Emeritus: Modern United States History

and

Jon Bridgman
Professor Emeritus: Modern European History
at University of Washington, Seattle

Contents

List of Abbreviations

ACLU	American Civil Liberties Union
AEF	American Expeditionary Force
AFL	American Federation of Labor
AIM	American Indian Movement
APL	American Protective League
CIA	Central Intelligence Agency
CO	conscientious objection
CO	conscientious objector
CORE	Congress of Racial Equality
CPI	Committee on Public Information
CPUSA	Communist Party of the United States of America
HUAC	House Committee on Un-American Activities
IWW	Industrial Workers of the World
MACV	Military Assistant Command Vietnam
MID	Military Intelligence Division
MOBE	National Mobilisation Committee
NAACP	National Association for the Advancement of Colored People
NATO	North Atlantic Treaty Organisation
NKPA	North Korean People's Army
NLF	National Liberation Front
NWLB	National War Labor Board
OPA	Office of Price Administration
OSS	Office of Strategic Services
OWI	Office of War Information
OWM	Office of War Mobilization
POWs	prisoners of war
ROTC	Reserve Officer Training Corps
SA	SturmAbteilung
SCLC	Southern Christian Leadership Conference
SDS	Students for a Democratic Society
SNCC	Student Non-Violent Co-Ordinating Committee
UAW	United Automobile Workers
UMW	United Mine Workers

USO	United Service Organization
WAAC	Women's Army Auxiliary Corps
WAVES	Women Accepted for Voluntary Emergency Service
WMP	War Manpower Commission
WPB	War Production Board
YAF	Young Americans for Freedom

World War I – United States Forces on the Western Front

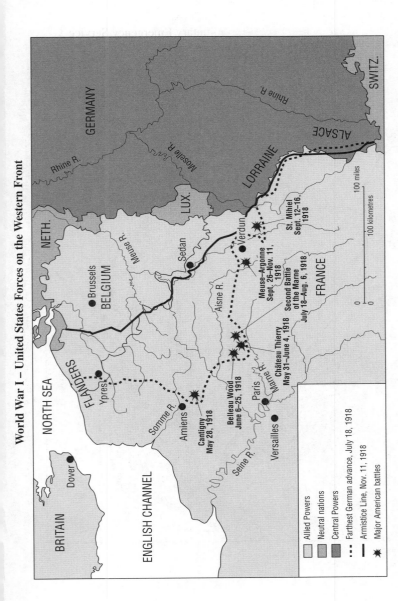

Adapted from The D.C. Heath U.S. History Transparency Set, 1994 Edition Volume II: From 1865. Copyright D.C. Heath and Company 1994

World War II – Pacific Theatre

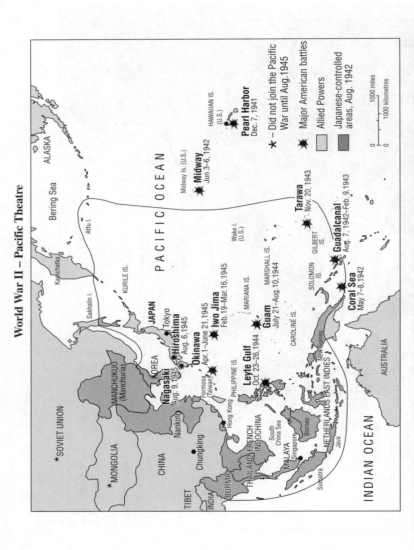

Adapted from The D.C. Heath U.S. History Transparency Set, 1994 Edition Volume II: From 1865. Copyright D.C. Heath and Company 1994

World War II – European Theatre

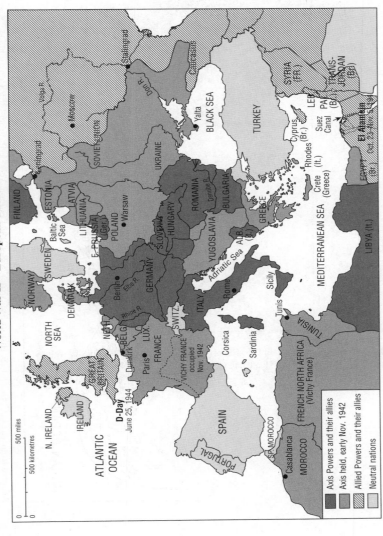

Adapted from The D.C. Heath U.S. History Transparency Set, 1994 Edition Volume II: From 1865. Copyright D.C. Heath and Company 1994

The Korean War

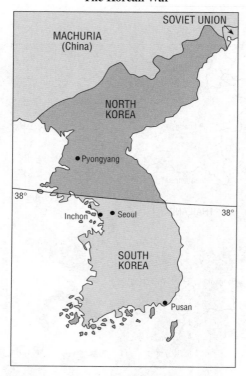

Adapted from The D.C. Heath U.S. History Transparency Set, 1994 Edition Volume II: From 1865. Copyright D.C. Heath and Company 1994

The Vietnam War

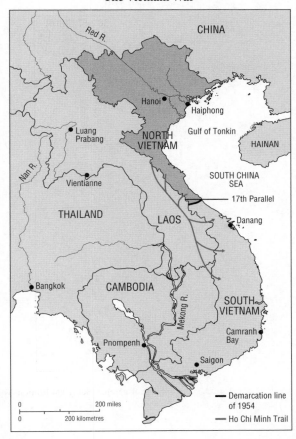

Adapted from The D.C. Heath U.S. History Transparency Set, 1994 Edition Volume II:
From 1865. Copyright D.C. Heath and Company 1994

1 Introduction

War as a subject of study and research has held a fascination for scholars for hundreds of years. As a result one can find books, articles, pamphlets and websites on many different dimensions of war. Authors have addressed issues such as why nations go to war, how wars are fought, the personal experience of war, the impact of war and the evolution of warfare itself. Subsequent scholars have drawn upon the work of others as diverse as Thucydides, Clausewitz and Keegan in an effort to come to some conclusion about the nature of war, whether that be about tactics or strategy, causes or consequences. Some writers revel in the details of battles or the minutiae of gun calibres, while others look at grand schemes and epic encounters. This book addresses the history of America's participation in the major wars of the twentieth century, looking at the factors that brought America into those wars, what contribution America made to fighting the wars and what happened on the United States home front as a consequence of being engaged in fighting a war. It also investigates the moral implications of those wars. It seeks to apply the wider ideas of the field of just war theory to the specifics of the United States' involvement in the four major wars of the 1900s. Is it possible, by looking at United States' participation in the First World War, the Second World War and at the wars in Korea and Vietnam, to come to some overall conclusion about the impact of those wars on America? How did these wars affect the government's foreign policy and what impact did they have on the home front? Ultimately one wants to know what these wars did to change America and how the United States' participation reflected its major concerns at the time. In order to do this it is perhaps helpful to look at these wars and their impact on the United States in terms of just war theory on two levels.

In just war theory the argument is made that there is a right and a wrong way to fight wars. The justice of war (*jus ad bellum*) theory relies on the basic idea that aggression is wrong and those countries that act aggressively and start wars are in the wrong. The justice in war (*jus in bello*) theory suggests that once wars have begun there is a right and a wrong way of fighting them. There are legitimate and illegitimate targets and participants. Within the theory there is now reference to how wars end (*jus post bellum*) suggesting that there is a right and a wrong way to bring the fighting to a conclusion. While this rather simplistic explanation of just war theory is further refined in the works of just war theorists, most people understand war at the basic level of justice of war and justice in war. It is the rules of war that we turn to when we discuss war, whether that be wars of the past or present. Although we may not articulate our beliefs by using the language of just war theorists, we do tend to pass judgements on governments and people with regard to their actions during war.

It is sometimes easier to recognise the bad behaviour of governments and soldiers than it is to explain it. For instance, most people would consider the news of atrocities or the mistreatment of prisoners of war in an unfavourable light. There are scores of examples from history of public outrage when details of events such as this are revealed. One has only to look at the daily newspaper accounts of the violence in Iraq in 2006–2007 and the unfolding story of mistreatment of Iraqi prisoners by United States and British forces to realise that these attitudes of outrage against injustice are very much alive today and not merely part of a theoretical investigation of historical events.

Furthermore, many years ago, Arthur Marwick, in his book *The Deluge: British Society and the First World War*, posited the suggestion that wars act as a catalyst for change. This could be both direct and indirect or short term and long term, but nonetheless wars have a profound influence on society. He suggested that 'underprivileged' segments of society especially are helped by their country's participation in war, mostly because in modern wars their labour is essential. If you combine Marwick's points with ideas about the justice of/in/after war, the question then becomes, can you apply the just war theory paradigm to the domestic front (*jus communitatis in bello*)? Is it possible to make judgements about the impact of war on the home front that directly challenge the notion of justice? One way of attempting to answer questions about the justice of war and justice in war in US history, as it applies to the major wars of the twentieth century, is to look at three elements of each war: how the war began, how the war was fought and the experience of those on the US home front.

One example of the application of just war theory can be found by looking at the fundamental principles of the justice of war. Just war theory relating to how wars begin (justice of wars) revolves around the idea of aggression. Those countries that are aggressors, and consequently initiate war, are seen to be fighting an unjust war. The rhetoric of governments involved in public discourse on specific wars often utilises the image of a just or unjust war. This is especially true when governments themselves become directly involved in the wars. This can readily be seen in the case of the United States and the major wars of the twentieth century.

In the First and Second World Wars, the United States did not get involved directly until several years had passed. These wars raged on while America proclaimed itself neutral. Neither Woodrow Wilson nor Franklin Roosevelt could declare war in the atmosphere of isolationism that prevailed within America. Both campaigned for a return to the White House while a world war raged (Wilson in 1916 and Roosevelt in 1940), declaring that they would not send American troops to fight in the European war. Despite the clear, naked aggression of the Central Powers in the First World War and that of the Axis governments in the Second World War, the American presidents did not try to precipitate American entry into these wars solely on the basis of the notion that they were unjust.

When events transpired to involve the United States in these two wars, the public discourses of the presidents changed. Their rhetoric of America fighting a just war was used to rally support and gather a consensus for participation in an ongoing conflict. While Wilson had called on Americans to remain impartial in thought as well as action at the outbreak of the First World War in 1914, by the time the United States entered the war in 1917 Wilson proclaimed that not only was the United States fighting a just war, it was also fighting a war to make the world safe for democracy, with the ultimate goal of fighting a war to end all wars. A war to end all wars is without doubt a just war. The aggressive act that precipitated this change in American involvement in the war was the German government's decision to reinstitute unrestricted submarine warfare in January 1917.

Over twenty years later Franklin Roosevelt was faced with a similar situation, although American neutrality was less forcefully argued once the war broke out in Europe. Before the United States entered the Second World War, government policy changed as the course of events in Europe unfolded. For example, America moved from neutrality as defined by the series of Neutrality Acts passed by Congress in the 1930s to supporting Great Britain and her allies through the institution of Lend-Lease and the destroyers for bases arrangement. Ultimately, as Roosevelt said, the United States could become the arsenal of democracy, without actually entering the war itself. So, even before the Japanese attack on Pearl Harbor, the president had begun to use the concept of the justice of war to describe the European conflict. In his Four Freedoms speech of 6 January 1941 he noted in relation to the wider war that 'the justice of morality must and will win in the end'. With the attack on the United States naval and air bases in Hawaii the full rhetoric of righteousness could be heard as Roosevelt declared that 'December 7, 1941 – a date which will live in infamy' witnessed a sudden and deliberate attack by the Japanese. He predicted that 'America in her righteous might' would win the war. In the subsequent declaration of war against Germany, Roosevelt assured Americans of 'a world victory of the forces of justice and of righteousness over the forces of savagery and barbarism'.

In the Korean War the goal was to stop aggressive communism. It was, once again, an unjust war started by a nation aggressively seeking to attack and destroy democracy. Faced with a supreme emergency the United States responded with a 'police action' that was war in all but name. The goal this time, under Cold War policy, was to contain communism, to keep an aggressive/expansionist nation in check. Yet it could not be a war for democracy since South Korea was a manufactured democracy and crossing the 38th parallel calls into question the whole issue of just war. But Harry Truman did not find it difficult to justify American participation. He noted that the North Koreans had acted wantonly and that 'a return to the rule of force in international affairs would have far-reaching effects. The United States will continue to uphold the rule of law'.

While to many the Vietnam War may seem less clear-cut in terms of obvious acts of aggression, that did not stop the United States from labelling the North Vietnamese as aggressors. The Gulf of Tonkin incident that set the scene for American commitment of military personnel may have been a mere apparition but at the time it was real enough for the American government to consider that it had reasonable grounds for retaliation, which took the form of another war. Lyndon Johnson noted that 'this is not just a jungle war, but a struggle for freedom on every front' and that the United States was 'determined to bring about the end of Communist subversion and aggression in the area'. In the Tonkin Gulf resolution, section one, Congress agreed for the need to 'prevent further aggression'. In fact, the term aggression was used to justify America's participation in the war in Vietnam in many documents and speeches. The State Department White Paper on Vietnam in 1965 was titled 'Aggression from the North', and in April 1965 Johnson stated that the United States was going to fight in 'defense of freedom'. Harkening back to Wilson and the outbreak of the First World War, Johnson also noted that 'we dream of an end to war. And we will try to make it so'.

However, when just war theory is applied to the justice of war, or how wars begin, it is meant to imply more than simply whose fault a war is, although this is a major part of the theory. Speaking about justice of war also relates to the subject of international law and neutrality in wartime. In addition, there are recognised categories of the justice of war that explain when rules can be modified, for instance what looks like aggression at the start of one war may actually be a legitimate pre-emptive strike, or aggression may justly occur when it takes place against a nation for humanitarian reasons.

Equally, the theory of just wars as applied to justice in war, or how wars are fought, encompasses a wide range of factors. It is not solely about the issue of who constitutes a legitimate enemy target and who qualifies as a non-combatant, although those are the basic tenets of the theory. It also can be applied to concerns about the methods of fighting wars, such as sieges and blockades. In addition, the concept of justice in war relates to technological advances applied to modern weaponry and even the morality of some weapons.

Justice after a war implies that the responsibilities of the victor and the rights of the defeated do not cease to exist once there has been a declared ceasefire or a negotiated armistice. Rather, it is imperative that the winning side takes steps to ensure that the peace itself is just and the settlements at the end of a war are morally sound. For example, the total destruction and obliteration of one's former enemy is not a legitimate way to end a war.

The question then arises as to why it is of interest to look at the United States' participation in the major wars of the twentieth century within the paradigm of just war theory. Most obviously it is because, as noted earlier, the government of the United States announced its participation in these, and other wars, using the words of just war theory. America spoke in each instance of fighting a just war. In each case, the First World War, the Second World War, Korea and Vietnam, the United States proclaimed that it was reluctant to go to war but had been provoked into war by acts of aggression on the part of others. The rhetoric used was one of pitting the righteousness of democracy against the evil of aggression, expansionism, fascism, imperialism or communism. Once the United States was engaged in these wars, public discourse revolved around the very essence of just war theory.

However, this book goes further and makes the case that just war theory needs to be applied to the home front in order to formulate a complete theory and in order to come to some conclusions about whether a democracy can be considered to be fighting a just war, using just means while at the same time promoting injustice at home. The concept of justice on the home front attempts to apply just war theory in a modified form to the internal workings of a democratic nation at war. When a government passes laws to curtail the civil liberties and civil rights of its own people, when it passes laws to stifle dissent and when these acts are upheld by the highest court in the land, can any war, for whatever reason, be truly just? Does the nation at war need to have the open, public debate and freedom of speech and action that is a part of daily life in the same country when it is not at war?

An analysis of the impact of war on the home front would not be complete, however, by only looking at the laws under which the home front is operating. It is also necessary to look at the social and economic impact of war itself. In total war or even limited war in the twentieth century, an economy harnessed to the engines of war has consequences that can be felt on the home front. On the one hand war may offer minorities a chance for economic improvement while at the same time raising tensions between races and ethnicities. War can spur minority groups to band together to work for positive change, but it can also help to incite a conservative backlash to changes in the status quo. As Arthur Marwick notes, the first and foremost consequence of war is the destruction and dislocation it causes. This was as true on the home front in the twentieth century as it was on the battle field.

This book is an attempt to apply just war theory to American participation in the major wars of the twentieth century. It is not meant to do this on a battle-by-battle basis, however. Instead, it will endeavour to bring together the main tenets of just war theory with the main events and incidents of these four wars. It is impossible, in a book of this size, to catalogue every detail of American participation in the four major wars of the twentieth century. This mammoth task has been undertaken in the past by numerous historians, and library and bookshop shelves are weighted down with volumes of military history that explore the topics of this book in far greater detail, many of which are noted in the bibliography here. The same can be said of books outlining, arguing and revising the theory of just war. It is by its very nature an incredibly complex issue with nuances and shades of grey that have stimulated debate since the days of Augustine in the fifth century, when he wrote on the issue of justice in war. This current work does not attempt to explore just war theory in all its permutations, such as international law, anticipations, interventions, utility and proportionality, supreme emergency or reprisals. Instead, what this volume seeks to provide, for readers who are unfamiliar with the topic, is a brief introduction to the ideas of just war theory, as applied to United States' participation in the major wars of the twentieth century. In addition, this work expands the usual territory of just war theory into the realms of the home front during war to test whether the application of the theory to the way governments treat their own citizens during war can provide previously unarticulated insights into the broader issue of just war.

Why is this important? Hopefully, this survey of America's wartime ethics in the twentieth century will equip readers with the knowledge necessary to stimulate discussion and investigations into other wars in the past as well as America's wars of the future.

2   The First World War

War dominated the close of the nineteenth and beginning of the twentieth century for the United States. As had the European nations before it, the United States pushed for and acquired an empire in the late nineteenth century. Equally important, the United States continued to exert its influence on other nations in the western hemisphere. These two forces combined in 1898 when the United States went to war with Spain over an island just 90 miles off the coast of Florida. The initial dispute in the Spanish–American War widened, however, from concerns over Spanish actions and dominance in Cuba to Spanish holdings in the Pacific. The war lasted less than four months but by the end of it the United States had acquired the Philippines, Guam and Puerto Rico. By the conclusion of what Secretary of State John Hay called 'a splendid little war', the United States was mired in its imperialist agenda.

After the quick defeat of the Spanish in the Philippines, the United States went on to fight a much longer war with insurgents who wanted independence for the Filipino people. United States military forces fought a guerrilla war with the Filipino insurgents until 1902 when the Philippines became part of the American empire. In the meantime, the United States had reneged on its initial promise of recognition of Cuban independence and instead initiated a system whereby the United States was free to interfere with and influence the Cuban governments' actions. Further imperialist ambitions manifest themselves in the Open Door policy in China (1899–1900) and the takeover of the Panama Canal Zone (1903). It remained to be seen if this foray into empire building meant a new attitude towards international involvement in a broader sense.

The turn of the century also witnessed changes on the American domestic front. A wide-ranging and diverse set of interests came together under the umbrella title of the Progressive Movement in the early twentieth century. It encompassed a large and occasionally contradictory set of reforms meant to improve the fabric of American society now that it had ended its frontier phase. Reacting to the human condition as it existed under the twin themes of industrialisation and urbanisation, the Progressive Movement tried to address specific issues that needed reform in order for specific groups of individuals to 'progress' under the flag of the United States. These wide-ranging reforms included the passage of legislation or the founding of organisations to improve specific problems. For instance, settlement houses sprang up in immigrant neighbourhoods in northern cities to help the assimilation of millions of newcomers arriving in the United States. Political reforms tried to make American politics more democratic and less corrupt. Labour reforms such as the 8-hour day and legislation against child labour addressed the conditions of the working classes. Unions grew, as did the emerging middle class. However, other reforms worked in different ways, backed by a more negative view of human nature and aimed at suppressing human vices. For instance, the campaign for prohibition gathered strength throughout the Progressive Era culminating in the passage of the 18th Amendment to the Constitution in 1918. Other groups worked to restrict the influx of immigrants, fearing the negative impact large numbers of Catholics and Jews from Southern and Eastern Europe could have on the American way of life.

While reformers were able to initiate some successful reforms during the Progressive period, other reformers laid the foundation for future gains. For instance, a group of reform minded African Americans and whites founded the National Association for the Advancement of Colored People (NAACP) in 1909 in order to push for racial equality. Faced with Jim Crow legislation and de facto discrimination, African Americans in the early twentieth century pushed for reforms and struggled to achieve equality. At the same time, American women renewed their call for gender equality. The industrialisation of America meant a surge in factory jobs some of which were filled by women, often immigrant women. Middle-class women also took on jobs as secretaries or teachers although these employment opportunities were mostly restricted to young, single women. This shift in circumstance and the influence of the Progressive Movement inspired the re-emergence of a woman's movement in early twentieth-century America. Before the outbreak of the First World War, many American women were campaigning for the right to vote. Yet as the storm clouds gathered over Europe, reformers within the United States feared that the outbreak of war would stop the push for progress.

BEGINNINGS

Europe was witness to intense rivalries in the late nineteenth and early twentieth centuries. In 1871, with unification, Germany continued to grow into an important industrial power. Germany's participation in the industrial revolution paralleled its participation in turn of the century European expansionism. Industrialisation required raw materials, and Germany, like Britain before her, went in search of an empire to supply the necessities of industrial growth. In the process of exerting its influence, Germany ran into conflict with other European powers. The long-standing rivalry between France and Germany over the Alsace-Lorraine region, annexed by Germany in 1871, was a continuous point of conflict. Elsewhere Britain grew increasingly concerned over Germany's growing naval capacity. In 1898 Germany launched a naval build up campaign and by 1912 Britain considered the German Navy to be a menace. British concerns about Germany's naval capabilities cost Britain a great deal of money as Britain competed with Germany's ship building campaign. In addition, Britain worried about Germany's imperialist push into Africa and the Near and Far East.

Over the years the continuous rivalries among European powers led to the establishment of an alliance system. In 1879 Germany allied itself with the Austria-Hungary Empire and, in 1882, with Italy. This Triple Alliance lasted until the outbreak of the First World War in 1914. The terms of the alliance were such that any country involved in a war with two or more powers could call upon others within the alliance for help. On the other side of the European alliance system, France and Russia agreed to an alliance in 1894; this was a most unlikely partnership initiated for the sole purpose of protection in the hostile atmosphere of Europe. All of these countries, Germany, Italy, France and Russia, were anti-British in one way or another. British imperial aims and its involvement in the Boer War at the turn of the century did not foster many European friendships. Yet the other European countries understood Britain's importance to the system. Her large navy and vast empire gave Britain a vital role in European affairs. In 1904 Britain and France decided to forget past differences and signed a treaty whereby they agreed to support each other against any third party although they called this an entente, or understanding, and not an alliance. In 1907 Russia signed a treaty with Britain thus completing the Triple Entente but also heightening Germany's sense of encirclement.

Eventually the peace of Europe was threatened and the alliance system put to the test by a series of crises in the Balkans and elsewhere. In the Balkans, one of the most volatile areas in Europe, the situation was complex. Many of the rivalries and hostilities went back for centuries. Part of the problem in the early twentieth century was the challenge to the declining Ottoman Empire led by Bulgaria, Romania and Greece. This left the area vulnerable to revolutionary forces. One such threat came from the small, landlocked country of Serbia, which was attempting to assert its influence. Austria had occupied Serbia's neighbour, Bosnia-Herzegovina, although belonging to the Ottoman Empire, since 1908. To the north, the areas of Croatia and Slovenia were also experiencing a period of increasing nationalism. Croats and Slovenes increasingly felt a kinship and worked together, formulating and promoting a pan-Slavic movement, which other Slavs living in Austria and elsewhere could join. Eventually Serbia became the centre of south Slav agitation in the region and, when Austria annexed Bosnia-Herzegovina in 1908, they protested to no avail. Larger European powers became involved in the area's conflicts through their connection with the Russian and Austro-Hungarian empires and through the alliance system. Russia supported Serbian claims in the area while Austria clearly hated the Serbian national movement.

The Third Balkan Crisis, which proved fatal to the peace of Europe, touched off the First World War. Several events occurred in the area, in rapid succession. First, Serbia claimed victory over Turkey in a confrontation in 1912. Second, in 1913, Serbia occupied Albania, gaining valuable territory along the coast although they withdrew within eight days. Then, on 28 June 1914 a Bosnian, trained by the Serbian secret society, the Black Hand, assassinated the heir to the Austro-Hungarian Empire. Gavrilo Princip shot Archduke Ferdinand and his wife while they were riding through the streets of the Bosnia capital, Sarajevo. The immediate outrage at this incident eventually died down everywhere within a week except in Vienna. Previously, as part of the alliance system, Austria had asked for Germany's approval for action against the Serbs. On 5 July, Germany gave its famous response to Austria's question of how far to go in responding to the Serb threat – 'be firm.' The Austrians interpreted this as having a free hand to do what they deemed necessary to crush the Serb nationalist movement. Consequently, Austria sent an ultimatum to the Serbs that included a list of 15 demands. At the same time, Austria secretly informed Germany of the contents of the communication, which Austria anticipated the Serbs would reject, and began to mobilise. The Austrians, having set a 48-hour deadline for a response, were determined to end the Serbian nationalist movement and, hence, save their fading empire. Russia had already warned Austria not to overreact to the situation. Serbia mobilised on 25 July but also agreed to the demands, asking only that the International Tribunal at The Hague undertake the investigation into the assassination. The Serbs were, ultimately, also relying on Russian backing should the situation deteriorate to the point of war. Russia, in turn, was relying on its entente with Britain and France. When consulted by the Russians as to the nature of any future action, France gave a blank cheque to Russia with declarations of war subsequently exchanged at a rapid rate.

Austria-Hungary declared war on Serbia on 28 July 1914, sure of German support although Russia and Germany were not yet at war. However, on 29 July Russia called men to arms on the German and Austrian frontier. On 31 July the Germans demanded that the Russians cease mobilisation but the Russians did not reply. The French and German governments began to mobilise their militaries on 31 July and 1 August, respectively. Eventually, on 1 August, Germany declared war on Russia and invaded Luxembourg. The German invasion of France followed on 2 August with a declaration of war on 3 August. Britain, during all of this, hesitated to enter into these manoeuvres despite the urgings of Russia and France to publicly declare support for the entente. Germany hoped Britain would stay out of the increasingly tense situation but this hope was unrealistic. On 2 August, Britain began mobilising and Germany petitioned Belgium for free passage through the country. On 3 August, when Germany declared war on France, it also sent troops into Russian Poland. As a pre-emptive strike, Germany launched its war against France through neutral Belgium and this violation of Belgium neutrality brought Britain into the war on 4 August 1914. One by one the other countries in the complex alliance system exchanged formal declarations of war, while Italy, Portugal, Greece, Bulgaria, Romania and Turkey stated their intention to remain neutral at this stage, with the United States declaring its neutrality on 4 August. The Great War had begun.

The situation in Europe deteriorated to the point of war for three main reasons: the alliance system, nationalism and German military leadership. Many people believed, throughout the early 1900s, that war was inevitable. Countries had been building armies, arms and alliances for the previous 30 years in an effort to avoid war but also because they anticipated war. By 1914 Europe was home to huge peacetime armies.

Compulsory military service for the men of many different countries meant most countries had large standing armies and troop reserves. At the beginning of August 1914 over 4 million men were at arms in Europe but by the end of the month this figure had grown to 20 million. Each country also had mobilisation plans put together by their war colleges and military experts so that they could react to threats quickly. The system of European alliances developed in an effort to keep a balance of power, yet both camps lived in fear of a war where allies would be needed. Germany needed Austria-Hungary and France needed Russia. Russia and Austria were old, dying empires and Germany, Britain and France were growing stronger and building upon their imperial bases. In 1914 the two armed camps were ready for a war, they just needed a reason.

Of equal importance in determining how the First World War began is the issue of nationalism. Most everyone agrees that the First World War could be felt coming. Nationalism was rampant and jingoism maintained nationalist fervour at a fever pitch. In the Balkans, ethnic national Serbs and Croats were struggling to exert their influence. Importantly, the Archduke Ferdinand's visit to Sarajevo in Bosnia occurred on 28 June, which was the anniversary of the destruction of the Serbian Army by Ottoman Turks in 1349. Serbian nationalism was on the ascendancy and the day was a time of heightened nationalism for the Serbs. Although Gavrilo Princip, a Bosnia student but a Serb nationalist, killed the archduke and his wife, most people held the Serbian government responsible. Nationalism fed, and was fed by, imperialism as well. Growing industries needed raw materials and natural resources, which to many Europeans meant acquiring an empire. Hence, national rivalries included rivalries for empire. There was a complete failure to see any international or pan-national economic interests among the European powers despite their economic interdependence. There was also a sense that life would be better after the war; in the early twentieth century many people still thought war was not all bad. One or two great battles would see an end to the conflict with a quick return to an uneasy peace. The German war plan predicted a defeat of France within six weeks. There was strong public support for the war that hinged on a miscalculation of the nature of warfare in the modern world. Technological inventions changed the face of war, yet few people understood this at the time. There were peace movements within the various participating nations, but these were less influential than the movements for action against perceived enemies.

The final issue in the outbreak of the First World War was the willingness on the part of the German military leadership to go to war.

Germany decided to gamble in its bid for world power status by urging Austria to attack Serbia, knowing the risk of general war. Germany was by no means the only country contemplating war; however, German willingness to embark on preventive war started the conflict. Most countries had war plans, which reflected the growth, in the late nineteenth and early twentieth centuries, of war colleges and strategic planning. Germany had a war plan known as the Schlieffen Plan, which recognised that any German war in Europe would involve fighting on two fronts: against both France and Russia. The basic premise of the Schlieffen Plan was for Germany to defeat France quickly by means of a surprise invasion through Belgium so that Germany could then turn and destroy Russia at leisure without spreading its resources too thinly. The problem, of course, was that Belgium was neutral, a neutrality that had been recognized by Germany in 1831 and again in 1839. Yet Germany decided to ignore that neutrality when it launched its attack. Germany suggested that its violation of Belgium neutrality was a military necessity brought about because of the large standing armies and rapid mobilisation of France and Russia. Equally important in Germany's decision to launch the Schlieffen Plan was a firm belief that the war would be over quickly. While Germany clearly did not anticipate the subsequent four years of slaughter that followed its invasion of neutral Belgium, equally clearly it was Germany that fired the opening shots of the war and that had the chance to de-escalate the situation but refused.

Still, most everyone expected a short war, that the two armed camps would meet and a decisive action would put an end to the conflict. Unfortunately, instead, the war dragged on for four years pitting the Central Powers of Germany and Austria-Hungary, against the Allied Powers or the Entente governments of Britain, France and Russia. Eventually the war expanded, with battlefields located on several continents and drawing other nations into the European power struggle including Japan, Italy, the Ottoman Empire, Bulgaria and, eventually, the United States. The Great War would see 65 million men in arms and over 30 countries involved. It eventually became a true world war.

For several years before this happened, however, the United States remained outside the official conflict. United States' involvement in the war would depend very much upon the war intruding upon its interests and many incidents occurred which tested American resolve to remain neutral. For instance, early on in the war, on 3 November 1914, the British essentially declared a blockade around Germany by proclaiming the whole North Sea a military area. Neutral ships could proceed if they first stopped in Britain to be escorted through to the Central Powers. The blockade was an attempt by Great Britain to utilise her best resource, the navy, to end the war quickly and break the stalemate. The blockade included the mining of the North Sea; however, Britain's blockade was illegal in international law. Nations involved in conflicts still had the right to conduct trade with neutral countries and Britain's blockade worked against neutral merchant ships. Britain's use of her navy and the laying of mines essentially closed down neutral trade to the Central Powers. Britain's actions affected any country trying to carry on normal commerce, including the United States. In addition, by expanding the list of what was contraband and seizing ships of other countries, Britain violated a range of international and maritime laws and the United States protested these actions.

Germany's response to the British blockade was to declare a war zone around Britain in February 1915. Germany could not blockade the island nation but instead opted for establishing a zone inside of which they could utilise the newly developed submarine by conducting unrestricted submarine warfare, which meant attacking ships without warning. The United States, as it had done previously with Britain, protested this proposed German strategy. Rules of engagement at sea existed in maritime and international law; however, there was a problem in applying these rules to the relatively new class of sea vessel, the submarine. Rules of engagement specified that in sea combat the attacking vessel should hail the ship, warn them of the attack, off-load passengers and take them on-board and then sink or seize the ship. The submarine was notoriously vulnerable to attack when it surfaced, much more so than other ships. It was slow moving, easily sunk, and had no room for passengers; hence, the rules of engagement could not apply equally to submarines. Clearly, the point of the development and use of submarines was for surprise attacks and the rules of engagement, as they stood, defeated the purpose of the vessel.

Britain went against international law in establishing the blockade because of the stalemate on land. Britain's best resource, its large fleet, was going unused and the blockade around Germany would put the navy to use and, hopefully, break the German will and subsequently win the war for Britain. On the other hand, Germany decided to go against international law by using unrestricted submarine warfare in an attempt to counter the British surface blockade. The German-declared war zone around Britain was, essentially, an undersea blockade. Both sides justified their blockades as necessary to break the stalemate in Europe and stop the bloodshed. Unfortunately, both actions also had the effect of injuring innocent non-combatants. The British blockade harmed the women and children of Germany. When food shortages occur in wartime, as they did in Germany due to the blockade, what food there is tends to go to soldiers first and then the civilian population. Equally, German submarines often targeted and sank ships on which innocent people travelled. While the Germans justified their tactic as an attempt to counter the British blockade, Britain declared the war zone illegal and moved to arm its merchant ships.

At the outbreak of the war in Europe US President Woodrow Wilson had admonished Americans to be 'impartial in thought as well as action'. However, as an avowed neutral nation, the United States was caught between Britain and Germany while the nature of the emerging sea warfare made strict neutrality impossible. The United States was unhappy with the British blockade since it interfered with neutral shipping. While contraband or supplies of war were legitimate targets of British ships, it also interrupted America's non-war related trade. The United States was not the only country alarmed by these actions. Norway and Sweden protested the British move as a breach of international law. On 18 February 1915, when Germany declared the waters around Britain a combat zone, the British responded by stating that no neutral ship would be allowed to leave or enter German ports. Wilson protested to the British over their actions and told the Kaiser that Germany would be held to strict accountability for its actions against neutral shipping and any loss of lives.

On 28 March 1915, the British steamer *Falaba* was sunk by a German submarine and one US citizen was killed. This was in violation of international law but a much bigger shock came on 7 May when a German submarine sank the ocean liner *Lusitania* killing 1198 of its 1959 passengers including 128 US citizens. The American people were outraged despite Germany's reminder that they had warned people not to travel on the *Lusitania* in advertisements in New York newspapers. In addition, the Germans claimed that the ship was a fair target since it was carrying arms or contraband. The British and American governments denied this charge at the time.

Although some Americans now suggested that the United States should enter the war, there was no overwhelming support among the American people for this action. Many Americans were still reluctant to fight in what most viewed as a 'European War'. While the sinking of the *Lusitania* led Wilson to send a note, on 13 May, asking Germany to deny the legality of the war zone, other Americans saw things differently. When Germany hesitated in its response, Wilson pressed for some kind of concession, which led William Jennings Bryan, Secretary of State, to resign as protest of Wilson's actions. Bryan stated his belief that 'Germany has a right to prevent contraband from going to the allies, and a ship carrying contraband should not rely on passengers to protect her from an attack – it would be like putting women and children in front of an army'. Yet there were others, including ex-President Theodore Roosevelt, who called for US participation in the war at most and for a campaign of preparedness at the least.

At this stage, however, the United States was not yet willing to declare war. Instead, it continued to declare itself officially neutral although strict neutrality no longer existed, if it ever had. After the sinking of the *Lusitania*, Americans were definitely pro-British, although the US government had always been leaning in that direction anyway. Eventhough Germany suspended unrestricted attacks, and in February 1916 apologised for the *Lusitania* and offered indemnity, it never acknowledged the illegality of its actions. Furthermore, the question of neutrality of the United States became even more problematic. US exports and loans to Britain and France increased throughout 1915–1916 while similar statistics for US trade with Germany shows a steady decline. US trade with the allies tripled during the period 1914–1916. The allies eventually became dependent upon American credit and trade. The submarines were, in essence, an attempt to redress this imbalance.

Meanwhile, both Britain and Germany launched propaganda campaigns within the United States to try and turn the Americans to their side by stressing the atrocities of the enemy. Britain was particularly skilful at suggesting that the Germans were uncivilised and barbaric in their pursuit of victory. The U-boat campaign tended to re-enforce these ideas. While the British blockade was equally illegal and produced the suffering of innocents, the German unrestricted submarine offensive seemed somehow to be more objectionable. The pro-British press in the United States tended to emphasise the concept of German or Prussian aggression as well as reporting alleged incidents of atrocities perpetuated by Germans on the Belgium civilian population. Yet, the United States was able to avoid going to war in part due to Germany's decision to refrain from the continued use of unrestricted submarine warfare in the aftermath of the sinking of the *Lusitania*. In 1916 the Germans signed the Sussex pledge which stated that merchant ships would not be sunk if the United States could get Britain to remove the blockade. The United

States was unable to get Britain to comply and the United States continued in trade that clearly favoured the allies, but the Germans honoured
the pledge anyway.

Yet the United States officially remained neutral in Europe. In part
this had to do with the preoccupation of the government with a growing
conflict with Mexico. In 1916 Mexican revolutionary Pancho Villa con-
ducted raids into the US territory of New Mexico, along the Mexican
border, killing several Americans. In response, the US government
sent troops to capture Pancho Villa and stop the incursions. Since the
American government had always seen the western hemisphere as part
of the US sphere of influence, and Pancho Villa had attacked American
citizens, there was very little debate in America about actions against
Mexico, unlike the discussions about United States involvement in
Europe. The punitive expedition of US troops, led by General John
Pershing, acted as a dress rehearsal for later mobilisation. In addition, the
US government continued to champion neutrality in 1916 because it was
an election year. President Wilson won re-election in a close contest on
the campaign slogan 'He kept us out of war.' Wilson had volunteered to
mediate an end to the European war and offered to negotiate for all sides.
He suggested that the European countries could stop the bloodshed by
agreeing to a 'peace without victory' and 'a peace among equals' in
which no one side was better off than the other. Wilson's idealism, his
belief in arms limits, freedom of the seas, a League of Nations, and the
end of empires, clearly showed through in his rhetoric. Both sides of the
conflict, however, refused to negotiate. In addition, while Americans
clearly stated their preference for staying out of the war, the US economy
experienced a war boom from 1914 to 1916. The United States benefited
economically from its position as a non-involved state.

Then, in early 1917, several events led to the US entry into the world
war. On 31 January Germany announced its plans to resume unrestricted
submarine warfare on the following day. By early 1917 Germany was desperate because of the British blockade and was hoping to end the war by
using submarine warfare before the entry of the United States could have an
impact. On 3 February Wilson severed diplomatic relations with Germany
as a protest against this reversal of policy and disregard of the Sussex
pledge. Within days US ships were attacked and sunk. Then the British
intercepted a telegram from German Foreign Minister Zimmermann
addressed to the German Ambassador in Mexico. The now infamous
Zimmermann telegram suggested that the ambassador should inform the
Mexican President that, if the United States joined the European war,

Germany would ally with Mexico and help it get back its lost territory in the southwestern United States. The British gave the telegram to the United States government on 25 February. Having argued with Congress about the government's official response to German submarine warfare, in late February Wilson asked for permission to arm merchant ships but Congress held back. At this point Wilson released the telegram.

When Wilson released the Zimmermann telegram to the American people on 1 March there was an immediate public outcry. The United States had just finished its war with Mexico and the telegram seemed to imply that Germany was colluding with one of America's enemies. Yet Congress still hesitated to act and adjourned in the face of the crisis. Then, in mid-March, German submarines sank three American merchant ships, which added to the public outrage. After this, on 20 March, Wilson's cabinet voted unanimously to support a declaration of war. On 2 April, Wilson addressed a special session of Congress. Wilson asked for a declaration of war so that America could enter into the conflict in Europe declaring that American participation in an allied victory would help to make the 'world safe for democracy.' The declaration passed the Senate on 4 April by a vote of 82–6 and the House approved it on 6 April by a vote of 373–50.

Wilson sold US involvement in the Great War to the American public as a crusade. Americans had the opportunity to fight in a 'war to end all wars.' All of a sudden the United States had gone from being an allegedly neutral country to being a country whose involvement in the war was based on the highest moral principles and would have a world changing impact. The goal of the United States was not only to re-establish the rules of warfare, including the rights of neutrals, nor only to end the slaughter, but America was also going to save the world and stop all future wars. On 6 April the United States formally declared war on Germany. From a Wilsonian and Progressive reform point of view, US involvement in the First World War would work to promote liberal, cap-italist ideals throughout Europe. In addition, by becoming involved in the conflict Wilson could take a place at the peace table and, hopefully, influence the future world order.

HOW THE WAR WAS FOUGHT

What the United States entered was a war unlike any war prior to 1914. On 3 August, when Germany invaded Belgium, the Schlieffen

Plan appeared to be working. The Russians, however, hit the Germans on the Eastern Front relatively quickly, which required German reinforcements and weakened Germany's position in the west. Germany rapidly found its lines of supply in the west were overextended. For the first month, however, Germany marched steadily towards Paris. This continuous battling soon wearied both sides as the Germans pushed west and the allies fought a running retreat. Then the French launched a counter attack at the Marne. This early major battle of the war, from 6 September to 10 September 1914, changed the whole face of war. The battle of the Marne ended the German advance and also demonstrated the high levels of casualties that future confrontations would involve with a resulting half a million casualties on all sides within three weeks. The Germans began a hasty retreat while each side switched to attempts at outflanking the enemy resulting in the 'race to the sea'. Eventually the battle line on the Western Front would extend 470 miles from Switzerland to the sea.

The Great War was the harbinger of the destructive capacity of humankind once it has enlisted the aid of twentieth-century technology. In past wars military commanders had relied upon the offence as the best possibility of winning. Military leaders in the First World War had not learned from the experiences of the United States in the Civil War where application of the old strategy of offence against increasingly deadly small arms and artillery fire only worked to produce extremely high casualty rates. The basic strategy of the First World War quickly became attack, shock and break through, a strategy utilised by Britain in the Crimean War in the mid-1850s. The reality of modern warfare, however, meant that the most important position in a prolonged war was the defensive. The First World War, after the initial battle of the Marne, quickly settled into a war of possession, but the possessions did not change very rapidly. Trench warfare meant that armies were immobile, making cavalries unusable. The machine gun dominated the whole war, which made it extremely difficult for foot soldiers (infantry) to advance. The result was a stalemate as each side dug in along trench lines that stretched for miles. While the trench system existed on other fronts in the war, it was never as extensive as on the Western Front. The Western Front would also turn out to be the area where American military forces served.

While the war was dominated by the use of artillery, machine guns and barbed wire, other military developments of the war, such as poison gas, U-boats, tanks and planes, involved inventions developed or utilised in order to bypass the stalemate and break through the trench system of the enemy. While U-boats and poison gas were readily utilised, military commanders adopted the tank and plane gradually and each had its own problems. The tank was initially very clumsy and the use of tanks as offensive weapons was not feasible at first. In addition, planes were used for reconnaissance and some bombing but aviation was in its infancy and the full utilisation of aircraft took time to develop. Poison gas depended upon wind speed and direction and could often inflict casualties on the side that launched it. Therefore, a variation of siege warfare prevailed and the outcome of the war rested more and more with the factories on the home front and less with great gains on the battlefield. The Great War produced the first modern, total war in which the side that could keep producing the materiel and supplying the bodies had the best chance of winning. As a result, the home front became as important as the battlefront.

In the early months of the war, on the Western Front, the war settled into a familiar pattern. The trenches that cover hundreds of miles were, at some points, only yards apart. The war became a war without flanks which meant that the only manoeuvre that military commanders thought possible was to break through enemy lines in a head-on assault. Battle after battle took on the same form: artillery barrages followed by direct frontal assaults across no-man's-land. This pattern characterised Ypres in October 1914 where 250,000 men tried to break through but failed. The answer, according to some strategists, was to employ more artillery for longer periods before the big push of infantry. This led to bigger and longer barrages but also failed to break the stalemate. The opposing side simply dug wider and deeper trenches.

For soldiers no-man's-land and the machine gun dominated their view of the war. The average machine gun could fire 450 rounds per minute and there was little escape from well-placed gun emplacements during an assault across no-man's-land. Tanks and planes, as noted earlier, were not quite ready or commanders lacked tactical schemes for their use on the battlefield. Hence, battles evolved into million men assaults with 1000 gun artillery barrages. These battles produced casualties at an astronomical rate. The war witnessed unheard of massive killing. As noted earlier, to counter the stalemate on the battlefield the military developed and used poisonous gas. Since artillery barrages did not clear the way for successful attacks on the enemies' line, poisonous gas was lobbed at the enemy trenches in an attempt to immobilise the opposition while the infantry attacked across no-man's -land. Poisonous gas brought on a slow death or disability by choking the victim. The Germans first introduced gas in April 1915 at Ypres at which time panic ensued in the allied lines. Canadian troops saved the allied position by standing their ground. Equally important, the German troops did not advance because they were afraid to go forward into the gas. While both sides introduced gas in an effort to break the deadlock, it failed in this goal. The invention of the gas mask helped to curtail its effects, as did countermeasures. In response, both sides developed more and more lethal types of gas including the deadly mustard gas.

The war continued in much the same way in 1915 as it had in 1914. The stalemate led the Allied Powers to take the war to the Dardanelles and Gallipoli in an attempt to win victories not forthcoming on the Western Front. Rather than break the war open these too ended in disaster. Then in May Italy joined the war on the side of the allies. The following year, 1916, became known as the Year of the Great Bloodletting. A series of long, drawn out battles took place on the Western Front. The battle at Verdun was a classic battle of the First World War. It raged from February to December and in these ten months war was reduced to a battle of attrition. The French held back reserves for the front at the Somme and yet they met a full German force at Verdun. The battle began on 21 February after a three-day bombardment. The Germans attacked and pushed the French back at first but then the French managed to retake lost territory. Little ground permanently exchanged hands yet the casualty rate was high. The Germans eventually gave up because their offensive force losses were as high as France's defensive losses. The two sides witnessed total casualties, referring to dead and wounded, of 500,000 for the French and 400,000 for the Germans.

To relieve the pressure at Verdun the British and French launched another attack, this time at the Somme. The 1916 battle of the Somme is probably one of the best known of the First World War. It began on 1 July 1916 and lasted until November, a total of four-and-a- half months. The main battle was a British assault aimed at the strongest field fortifications ever built, a fatally bad tactic. An unprecedented artillery barrage preceded the battle, which lasted a full week building up to the final assault, on 1 July, when nearly 250,000 shells hit the German lines. The barrage was so large that it was heard in north London. The casualty rate was high from the opening battles yet commanders continued the battle for over four months. Advancements were minimal and gains often held for only a short while. It was during the Battle of the Somme, on 15 September, that the first tank appeared in battle, but it broke down quickly and few commanders took the tank seriously at first. It was finally used to good effect in November 1917. Yet by the end of the battle of the Somme, in November 1916, casualty rates were extremely high and nothing had been achieved. The German losses totalled 500,000, British losses equalled 400,000 and the French suffered 200,000 casualties. Of these the British dead stood at 95,000 while 50,000 Frenchmen had been killed, putting the allied death toll at approximately 145,000. Over 164,000 Germans died. These death rates are almost impossible to comprehend. The overall death toll at Verdun, added to the death toll of the Somme, equalled approximately 960,000 men; almost 1 million men killed in just two battles on just the Western Front in just one part of one year of the war. Another 1 million or more were wounded. Other fronts in 1916 and other years had similar or higher casualty figures.

Some scholars have suggested that the Western and, especially, Eastern Fronts provide a classic study in bad leadership. Commanding generals were often more concerned for their reputations and the easy life behind the trenches than for easing the suffering of the men on the battlefield. What this meant was that few leaders looked for ways around the stalemate other than throwing more men at the front line. In contrast, the infantry soldier awaited his fate on the battlefield in trenches filled with mud, lice and rats. In this analysis, the commanders were stuck in nineteenth century military thought and unable to conduct a modern war. Others have suggested that the high battlefield casualty rates of the First World War owe more to the deadly effects of modern weaponry. More recent scholarship shows that the war was not quite as static as previously believed. By the end of 1915 and into early 1916 Germany had advanced 300 miles on the Eastern Front and come to dominate southeastern and central Europe. Germany also occupied Belgium, had gained ground in northern, industrial France and defeated Serbia.

Despite these examples of wartime gains on the part of Germany, the Western Front was more or less a deadlock between the Allied and Central Powers. However, the nature of the conflict changed dramatically in 1917, which turned out to be a propitious year in the war. In April 1917 the United States declared war on Germany, and Russia withdrew from the conflict, in part as a result of loss of lives in the war. In February the Russian Army had experienced a mutiny and there were bread riots in the civilian population. The czar was eventually overthrown and by November 1917 Lenin and the Bolsheviks had seized power. In March 1918 the Russians signed a treaty with Germany which recognised the independence of Poland, Finland and the Baltic provinces. Hence, just as the United States became involved in the European conflict Russia withdrew, which meant that Germany was able to concentrate its efforts on the Western Front.

Although a preparedness campaign had begun, which sought to increase the size of the army and step up production of armaments, the United States was amazingly unprepared for the fight when it declared war on 6 April 1917. When the United States entered the war in Europe its army was only the seventeenth largest in the world with 120,000 enlisted men and a National Guard numbering another 80,000. America needed time to enlist and train large numbers of men before it could contribute to the fighting in Europe. In order to address this situation, the US government instituted the Selective Service System or conscription of soldiers just a little over one month after the declaration of war with Germany. Britain had not instituted the draft until 1916, instead going through the first two years of war with strictly volunteer soldiers. Eventually the draft became necessary in Britain, however, because volunteers tended to be skilled workers, or those whose civilian talents helped in the war effort. A similar situation developed in the United States where the greatest enthusiasm for the war came from the best-educated section of society.

The first step in conscription was to register men between the ages of 21 and 30 on 5 June 1917. The age range later expanded to include men from 18 to 45 years of age. As the June deadline approached, the government was afraid there could be draft riots, as had happened during the Civil War. Hence, Wilson and other officials took pains to avoid calling it a draft, instead they referred to it as 'a selection from a nation that has volunteered in mass' and they used the term service repeatedly. Some Americans were in favour of conscription because they worried that the government would have to whip up emotions and patriotism to get enough volunteers and the country would become even more jingoistic. However, on the first day of the draft over ten million men registered at one of 4000 local draft boards in an atmosphere of calm, despite officials' initial fears. In total, 24 million men registered through the draft and received classification according to their fitness for combat and other military duties. Once all men had registered the government drew numbers and a call to service order was established. Men with dependants were exempt initially, which resulted in a marriage boom in 1917. The act also called for the exemption of skilled and essential workers in both industry and agriculture. Conscription resulted in 2.8 million men being conscripted with another 0.7 million men volunteering to become soldiers in the US military. Of these, approximately 2.5 million men served in the American Expeditionary Force (AEF) overseas.

When the United States entered the war in 1917 the situation on the Western Front was difficult for the allies. Germany's U-boat campaign was sinking merchant shipping at a worryingly high rate. The spring offensives by the French had led to huge losses again, which resulted in a short-lived mutiny in the French forces. In addition, the British were also at a stalemate again. In these circumstances the western allies wanted to see American troops in action as soon as possible, hopefully in positions of support to already established French and British commands. However, the United States entered the war as an associate power, not a full part of the alliance. This reflected the long-held concerns of America, first voiced by George Washington in his farewell address, against getting involved in entangling foreign alliances. Wilson wanted very much to participate in the war but only in order to influence the peace. He wanted the United States to be able to act independently in terms of its contribution to the military struggle taking place on the European continent.

With this in mind, the US military effort in Europe was directed by General John J. Pershing. General Pershing, or 'Black Jack' Pershing as he was known, had overseen US forces in the skirmish with Pancho Villa in Mexico in 1916. Since he was a long-time veteran of American military actions, Wilson appointed him as overall commander of the AEF in Europe. Pershing quickly asserted his plan to uphold the US strategy of a separate command for the use of American troops independently of British and French control. Pershing left for Europe on 28 May 1917 and, eventually, 2.5 million Americans followed. The overall US strategy called for a training session that would eventually see the utilisation of American troops in 1918 to break through the German line at Lorraine-Metz. The first draftees, however, did not begin training until September 1917. Yet the first troops, members of the regular army, went over as early as late June 1917 but lacked sufficient experience, requiring several months of training in the Lorraine area. While Pershing was unimpressed with allied strategy and determined to fight independently, small contingents of American troops did eventually serve with British and French forces for short periods prior to the first full-scale attack by US forces. They did not see any fighting until October 1917 and then only in a limited capacity. The training in trench warfare, deemed essential by allied commands, took time and indicated how ritualised the fighting had become.

Finally, in early 1918 the US military saw its first major combat of the First World War. The Germans launched a campaign to break the allied lines and Americans saw action on a limited scale at Amiens in March 1918 and on a much larger scale in June at Chateau-Thierry and Belleau Wood. The fresh American troops in large numbers helped turn the German offensive around at their final push at Rheims. Then the allies launched their own offensive in July 1918 at the Marne and the Somme. And finally, Pershing led an American offensive in September on the river Meuse. The offensive eventually pushed forward into the German held territory but at the same deadly cost of the earlier battles of the First World War. The AEF and Pershing experienced huge artillery barrages followed by large-scale offensives at established enemy emplacements.

The American military had changed dramatically throughout the course of US involvement in the Great War. As a direct result of the draft, information on the state of the nation's health emerged. As in Britain, when young American men registered for the draft a cross-section of society appeared before medical and other examiners. It was from this evidence that Americans learned that some of their fellow citizens were underfed and undernourished and that the level of literacy and standard of living in the United States varied greatly.

In addition, the draft applied to both black and white men, although their experiences differed greatly because the military was highly segregated. The army discriminated against African American troops in many ways including restricting them to certain jobs, usually associated with supply. Most blacks performed menial tasks as stevedores and labourers with only one in five black troops sent to France, seeing combat. As would happen in subsequent wars, African Americans made up a larger percentage of the draftees in proportion to their size in the population. For instance, while blacks made up just over 10 per cent of the men who registered for the draft, they subsequently provided over 12.5 per cent of draftees. In addition, racial violence marred black participation in the war effort. For example, black troops rioted over problems with Jim Crow laws in Houston, Texas on 23 August 1917. Many race problems resulted due to the location of military training centres in the South because of better all year weather conditions for training. Blacks from northern cities, who ended up training in the South, were used to more freedom in the North and found it difficult to adapt to life under Jim Crow laws. In the Houston riot 17 whites were killed while 13 African Americans were court-martialled, tried and hung.

The other changing face of the military included the participation of women who served in the US military services throughout the conflict. At the outbreak of war in April 1917 there were 403 women serving in the Army Nurses Corps. By the end of November 1918 there were 21,460 females working in this capacity with 10,000 of these serving overseas with the AEF. They mainly served at US military bases but also saw duty at evacuation centres and front line hospitals. The women saw service in numerous locations outside the United States including Hawaii, the Philippines, on ships and in Europe. Women also served in the navy as nurses with a peak participation rate of 1386 in 1918. An additional 12,000 women enlisted in the United States Navy and Marine Corps serving as clerical workers and telephone operators. Additionally, thousands worked as civilian volunteers for the military and the medical profession. The jobs they filled were similar to those that women had been moving into in the private sector prior to the war. The vast majority of women, who served in the military or as auxiliaries, were white, lower middle class, previous wage earners who were often self-supporting. The women's work with the AEF, often described in domestic terms despite taking place in the masculine arena of war, included performing domestic tasks. For example, canteen workers, mostly volunteers with the YMCA, YWCA and Red Cross, were meant to bring a touch of home to the overseas soldiers. Approximately 6000 women worked as canteen workers in the European theatre fixing meals, handing out doughnuts and coffee, mending clothes and so forth.

The United States' entry into the war acted to turn the tide. The expanded military, with the inclusion of blacks and women, and America's unhindered economy, ability to convoy supplies, and introduction of fresh troops to the battlefield helped to secure an allied victory. By November 1918 the allies had gained the upper hand but the cost had been great. An armistice was negotiated and a ceasefire took place at the 11th hour on the 11th day of the 11th month of 1918.

US HOME FRONT

During the war, numerous issues and events dominated the American home front, which collectively challenged notions of American's civil liberties. In the United States the Progressive Era preceded the First World War I. With the outbreak of war in Europe in 1914 many reformers worried that US involvement would adversely affect the reform spirit. In an atmosphere of heightened nationalism and patriotism, calls for reform could be misconstrued. Indeed, the war did have a major impact on reform as the definition of what it was to be an American and what

America should be was redefined. Patriotism replaced reform and the consequences were severe for some sections of American society. From 1914 to 1917, before the United States became involved, Americans watched the war in Europe and developed strong opinions about the conflict. Propaganda came of age in the First World War, as governments created agencies to regulate the flow of information and to promote the war effort. This selling of the war took many forms. For instance, when the United States entered the war the government produced the now famous "Uncle Sam Wants You" poster for recruitment purposes. Other campaigns included the admonishment to American citizens to conserve both fuel and food and to buy Liberty bonds to help finance the war effort. The government also targeted women directly as shortages in labour took place. They were recruited in the war effort by the use of posters and pamphlets asking them to help both at home and by taking wartime jobs vacated by men serving in the military. In other words, an atmosphere of heightened patriotism and conformity spread throughout America.

The US government wanted a consensus about the war to reflect a unity of purpose within America. To help achieve this Wilson's government set up the Committee on Public Information (CPI) in April 1917, headed by journalist George Creel. Among other things, the CPI began by printing and distributing 75 million copies of pamphlets, which tried to explain US involvement in the war. The CPI set up travelling exhibits on the war and issued over 6000 press releases to newspapers. In addition, the CPI created a Speaker's Bureau whereby a reserve force of 75,000 speakers was on hand to give short talks within communities across America. Known as 'Four Minute Men', these speakers visited schools, community clubs and churches to detail the latest war news and urge support for the government's war effort. At first the CPI's role was purely informational, offering facts about the war, but eventually it became a propaganda machine.

The CPI added to the wartime patriotic push for conformity by suggesting that everyone should report 'the man who spreads pessimistic stories, cries for peace, or belittles our efforts to win the war'. The CPI sponsored the making of films, which at first focused on positive images such as 'Our Colored Troops' but later took a more negative approach towards describing the war, producing titles such as 'The Kaiser: The Beast of Berlin'. Many Americans were uncertain as to the causes and aims of the war and conservative elements within the United States used this ignorance to promote patriotism. From the government's point of view, the need for consensus and harmony was paramount. Hence, there were also patriotic films released such as the 1918 'Pershing's Crusaders'.

Even with the surge in patriotism after the Zimmermann telegram, the US government found it necessary to cultivate or manufacture public opinion favourable to the war. This, coupled with Wilson's need for unity, translated into a crackdown on civil liberties that government officials believed the large ethnic mix and isolationist temper within the United States necessitated. The government manipulated public opinion and stepped up the movement for Americanisation of immigrants, in order to create a consensus in favour of the war. To do this the government criminalised 'wrong' ideas and dissenting associations. There had been conservative pressure to curtail the activities of certain minority groups before the war but now conservatives could label dissent as a criminal activity. Mainstream labour and business voluntarily gave in to governmental pressure for consensus and, as a result, as is often the case in times of war, the powers of government increased.

Groups targeted for suppression before the war included the Industrial Workers of the World (IWW) or Wobblies, the Socialist Party, anarchists and radical labour. However, due to the nationalist fervour of the war era, the federal government could be much more overt in its goals of suppression in the name of wartime necessity. It was in this context that the First World War brought the issue of civil liberties into the national debate. This debate revolved around whether the issue of suppression of civil liberties was a legitimate concern when the government faced the task of waging war. Some citizens saw the pursuit of subversive elements within American society as reasonable. Still, others saw governmental moves aimed at suppression of ideas and opinions as a substantial new threat to citizens and to the constitution. This latter group did not fail to note the irony of a democratic government working to suppress freedom and civil liberties at home while fighting a war abroad in the name of making the world safe for democracy.

Unfortunately, the government's insistence that suppression of civil liberties was legitimate in order to successfully prosecute the war inadvertently gave validity to hate groups and vigilantes who felt they were supporting the government's views when they attacked alleged dissenters. This approach was re-enforced at the highest levels with the establishment of the Military Intelligence Division (MID) by the army general staff in 1917. The purpose of the organisation was to locate German spies and saboteurs. However, the system that eventually emerged also began to investigate American citizens suspected of enemy sympathies. Whereas foreigners and recently arrived immigrants from enemy nations may have been legitimate targets of investigation, the MID also looked into the background and activities of American citizens. Most often targeted groups included labour unions, Socialists, pacifists and civil rights advocates. Eventually, the MID worked with law enforcement officials and local police departments as well as the Federal Bureau of Investigation (FBI) to locate subversives. These agencies also recruited vigilante groups to participate in raids and arrests. This led to the suppression of local labour disputes and racial controversies.

The foundation of many conservatives' concerns rested on the fact that America was home to millions of recent, as yet unassimilated, immigrants. US involvement in the war quickly led to a push for faster assimilation or Americanisation of these foreign elements. Underlying this push for 100 per cent Americanism was a general concern over the shift that had taken place in immigrants' origins since the 1880s. Since that time, fewer immigrants arrived from Northern and Western Europe and more came from areas of Southern and Central Europe. Prior to the outbreak of war many nativist Americans had suggested these 'new' immigrants were too different; they were radical, they were Catholic or Jewish, they were peasants, and, it seemed, they could not assimilate. The war added to this concern and increased the perceived need for homogeneity as well. Hence, the middle-class public attitude towards immigrants shifted from the Progressive Era push for education to the wartime mood of repression or forced assimilation. The government and spokespersons of the day outlined the dangers of allowing hyphenated Americans to remain unassimilated. Even Wilson, a long-time Progressive, suggested the need for 100 per cent Americanism.

Yet ironically, the targets for most anti-immigrant feelings during the war were those immigrants or Americans of German ancestry. Prior to the First World War Americans viewed Germans as part of the desirable 'old' immigrant population from Western Europe; however, with United States involvement in the war, the attitude toward Germans changed. The irony of this situation becomes even more acute when one remembers that many of these immigrants had fled to America to get away from arbitrary state action. Yet German Americans became the targets of vitriolic campaigns. Actions against anything German included the trivial when Americans began to call hamburgers liberty sandwiches and sauerkraut liberty cabbage. The actions of the governor of Iowa were far more serious, however, when he forbade the speaking of German in public. Most distressing were the incidents of violence that occurred. For example, in April 1918 in Collinsville, Illinois, Robert Prager, who had been born in Germany but lived in the United States and had tried to enlist in the US Navy, was seized by a crowd, stripped, bound in the American flag, dragged through the streets, and lynched. At the trial his killers wore red, white and blue ribbons and the jury took 25 minutes to find them not guilty. The government's attitude towards dissent coupled with the presidential campaign for 100 per cent Americanism bred suspicion, intolerance and vigilantism.

Organised labour proved to be another target of the nationalist fervour unleashed by US participation in the war. This anti-unionism was linked to concerns about immigrants since immigrant labour made up a large part of America's industrial work force. In addition, radicalism had long been associated with immigrants and radical ideas were especially worrisome after the Bolshevik revolution 'unleashed' communism. Furthermore, Socialists had proven their unpatriotic stance by denouncing the war in their campaign to attract American workers. They claimed the war was a capitalist quarrel and had little to offer the working man. Before the United States entered the war, the Socialist Party attracted those who were against the war and made substantial gains up to 1917. However, once the United States declared war on Germany the party split. In addition, the IWW came out against the war, which it too labelled a capitalist conspiracy that would benefit only big business. The Wobblies were more militant than the Socialists and often called for sabotage of industry to impede the progress of the war. Still other labour groups, such as the United Mine Workers (UMW), resented the government's use of the war as an excuse to suppress or break strikes that were dealing with legitimate labour issues.

From the government's point of view, radical unions and dissident parties threatened the mobilisation of US industry for the war effort. Also, dissident voices made it hard for Wilson to continue to define the war as a popular democratic struggle. From organised labour's point of view the government stance against Socialists, the IWW and other radical labour movements had major side effects since it allowed management and business to label all labour unionisation as traitorous. Labour worried that voicing legitimate complaints about hours, wages and conditions would now be seen as disloyal because of the war. Strike action could also be seen this way. Moreover, the American Federation of Labor (AFL) with Samuel Gompers as President did not help the Socialist or IWW position. Gompers had always opposed socialism and when the United State entered the war Gompers pledged labours' support, which subsequently split the labour movement. He, however, saw his main mission as leading the fight for workers against the Socialist Party. Hence, Gompers joined with the government and the Committee on Public Information to use propaganda to guarantee a consensus of support for the war.

One result of all this intolerance and nationalist rhetoric was a series of governmental raids on IWW halls in September 1917 just five months after America entered the war. The process resulted in nearly 200 IWW members in Illinois, California and Oklahoma being arrested, charged and convicted. These raids, in turn, fed vigilantism in Butte, Montana; Cincinnati, Ohio and Centralia, Washington where lynching and beating of Wobblies took place. Many prominent Americans came out in support of these actions including Teddy Roosevelt, members of the clergy and university professors. Historian Richard Hofstadter has suggested that during war:

What had been tolerated becomes intolerable now.
What had been wrongheadedness was now sedition.
What had been folly was now treason.

This desire to see dissent controlled led to censorship of the press, punishment of those who interfered with the armed forces' recruitment and conscription, and control of the mails to prevent distribution of treasonable materials. A series of acts passed by Congress, which ultimately violated citizens' civil liberties, would hopefully ensure a better chance of maintaining a consensus for American participation in the war.

One of the first acts Congress passed was the Espionage Act of June 1917. Postmaster General Albert Burleson, already intolerant of dissent and alleged subversives, was authorised to ban from the mails or post any material violating the act or advocating treason, insurrection or forcible resistance to any law of the United States. This law was, in effect, censorship and, as such, created a censorship board that banned certain journals from the mails in direct violation of the first amendment. Of special interest and concern, under the Trading with the Enemies Act of October 1917, were foreign language newspapers. In fact, any mail or correspondence to foreign countries was subject to inspection. The act gave Postmaster Burleson almost total control over the foreign language press by requiring the submission of English translations in advance of publication for all articles or editorials referring to the government, belligerent nations or conduct of the war. The result of the adoption of this act was the closing down of many foreign language newspapers that served the immigrant community. It also forced the remaining foreign language newspapers into offering uncritical support of the US government.

Surprisingly few people protested against the acts or against Postmaster General Burleson. Attorney General Thomas Gregory, in charge of enforcing the Espionage Act, oversaw the conviction of people for discussing the constitutionality of conscription or for suggesting that bankers were behind the war. Conviction on either count could lead to three-year prison terms. Yet another act, the Sedition Act of May 1918, prohibited any disloyal, profane, scurrilous or abusive language about the form of government in the United States, the constitution, the flag or military uniforms. Its purpose was to suppress views of Socialists, pacifists and radicals. Of special interest as well was the Non-Partisan League, a movement of agrarian radicalism that was thoroughly against the war. Vigilante movements grew alongside these pieces of legislation. In the spring of 1917 the American Protective League (APL) was established and worked closely with Attorney General Thomas Gregory as a system of citizen spies. APL members spied on their neighbours and fellow workers and reported anyone violating the wartime laws to the local FBI.

Unsurprisingly, these acts were eventually tested in the Supreme Court but not until the war had ended. *Schenck v. United States* (1919) challenged the Espionage Act. Under the terms of the act Charles Schenck was arrested for encouraging resistance to the draft. Schenck also happened to be an official of the Socialist Party. He had sent a pamphlet to draftees suggesting that conscription was unconstitutional. In this case Oliver Wendell Holmes wrote his now famous clear and present danger opinion, claiming that during times of war, when there is a clear and present danger, governments are free to restrict the liberties of citizens as and when necessary. The Supreme Court upheld Schenck's conviction despite criticism that the act itself, and the court's decision, ignored basic issues of free speech. In the case of *Debs v. the United States* (1919) the Supreme Court upheld Eugene Debs' conviction and imprisonment under terms of the Espionage Act for giving an anti-war speech. Debs was a member of the Socialist Party and the railway workers union who, ironically, gained over one million votes when he ran for President in 1920 from his federal jail cell in Atlanta.

However, the tide eventually began to turn. In the case of *Abrams v. United States* (1919), justices Holmes and Louis Brandeis condemned the wartime conviction of Abrams under the terms of the Sedition Act. Jacob Abrams, an anarchist and Russian immigrant, had distributed pamphlets calling for a general strike to denounce US intervention in Russia during the revolution. Holmes and Brandeis, however, were representing the minority opinion when they suggested that his conviction was unsound and that he did not present a clear and present danger. Holmes also went further by suggesting that freedom of speech and the airing of dissenting opinion could be better for society than the repression of speech, yet a majority on the Supreme Court upheld Abrams' conviction.

The prosecutions under these acts amounted to a concerted attack on free speech and civil liberties. The general reaction against this repression was weak, often because vocal protest could bring more repression. No immigrant organisation made any concerted effort to fight for civil liberties although there were individual exceptions. Oswald Garrison Villard, a German American journalist, spoke out against the government's actions, noting 'the right to criticize the government is never more vital than in wartime'. However, the majority of Americans supported the use of censorship to preserve national security. Since the Alien and Sedition Act of 1798 when President John Adams imprisoned dangerous enemy aliens without trial, loyalty had been defined in such a way as to outlaw certain behaviour. In the First World War era those Americans who opposed US preparedness for and, later, participation in the war tended to be Irish Americans, German Americans, Socialists, political radicals, pacifists or Progressives. The subsequent campaign for 100 per cent Americanism reflected an out of control patriotism or jingoism. The debate over what was loyal became so heated that it drowned out minority opinions, which had major implications for the post-war period.

During the war the air of intolerance continued with the Threats Against the President Act of February 1917, which targeted people who knowingly or wilfully made written or spoken threats to the life or body of the President. It was a small step from threatening the President to criticising the President and Americans against the war had to tread carefully. Wilson rallied support for the idea of federal repression by suggesting it was a small price to pay for a unified front. This argument contended that it was reasonable for people to give up their freedoms under the circumstances. As noted earlier, the Supreme Court tended to back the government. Oliver Wendell Holmes, in the *Debs* case of 1919, wrote: 'when a nation is at war, many things that might be said in times of peace are such hindrance to its effort that their utterance will not be endured so long as men still fight'. The national interest, in other words, prevails over individual liberties. Although Holmes would later dissent from his own 'clear and present danger' formula, the consequences of these acts and the Supreme Courts' backing was to suppress liberals and dissenters within America and leave conservatives and reactionaries in power. It also, however, moved reformers to create the American Civil Liberties Union (ACLU) in 1920, an outgrowth of the wartime American Civil Liberties Bureau, in order to protect the Bill of Rights, including the freedom of speech.

However, another act, passed in May 1917 and upheld by the Supreme Court in 1918, brought the issue of individual rights into a different debating arena. Under the terms of the Selective Service Act some argued that the draft or conscription was the ultimate violation of an individual's civil liberties by forcing people to serve in war. Others pointed out that military service in defence of one's country was a small price to pay for the democratic rights and freedoms one receives as a citizen of the state. While the government did not experience a major backlash against the institution of the draft, this could be because it tried to head off any possible criticisms of the selective service system by instituting the series of repressive pieces of legislation discussed earlier, such as the Espionage Act of 1917. In fact, those who spoke out against the Selective Service Act, such as Emma Goldman and Eugene V. Debs, were arrested.

The draft highlighted the concomitant issue of conscientious objection (CO) to war. The Selective Service System recognised religious beliefs as the only legitimate reasons for refusing to fight and based its acceptance of CO status on an individual's membership in one of the 'historical peace churches'. In such cases the government offered alternative service to substitute for combat. Approximately 64,000 men claimed CO status, but not everyone based his claim on religious belief, some proclaimed their non-combatant status as part of their political beliefs. Local draft boards registered 57,000 COs officially and of these, approximately 21,000 were inducted into the US Army and sent to training camps. Of these, approximately 16,000 gave up their right to CO status after experiencing treatment aimed at humiliating and shaming them into combat service. A few absolutists, however, refused to join the army at all and over 500 went to prison. There were also a number of draft evaders, estimated at 330,000 in total, about half of whom were eventually caught.

While the war propelled Americans into participation in the war effort in the form of military service, the war also had a direct impact on various segments of American society. For example, as a direct result of the First World War a great migration of African Americans took place from the agricultural and rural South to the growing industrial cities of the North. Labour shortages and the expansion of industry provided opportunities for work in the North. As African Americans moved they experienced more freedom than in the South. The war curtailed immigration from Europe, and this, combined with the institution of conscription, meant that industry experienced a labour shortage. African Americans were able to take advantage of this although they ran into trouble with labour organisations, which often viewed them as scabs. In addition, African Americans faced housing shortages and other problems such as segregation in the North. Despite this, northern industry actively recruited African Americans as early as 1916 and by 1920 an estimated half-a-million blacks had moved north. Southern whites attempted to resist this movement, often through coercion, for fear of losing a cheap labour source. Even the federal government, through the Department of Labor Employment Service, at one point suspended assistance programmes to southern blacks headed north. Wilson was very much a southerner and was sympathetic towards maintaining segregation. He had screened DW Griffith's *Birth of a Nation* (1915) in the White House and approved the movie. Hence, while economic forces worked to improve conditions, African Americans could not expect much help from the government or official agencies when confronted with prejudice, racism or discrimination. Unfortunately, the problems associated with the changing circumstances for African Americans often led to violence.

On 2 July 1917 a race riot occurred in East St. Louis, Illinois. It started over labour issues as a direct result of the influx of African Americans to the city. By the time the riot had ended, 39 blacks were dead. Despite the violent nature of the conflict there was no federal intervention. The problem stemmed from blacks' movement north into segregated cities with very small areas of black housing which quickly became overcrowded with black neighbourhoods expanding and encroaching into white areas. The end of the war did not ease the situation; by 1919 a total of over 60,000 African Americans had moved to Chicago and a race riot erupted there on 27 July. This violence lasted 13 days and involved roving black and white gangs who launched violent attacks on their counterparts. By the end of this riot 15 whites and 23 blacks were killed. There were other riots in 1919 in Knoxville, Omaha, and Washington D.C. Approximately 200 African Americans were killed during the war era within the United States, yet however short of perfection the situation, the move to the North did mean more opportunities for blacks. By 1920 approximately 1.5 million African Americans were working in the North. They had access to political power denied them in the South under Jim Crow, and their recruitment into industry in the First World War gave them a toe hold in previously denied areas of employment. They also joined organisations such as the NAACP, whose membership doubled from 1918 to 1919, as part of a push for African American civil rights.

The wartime experience of women could also challenge the structures within American society and American women made some gains with the US entry into the war. From the outbreak of war in Europe in 1914 until the end of the war in 1918, women played an active role. The exact nature of their participation, however, was as varied as their economic and ethnic backgrounds. Some women, including many Progressive reformers, worked with anti-war and peace organisations when the war began. The Women's Peace Party, for example, was a large and influential organisation that combined both peace sentiment and reform impulses. Equally, there were women who believed in preparedness and in the entry of the United States into the conflict. Other women participated in the war effort by working for relief agencies and government departments that attempted to co-ordinate women's voluntary services. As with the women's movement before the war, women varied in their opinions towards the war and towards its potential impact on the suffrage movement. Still, women made many practical contributions to the war effort through their participation in war work, although their work was limited and brief.

Over one million women entered into war work but only a fraction of these were first-time workers. Women were very hopeful about gains they could make in the war and the establishment of the Woman's Bureau in the Department of Labor seemed to suggest new government attitudes towards the female work force. However, most women who worked during the war were women who had worked before the war. For the most part they were single, few were in heavy industry and most lost their jobs when the war was over. In addition, women continued to be paid less than men although they often took on 'male' jobs and labour unions opposed women in industry. Surprisingly, in 1920 women were a smaller percentage of the labour force than they had been in 1910. However, in 1920 the United States finally ratified the 19th Amendment to the constitution giving women the right to vote. The First World War gave the last, necessary push, as a reward for women's support and help during the war, to the passage of this amendment, which finally gave women full political equality.

The war brought other benefits to the home front. The boom economy of the First World War resulted in high employment figures and an over-all increase in real wages. In addition, despite the government's move against radical labour, membership in less radical trade unions increased from 2.7 million in 1916 to over five million by 1920. The mainstream unions' pledge to hold off strikes for the duration of the war, as had the AFL under Gompers, was helped by the pro-labour views of the govern-ment's new National War Labor Board, which recognised the right of workers to organise and push for improvements in the work place. The Progressive reform spirit continued in some ways with the adoption of the 8-hour day as standard by the end of the war. It seemed as if the war brought both significant progress and repression to the American people.

THE CONSEQUENCES

The war years had witnessed considerable and far-reaching changes on both the battle and home fronts. The post-war world would reflect many of those changes, which became apparent in the days immediately fol-lowing the armistice. Considering the nature of the war, and the long, extended battles over the years, the war ended rather abruptly. The German high command had seen the end approaching and the military informed the government that the war was not winnable. The German Foreign Office made peace overtures to the allies and eventually Germany surrendered. The Germans moved quickly to establish a parliamentary system to curry allied favour and made their offer of peace based on Wilson's Fourteen Points, which he had outlined in early 1918.

While the Germans were hoping to surrender to Wilson's programme, this idealistic agenda belonged to Wilson alone and not the allies. When discussing Wilson's Fourteen Points, Georges Clemenceau of France noted that even God only had ten. It became clear quite quickly that the allies had completely different post-war agendas. For instance, the first of Wilson's Fourteen Points called for 'open covenants of peace, openly arrived at'. This was an attempt on Wilson's part to forestall any future conflicts associated with secret negotiations and secret treaties as had been experienced during the First World War. At various times during the war, each side in the conflict had been in need of more help. For exam-ple, Germany and Austria-Hungary signed alliances with the Ottoman Empire in 1914 and Bulgaria in 1915. Italy had been courted by both sides, to the point where the Italian people were split evenly over which side to join. In 1915 the Italian government signed a secret treaty with Britain, with Italy agreeing to give up parts of the German empire. Britain and France also signed a secret treaty with Russia over the Dardanelles. Each side fed on ethnic rivalries in the Balkans and made promises about the post-war world in order to gain wartime advantages. Wilson believed that these secret negotiations served to feed and not end the conflict and wanted to see an end to their use. Many of his other points, such as guaranteed freedom of the seas and self-determination of countries, had similar roots in pre-war and wartime events but also generated opposition from one or more of the allied governments.

Eventually the victors came to Paris from January to May 1919 to negotiate the treaty signifying the end of the war. At this point the world was in flux, the war that had just concluded brought about the end of the great empires of Europe. Gone were the Russian, Austro-Hungarian, German, and Ottoman Empires. The world had also witnessed the rise of communism when, in November 1917, the Bolsheviks successfully negotiated their revolution in Russia. Elsewhere in world the forces that had participated in the war were also changing. There were race riots in Korea, China launched a revolution, and India was witnessing the rise of Gandhi. Many people felt the need to re-establish order in the world since there seemed to be so much chaos.

It was in this atmosphere that the Big Four met in Paris. Wilson for the United States, Clemenceau for France, David Lloyd-George for Britain and Vittorio Orlando for Italy came together to negotiate some kind of settlement for the war. Wilson based his negotiations on his Fourteen Points agenda. Lloyd-George represented the right wing of British politics, which hated Germany and sought to protect Britain's ships, their biggest international asset. Clemenceau of France also hated Germany and much of his agenda revolved around the notion of revenge for the unspeakable horrors and loss of life that France had experienced with wartime reparations high on his list of negotiating topics. Orlando, representing Italian interests, was out to get whatever he could which would improve Italy's position in the European equation.

The ultimate outcome of the negotiations was a compromise of Wilson's ideas. British economist John Maynard Keynes called Wilson 'a blind and deaf Don Quixote' because Wilson's idealism, as embodied in the Fourteen Points, did not mesh with the realpolitik of the European situation. The result of the deliberations was the document known as the Treaty of Versailles. The Treaty was a dictated treaty whereby Germany was never consulted but was expected to bear the brunt of the burden for the war. The Treaty of Versailles created new countries out of the old territories of the Austro-Hungarian Empire, namely Czechoslovakia and Yugoslavia. The establishment of these nations rested upon the ideal of popular sovereignty whereby the people of the area voted to establish their governments. The treaty stripped the defeated nations of their colonies with the area of Alsace–Lorraine returned to French control. Furthermore, the only nation required to disarm was Germany and Germany was expected to pay a $15 billion indemnity for the costs of the war with the possibility left open for further reparations. The allied nations also inserted a war guilt clause in which they forced Germany to take responsibility for all of the slaughter of the war. The victors laid the blame for the loss of life and destruction of the Great War at Germany's feet. Finally, the Treaty established the League of Nations as an international forum for discussion and settlement of future disputes between countries. Once the negotiators finalised the Treaty in Paris, Wilson launched his campaign for ratification in the United States. The Senate, however, refused to ratify the treaty and, consequently, America never joined the League.

The prevailing attitude in the United States, after the war, called for a return to domestic concerns. Foreign policy became a strictly hemispheric and imperialist question. Yet the consequences of the First World War were enormous. On a purely statistical level, the number of soldiers killed exceeded that of all other wars known to history. The published lists of those killed in action, or who died of wounds received in action, seemed endless. Yet final calculations can only be approximates. Not all the victims of the war were soldiers; for instance, more Serb civilians died (82,000) than soldiers. For the US military, more soldiers died of influenza (62,000) than were killed in battle (53,000). More than one million Armenians were massacred between 1914 and 1919. The number of German civilians who died due to the Allied blockade totalled an estimated three-quarter of a million. The Central Powers (the losers) lost 3,500,000 soldiers on the battlefield while the Allied Powers, the winners, lost 5,100,000.

The other consequences of the First World War were equally far reaching. Often labelled the first modern war because of the introduction of certain technological innovations such as poison gas, tanks and airplane and the deployment of massive armies, the Great War is more accurately described as the first total war. The various nations involved in the conflict not only had to mobilise their military but also their economies. Governments took over control of war production, creating massive bureaucracies in the process. Civilian populations became part of a huge mobilisation for war that included the use of the draft to guarantee a continuous supply of soldiers for the large battles but also included the mobilisation of labour to work in the factories that provided the materiel of the war. Perhaps the First World War is best described as the largest industrial war to that date.

As noted, the First World War heralded the destruction of the great empires of the nineteenth century. By war's end the Austro-Hungarian, Ottoman and Russian Empires were gone. The Russian Revolution occurred, in part, because of the war, which in turn led to the long-term, post-war struggle between communist and non-communist countries. Yet the end of the war also brought about the creation of several new democratic states. The Baltic states of Estonia, Latvia and Lithuania emerged, as did the states of Yugoslavia and Czechoslovakia. Austria and Hungary came into existence based on the principal of self-determination, and other areas expanded their territory as Germany and Russia lost some of theirs. In terms of international power and influence, the United States came out of the war as a recognised major economic and military power. It was the beginning of the rise of the United States and the decline of Europe, both economically and militarily, that would continue after the Second World War.

While some scholars credit the war with bringing about a growth in democracy, both in the creation of democratic states and in the expansion of democracy to previously denied sections of society such as women, others blame the war for the death of a lost generation, the survivors of which never fully recovered from the horrors of large-scale industrial war. Part of their concern was the emotional impact of the war. For many survivors the rallying cry was 'never again.' Never again could man be allowed to wage war at such a level and at such human costs. Many diplomats believed that the Treaty of Versailles would help ensure that this did not happen again. However, within the pages of this document lay the seeds of another war. The war guilt clause and reparations forced upon Germany would eventually give rise to problems in the 1930s. Some scholars have suggested that the war in Europe lasted from 1914 to 1945, with a 21-year peace in the middle.

Still, some scholars see wars as democratising events: ex-colonies became free, new countries emerged based on self-determination and the League of Nations was formed to stop unrestricted empire building. On the US home front African Americans and women emerge from the war, not as equals to middle and upper class white men, but further along the road to equality than they had been at the beginning of the war. Organised labour, at least the trade unions of skilled workers, had finally been recognised with the 8-hour day becoming standard practice. In addition, as a direct result of the war, on the home front more government control existed in some industries such as telegraph, telephone, railroads and shipping. However, big business was even bigger and the government had given out anti-trust exemptions. Moreover, the government had restricted civil liberties to an unprecedented level, although this meant that, after the First World War, civil liberties became a legitimate issue in public discourse. Hence, some historians have argued that the war helped in spreading democracy not only abroad but also at home and that the war was a catalyst for positive social change.

The immediate aftermath of the war in the United States, however, puts this argument in a different perspective. The attack on dissent witnessed on the American home front during the First World War continued after the war. The Red Scare of 1919–1920 swept across America and continued the attack on radical and minority voices. As noted earlier, race riots occurred in 1919 in the United States and attacks on African American veterans occurred. In addition, fear of communism or bolshevism resulted in numerous conflicts across America as labour strikes erupted in 1919. In December the government deported approximately 150 Russian-born individuals for fear of their radicalism. The fear continued in 1920 with federal and local governments raiding the headquarters of various organisations followed by more arrests and deportations. The Attorney General, A. Mitchell Palmer, lends his name to these raids but the sentiment behind them was widespread across the United States. Despite the violation of citizenship rights that produced these attacks, little protest occurred. The scare faded as quickly as it had appeared but the American people were left exhausted. The Presidential election of 1920 saw Republican Warren Harding elected based on his pledge to return American society to 'normalcy' after the chaos of the Great War, ending most hopes for future liberal reforms.

3 The Second World War

THE INTERWAR PERIOD

The interwar period, from 1919 to 1939, was dominated, in both Europe and the United States, by issues related to the economy. In Europe the war had left most belligerents' economies in ruins. Germany was especially hard hit with the call for reparations posing an added burden to its post-war recovery. The United States, however, had come through the war relatively unscathed to emerge in the post-war world as a major economic player. Consequently, many European governments turned to the United States to secure loans in order to rebuild. A complex web of loans, loan repayments and reparations helped to entwine the economies of Europe and America, which meant that any problems in one area could spread to another. Germany's immediate post-war slump in the early 1920s led to years of hyperinflation and German citizens found that literally whole wheelbarrows full of Deutsch marks could go towards purchase of small, essential items.

For the most part America looked inward in this period. The Republican Party dominated the White House in the 1920s and big business became even bigger. American society witnessed a flourishing of cultural trends that had an impact on everything from literature and the arts to the emergence of Hollywood and mass advertising. The decade also witnessed the beginnings of a consumer culture that fed on the overall prosperity of the post-war period. Unfortunately, the seeds of future economic problems were also present and would blossom into a depression. By the late 1920s the bubble burst for everyone, including Europe, and in 1929, with the Wall Street Crash, the United States entered into its worst depression in history. Republican President Herbert Hoover tried to address the economic situation without resorting to massive federal intervention but his efforts failed. So, in 1932, the American people turned to the Democrats for a solution to the problem and, in November, elected Franklin D. Roosevelt to the Presidency.

Roosevelt's inauguration in 1933 heralded the launching of the New Deal, intended to end the problems of the Depression and relieve the suffering of the American people. The year 1933 was also the worst year of the Depression with unemployment at 25 per cent. Under FDR's direction many new agencies appeared, governmental bureaucracy increased and he and his advisors introduced a series of solutions to specific problems that were tested, then maintained or abandoned. These governmental policies of the New Deal era made winners out of some Americans and losers out of others. For instance, the Depression hit women hard. Though more women went to work during the Depression than before, they tended to do so because they had to; men had lost jobs. Yet many New Deal agencies often ignored women and women's jobs. For example, women's work in domestic service was untouched by New Deal policies like Social Security. In addition, when some government agencies did recruit women, as with the Works Progress Administration, they paid women about 60 per cent of a man's wage. African Americans fared least well of all groups having been hardest hit by the Depression. Whereas average unemployment rates for the United States as a whole during the worst years of the Depression were an estimated 25–30 per cent, for African Americans this rate was as high as 50 per cent. Often New Deal legislation hurt African Americans rather than helped, such as the Agricultural Adjustment Act that forced many tenant farmers off the land. Social Security did not apply to agricultural workers or domestic servants, and other agencies, such as the Civilian Conservation Corps, were strictly segregated. The New Deal also lacked any serious civil rights legislation.

However, by the end of the New Deal the United States had moved some way forward from its laissez faire attitudes towards poverty and the poverty-stricken. Overall, America was more liberal at the end of the New Deal than it had been at the beginning of the Depression. The government was closer to a welfare state than it had been and the establishment of New Deal agencies led to a more centralised and bureaucratised government.

In terms of foreign policy, in the 1920s and early 1930s international relations in Europe were dominated by the concern that never again would Europe be plunged into war. Foreign policy tended to focus on retreat with less money spent on arms and governments negotiating treaties limiting their military strength such as the Five Power Naval Limitations Treaty of 1922, which curtailed the naval forces of Great Britain, France, Japan, Italy and the United States. This attitude of avoiding war by limiting arms or controlling behaviour was epitomised by the Kellogg–Briand Pact of 1928. Frank Kellogg, United States Secretary of

State and French Foreign Minister Aristide Briand formulated the pact, which renounced war as an instrument of national policy. The Kellogg–Briand Pact reflected two things: the firm desire on the part of most nations involved in the devastation of the First World War that it should not happen again and a firm belief in the perfectibility of mankind. This last point suggested that the force of law and public opinion could eliminate war, which entailed a strange combination of idealism and legalism. Fifteen nations signed the Pact initially, led by the United States, France, Great Britain, Germany, Japan and Italy. All those countries that signed the Pact pledged not to wage war except in situations of self-defence, with self-defence going undefined. Within 5 years over 60 countries had signed the agreement.

However, the Kellogg–Briand Pact was not as idealistic or foolish at the time as it might seem with the benefit of hindsight. Immediately after the First World War there was reason for optimism. In the early post-war years it seemed to many leaders in the western world that democracy had been triumphant. New democracies dotted Eastern Europe and in the 1920s Germany and Japan appeared to be working to become democracies in their own right. The Fascism of Benito Mussolini in Italy posed little or no threat at first and, although communism existed in Russia, this too seemed to be non-threatening. After 1929, however, economic depression spread throughout the international scene and democracy appeared to be on the defensive. By 1933 it looked as if the non-democratic states were doing things, making forward strides to end their economic problems. These states appeared to be active and their activities often revolved around military programmes.

BEGINNINGS

The circumstances that culminated in the outbreak of the Second World War arose over the course of a decade prior to the exchange of official declarations of war. However, as with the outbreak of the First World War, the United States was late to enter the conflict. During this time various nations interacted with each other independently, rather than as a group. The League of Nations failed to materialise as an organisation that would act collectively to either settle disputes or defend countries under threat. Ultimately, the aggressive nature of several countries pushed the world into war.

Unrest characterised the post-war period. In Italy there was an economic depression much earlier than in some other European countries, with numerous industrial strikes and armed young men in black shirts known as Fascists clashing with communists. In this atmosphere Benito Mussolini rose to power, managing to seize control of the government in 1922 and, under the banner of fascism, proclaiming a return to law and order. He was backed by many people in the wealthy classes whom he courted by calling on their strong feelings of patriotism and nationalism. The government granted him full emergency powers for one year so he could restore order and make reforms. Once in power, however, Mussolini took control and proclaimed himself leader or Il Duce. Within a few years he overrode the Italian Parliament, censored the press, destroyed labour unions, outlawed strikes and abolished all parties except the Fascist Party.

The Fascist philosophy denounced democracy, liberalism, free trade, capitalism, Marxism, materialism and socialism. It preached national solidarity and state management of the economy. Mussolini organised the syndicalist or corporate state where the government set the working conditions, wages, prices and policies although ownership was still in private hands. Hence, as long as they made profits, wealthy industrialists could and did back Mussolini. To Mussolini his dictatorship was one of the state over many co-operating classes. This form of leadership did not keep depression away but it did give people a sense of psychological exhilaration – of things getting done. All the while Adolf Hitler closely watched Mussolini's gains. In 1935 Mussolini's Fascism turned aggressive and he launched an attack on Ethiopia. Ethiopia's leader, Haile Selassie, went to the League of Nations to plead for help but the League ignored his calls for international intervention against aggression. Although many nations and individuals looked upon Ethiopia with sympathy, no one wanted to risk war by trying to save Ethiopia's sovereignty. This failure to respond to the aggression of a totalitarian state occurred again in the lack of response to Hitler's expansionism.

Germany was a large industrial state even after its defeat in the First World War. The German economy, however, suffered severely in the depressions of the 1920s due, in part, to the reparation demands of Britain and France and the foreign loans it required to meet these obligations. The Great Inflation of 1923 saw many Germans struggling to purchase mere necessities. It was in this atmosphere that the rise of the National Socialists occurred; however, the eventual triumph of the National Socialists did not happen overnight. In the 1920 elections

90 per cent of the German people voted democratic, 7 per cent communist and only 3 per cent National Socialists. Yet by 1929 and the globalisation of the depression more and more people were looking for solutions to their problems. By 1930 the National Socialists were able to gain 6.5 million popular votes and by 1932 they were the largest single party. Although they did not have a majority because of the existence of multiple parties, they clearly held a position of power.

The man, of course, most associated with this party and this power was Adolf Hitler. Hitler was a superb orator and a good political organiser. He also knew how to play on the fears of the German people through his National Socialists German Workers Party. Hitler came fully into power in January 1933 in the same year that Franklin Roosevelt took over the presidency of the United States. The German governmental hierarchy appointed Hitler Chancellor as a way for them to exert some control over his actions; however, from his position as Chancellor Hitler seized dictatorial powers and proclaimed himself leader or Fuehrer. Hitler had clear plans for his Third Reich or Empire, which he hoped to achieve through foreign policy. His main aim was to undo the Versailles Treaty, which meant remaking the military, re-establishing Germany as a world power and embarking on a campaign of conquest to provide Lebensraum or living space for his fellow Germans. He focused this campaign to the East at first but planned that this would eventually lead to a German-dominated Europe and rest of world. Hitler hoped to achieve his aims through his three-step plan for Germany.

First, in 1933–1934, Hitler launched his Gleischaltung plan for making equal or levelling society. This translated into the establishment of one party, one workers' union and so on. This was the first step in producing a totalitarian state that frowned on individualism and individual rights. It was also in these years that Hitler moved to tighten his control of the government. On 30 June 1934 he had the leaders of the SturmAbteilung (SA) or storm troopers, potential rivals, executed in what became known as the Night of the Long Knives. Hitler then went on to establish the Gestapo, the people's courts, concentration camps and the Hitler Youth as a means of consolidating his control. He managed to gain complete control of the party with a unified nation behind him. Hitler put the people to work through government projects such as construction of the autobahn and thus gained the support of the people. With his position solidified he furthered his vision of a triumphant Germany by launching his anti-Jewish programme in 1935. With the establishment of the Nuremberg Laws, a racist attack on the Jewish population of Germany, Jews lost their citizenship and their civil liberties.

Hitler's second step in his plan for Germany began in 1935 with the push to build up the military. In March of that year Hitler announced to the world that Germany was no longer bound by the Treaty of Versailles. He gambled that his European neighbours would not respond in a physical way to his declaration and he won the gamble. Then, in 1936, Germany re-militarised and occupied the Rhineland, helped Fascists in the Spanish Civil War, signed an anti-communist pact with Japan and Italy, and announced the Rome–Berlin axis of power in Europe around which the rest of the world would revolve. By the end of 1937 Germany had one of the best militaries in the world with the Luftwaffe, in particular, setting the standard for other air forces.

The third or final stage in Hitler's plans called for expansion and began in 1938. In February Hitler announced his programme of Anschluss or annexation of Austria. Without resistance Hitler annexed Austria to Germany in what became known as the Blumenkreig or Flower War because of its bloodlessness. He next set his sights on the takeover of Czechoslovakia by suggesting that Germany wanted to annex the Sudetenland area of Czechoslovakia because the area was full of Germans. The Sudetenland was also, however, the area of natural defence for Czechoslovakia, the easiest place to fortify and held most of Czechoslovakia's industry. To complicate matters, Czechoslovakia had treaties with Britain, France and the Soviet Union. In September 1938 a meeting took place between British Prime Minister Neville Chamberlain, French Prime Minister Edouard Daladier and Hitler in which Chamberlain and Daladier agreed to let Hitler 'have' the Sudetenland in exchange for a promise that Hitler would stop his aggression. Hitler willingly signed this Munich Agreement and Chamberlain returned triumphant to England declaring 'peace in our time.' Many people praised this policy of appeasement towards Hitler as a means of staving off war. Unfortunately, with German occupation of the Sudetenland Czechoslovakia was defenceless, and, in March 1939, Hitler took the rest of the country and the brief life of appeasement was over. The following month Mussolini used this opportunity to seize Albania. Then, to consolidate his plans for war in the west, Hitler signed a peace treaty with the Soviet Union in August 1939. This alliance shocked the world. Few people had foreseen this partnership but from Hitler's point of view, once his eastern flank was secure, he felt more confident about launching a further attack that had the potential to lead to war with Britain and France. On 1 September 1939 Germany invaded Poland, ostensibly over the issue of securing Danzig and access to the sea via the Polish corridor. The world was standing on the brink of world war just 20 years after the end of the last one.

While aggression was changing the map of Europe and North Africa, the Japanese had already launched their own campaign of aggression in the Pacific. The control of power in the Japanese government resided with the Cabinet and with the military. In the 1930s the military was able to assert overall control and began to lead Japan down the road of expansion. In 1931 Japan invaded Manchuria renaming it Manchuko. Similar to previous acts of aggression by Italy in Ethiopia and Germany in Austria, there was no forceful response from the rest of the world. Japan proclaimed its interest in establishing the Greater East Asia Co-Prosperity Sphere to redress past European imperialism. Under this scheme Asia would be for Asians with Japan dominating the region. Japanese spokesmen forcefully denounced the colonial greed in the Pacific of European nations such as France and the Netherlands.

In 1936 Japan, disregarding previous international agreements on arms limitations, began building its military and signed the anti-communist treaty with Germany and Italy. In 1937 Japan attacked China and Chiang Kai-shek and the Nationalists fought to resist the Japanese advance with little help from outside. The Japanese began moving south in their rush to expand. As an island nation they proclaimed their need for raw materials and they insisted on the need to gain control of natural resources in order to reduce their dependence on western countries. During all of this aggression and expansion there was still no meaningful response from the rest of the world.

While Japan, Italy and Germany began their campaigns of aggression in the 1930s, other countries were more pacifistic. Many theories of war circulated after 1918 and certain belief systems developed, which hindered nations' responses to the naked aggression of states such as Germany and Italy. For instance, one school of thought clearly believed that arms caused wars, which led to a massive cutback in militaries and military spending immediately after the First World War. Of equal importance was a belief, on the part of Britain and France, that there was little need for large armies. Instead, the English Channel in Britain's case and the Maginot Line for France made attack by an aggressor unlikely and war avoidable. In addition, many people in Britain and France felt that they would do whatever it took to avoid war in the future after the immense slaughter of the First World War. France had lost half of its men between the ages of 20–30 in the First World War. The social impact of this devastation was great and clearly did suggest a literal 'lost genera-tion.' Britain was equally unwilling to contemplate future wars as noted in 1933 by Oxford students who vowed to never take up arms for Britain. The idea of 'never again' was pervasive and persuasive.

Finally, hand in hand with the view of never again and the anti-war campaigns, there was a firmly held belief that aggression could be stopped by other means. The Treaty of Versailles had established the League of Nations as a forum for nations to discuss their differences. Unfortunately, the League failed when it came to stopping aggression as witnessed by its lack of response to Haile Selassie's powerful pleas for Ethiopia. While the League had little will to react, it was also ignored by the main aggressors when they resigned, Japan in 1933, Germany in 1934 and Italy in 1937. Furthermore, the 1928 Kellogg–Briand Pact clearly indicated thinking among post-First World War nations that laws could influence the behaviour of nations. Unfortunately, although many nations signed the Pact, there was no means of enforcing the sentiments of the pledge. Still others believed that negotiation was a means of avoid-ing all out war, which explains the euphoria that greeted Neville Chamberlain's return from Munich. Yet none of these methods or beliefs worked. As a last resort the European powers knew they had one method that, though it might not avoid war, could make the cost of war too great a price for some nations to pay; the old alliance system. However, the old system of alliances was thwarted when Stalin signed the peace pact with Hitler and the Soviet Union and Germany became allies. All of the meth-ods of avoiding war had failed. Once Britain and France realised that Hitler planned further aggression and could not be trusted they began to re-arm in earnest but it was a case of too little, too late. Meanwhile, on the other side of the Atlantic, the United States looked on.

Although the United States eventually responded to events in Europe and Asia, the response was limited and slow in coming. Throughout the 1930s, as these totalitarian governments seized power and then launched aggressive warfare, the United States followed a line of neutrality. To most Americans it was clear that America had not achieved its goals in the First World War. Attempts to apply Wilson's rhetoric had failed and the world was not safe for democracy and war had not ended. In fact, people were beginning to call into question the causes of the First World War. Investigations looked at the origins of the Great War and many people came to believe that the war had begun as a result of the wishes of arms merchants and bankers. A Gallup poll in 1937 recorded that 70 per cent of respondents thought the United States should have stayed out of World War I. Many nations owed the United States money from their war debts and they were not paying them back. The age-old prejudice against Europeans was also to play a part in American neutrality with many Americans believing that Europeans could not be trusted. As was the case in Western Europe, a large peace movement existed in the United States that lobbied and petitioned for US neutrality. The United States had stayed out of alliance systems since the Revolutionary War and meant to stick to that policy. Finally, the United States was in the throes of the worst depression in its history re-enforcing most Americans' belief that the United States had its own problems to deal with; the problems of Europe or Asia had very little to do with them.

Franklin D. Roosevelt found himself in similar circumstances as had Wilson 25 years earlier. Europe was heading for war and everyone in America, from Congressmen to the voters, seemed to be telling the President that they did not want to see the United States pulled into another European war. There was a powerful peace movement within the United States and the system of elections, both presidential and off-year, ensured that elected officials heard from voters frequently and the voters were clearly saying 'stay out' of this coming war. This attitude, as well as the perceived reasons behind United States' involvement in the First World War, clearly influenced the passage of a series of Neutrality Acts throughout the 1930s. Each act reflected American concerns about involvement in the First World War. The first Neutrality Act, passed in 1935, banned arm sales to nations at war and stated that travel on ships of warring nations occurred at a citizen's own risk. In 1936 the Act was amended to also ban loans. In 1937 Congress passed the Neutrality Act that instituted the policy of cash and carry whereby exporters needed to carry away goods on their own ships and pay cash when they bought anything in the United States. This last act would hopefully avoid problems with debt as well as leaving United States shipping free from any possible entanglement with belligerent ships. The hope was that no American merchant ships were going to be attacked and sunk, inadvertently bringing the United States into any European conflict. At the same time, Franklin Roosevelt began building up the United States military with an increase in military appropriations as early as 1938, although, by 1939 the United States had only the 16th largest army in the world consisting of 270,000 regular army troops. This was a level behind not only major powers such as Britain, France and Germany but also Yugoslavia, Turkey, Romania and Poland.

Then on 1 September 1939 Hitler ordered the invasion of Poland and on 3 September Britain and France declared war on Germany. Slowly, very slowly, attitudes began to change in the United States. By November of that year, there was a relaxation of the cash and carry policy as it applied to allied shipping by including the sale of arms, previously embargoed. In 1940 Roosevelt ran for an unprecedented third term in office. Although Roosevelt was a supporter of Britain he knew that he had to wrestle with public opinion and an 'isolationist' Congress. Hence, Roosevelt ran a very careful campaign in which he pledged, much as Wilson had in 1916, that no American boys would be fighting overseas. Roosevelt won re-election although the result might have been more doubtful if it had not been for the shadow of war. Still, Roosevelt slowly began to manoeuvre America into a position whereby the United States was anything but neutral in terms of the conflict in Europe.

In September 1940 Roosevelt negotiated a 'Destroyers for Bases' deal whereby Britain received 50 old United States Navy destroyers in return for the lease of bases in the western hemisphere. Roosevelt was able to convince the American public that this was a good deal and that it was a one-off exercise. He also managed to get Congress to pass the Selective Service Act in 1940. It was America's first peacetime draft but Roosevelt told the American people that it was necessary as a means of preparedness for the unexpected. Congress passed the Selective Service Act in September 1940, which allowed for the registration of men between the ages of 21 and 36 (later expanded to 18–65). Initially, balloting selected those who would serve for one year but later this expanded. Sixteen million men registered in the first month, with 600,000 taken into the military that year. In March 1941 the United States Congress approved Roosevelt's suggestion of Lend Lease in order to aid the allied war effort against German aggression. Again, Roosevelt worked to reassure the American people, this time by using the garden hose analogy. Roosevelt suggested that a person might not risk their life to put out a fire in their neighbour's house but they would surely lend him a hose to do it himself. As early as December 1940 Roosevelt proposed that while the United States would not fight in this war it could act as the arsenal for democracy by supplying forces opposed to Hitler.

Also in 1940, Japan signed a defensive pact with Germany and Italy and began its expansion into areas south of China. The United States finally responded to this aggression by initiating sanctions. At first the United States refused to sell scrap metal and petroleum to the Japanese although aviation fuel was not included in the sanctions until later. Undeterred, Japan continued to expand into Southeast Asia in July 1941 in search of oil and rubber. The United States responded to this act by freezing Japanese assets in America. While the Japanese had been continuing their expansion throughout Asia, things had been going extremely badly for Britain in the war in Europe. It was in this atmosphere, in August 1941, that Franklin Roosevelt met with Winston Churchill and the two formulated the Atlantic Charter. The Charter laid out a mutually agreed agenda for Britain and the United States with a vision of a post-war world that included a pledge of support for the four freedoms: freedom of speech and religion and freedom from want and fear. Very much like Wilson's Fourteen Points, the Atlantic Charter looked to a post-war world without war. With US support of Britain increasing, it looked as though America's so-called neutrality was evaporating, if it had ever existed. However, in September 1941, when an extension of the Selective Service Act came to a vote, Congress passed the bill by only one vote, illustrating the strength of isolationist feeling in Congress as late as 1941. Yet, by then the United States had decided to challenge Japan and demanded that the Japanese cease their invasion of Southeast Asia and withdraw from China leaving Japan with few options.

Then, on 7 December 1941, when the Japanese attack occurred at Pearl Harbor, the debate ended. The initial attack killed 2400 and sank eight US battleships. The Japanese also attacked other areas in quick succession including Wake Island, Guam and the Philippines. The war then became a true world war when the United States declared war on Japan on December 8 and the other parties, both Allied and Axis, exchanged declarations of war over the next week, with the notable exception of the Soviet Union and Japan.

HOW THE WAR WAS FOUGHT

For two years the war in Europe remained a European war. Once Hitler defeated minimal Polish resistance he divided the country with Stalin. Then, from September 1939 to May 1940, not much happened in Europe giving rise to terms such as the Phoney War, Bore War or Sitzkreig to describe the conflict. There was a sense that both sides were catching their breath and building up for the big push. In Spring 1940 the Germans went on the move and on 9 April they overran neutral Norway and Denmark. On 10 May Germany entered Belgium moving on swiftly to the Netherlands, Luxembourg and Northern France. Hitler's Blitzkrieg or Lightning War was no match for the small European countries and the German Army quickly circumvented the Maginot Line. From the end of May to 4 June a flotilla of boats evacuated over 330,000 British and allied soldiers, cut off in Northern France at Dunkirk. On 22 June 1940 France surrendered to Germany with the North enduring occupation and the South functioning under the collaborating Vichy government. It took Hitler just six weeks to solidify his control over Western Europe. Once it was clear that Hitler would win, Mussolini moved in to attack France, Greece and the British in North Africa.

At this point Hitler turned his attention to Great Britain. He began probing British air defences in July and then in mid August 1940 Germany initiated the Battle of Britain. Head of the Luftwaffe Hermann Goering tried to destroy the Royal Air Force (RAF) fighter command as a prelude to invasion. Although he came close, the RAF was able to hold off Goering's Luftwaffe with the help of radar. Germany lost 602 aircraft to Britain's 260 while the battle ensued. Eventually Germany switched tactics and, instead of going after fighter command, they began to bomb British cities in the hopes of breaking the people's morale. The Germans bombed London first and then other cities, switching to nighttime raids for maximum psychological effect.

By the end of 1940 France was out of the war and the resistance movement was not well established. While the Free French carried on outside the borders of their country, it was unclear who was in charge of these limited forces. Britain was holding out but just barely and its survival was in doubt. The Soviet Union, however, had been on the move. As well as moving into the eastern half of Poland, it had taken over the states of Latvia, Estonia, Lithuania and the eastern region of Rumania in the Balkans. Then, in June 1941, Hitler attacked the Soviet Union taking leader Joseph Stalin and others completely by surprise. By the end of 1941 the Nazi's were a long way into Russia, Leningrad was under siege, the German Army was 25 miles from Moscow and Stalingrad was within their sights. The future of Europe looked grim. The Germans were able to make these huge gains with minimal resistance and at small cost due to the way the war was fought.

From its very early stages the Second World War was clearly not going to be fought in the same way as the Great War. The Second World

War proved to be a war of movement rather than stalemate. By 1939 the tank and the airplane were no longer in their infancy and they added mobility to war. The German Army developed its tactic of Blitzkreig, or Lightning War, to a fine art. Tanks would accompany and protect advancing infantry, which allowed the Germans to make rapid forward movement, capturing everything in their path. Having led the way in air corps development in the 1930s, the Luftwaffe controlled the skies. The continued resistance of Great Britain and its island nation status meant that the second major technology of the Second World War was utilised to full effect, the long range bomber. In the Pacific the Japanese made swift advances as well. They too had shown the advantage of air power, albeit provided by aircraft carriers, through their devastating blow at Pearl Harbor. They continued to utilise the element of surprise by attacking, in rapid succession, a series of European and American held strongholds and strategic islands throughout the Pacific. The Japanese dominated and were able to make great gains at very little cost. They took Singapore in February 1942, the Philippines in April and May, with victories in Burma, Malaya and New Guinea as well. Eventually their sphere of domination extended from the Japanese home islands to the Gilbert Islands and included Thailand and Borneo. They appeared unstoppable.

The United States, having joined the fight and begun to work with Great Britain and the Soviet Union against Germany, Italy and Japan, could bring American wealth and abundance of resources to bear on the enemy. When the United States did go to war the Selective Service Act was modified to make the length of service 'for the duration'. The draft would eventually recruit 10 million men, mostly for service in the army. Another 6 million or so men and women would volunteer, usually joining the Army Air Corps, navy or marines. African Americans were included in the selective service requirements but also volunteered for military service. However, they entered into a highly segregated institution. The Marines and Army Air Corps refused to enlist African Americans and the navy only allowed them in the lower decks, particularly working in the mess. African Americans could serve in the army but only under rigidly segregated circumstances and were usually in non-combat units overseen by white officers. While the government did not draft women during the Second World War, it actively recruited them, especially with the establishment of various auxiliary branches of the armed forces. Congress established both the Women's Army Auxiliary Corps (WAAC) (later replaced by the Women's Army Corps (WAC)) and naval equivalent Women Accepted for Voluntary Emergency Service (WAVES). In total over 350,000 women saw military service of some sort, mostly in medical or administrative posts although a minority of women also worked as pilots, mechanics or drivers. Their function was to fill suitable roles that could then release men for combat.

However, while the allies now had the resources to win eventually, during the first six months of 1942 the outcome of the war was not at all clear. The spring of 1942 especially represented the dark days of the war for the allies. Hitler was extremely secure in early 1942 and the Japanese continued to gain territory in the Pacific. In North Africa, the only arena where British and German troops met, German Field Marshal Irwin Rommel dominated. He drove the British out of Libya taking Tobruk in June then moving on to El Alamein. In an area once dominated by the British and French empires, access to the Nile and the Suez Canal looked vulnerable. In addition, the Germans were dominating in the Atlantic, where they were sinking merchant shipping at an astronomical rate. An estimated 1000 allied ships had been sunk by the end of 1942. The tonnage lost was devastating for the United States but even more so for Great Britain. The Germans also advanced into Russia where the army of the Third Reich held on through the winter of 1941 and by the spring of 1942 looked ready to push further east. The allies worried that Russia could not survive another assault of equal force to that of the autumn and winter of 1941.

In the meetings that took place between the United States and Great Britain to discuss strategies, Roosevelt and his advisors were able to assure Churchill that the United States, though committed to the war in the Pacific, wanted to pursue a strategy of dealing with the European war first. The isolated nature of the Japanese strongholds meant that they could wait whereas the dire circumstances in Britain and the rest of Europe needed immediate attention. Hitler appeared to be the bigger menace in early 1942. As 1942 progressed, however, the first cracks in the axis advances appeared and the allied side began to record some gains.

In the Battle of the Atlantic the allies were learning how to counteract the German attacks. Newly developed patrol planes could fly further to protect shipping as it headed out to sea. The allies also learned to use convoying and counter measures more strategically. The situation began to ease by mid-1942 and, although losses were still remarkably high, they were declining. As the war continued and the United States went into full production, America was able to outproduce the sinkings. The allies also took advantage of radar and sonar to avoid and detect German

U-boats bolstered by the secret intelligence gathered through Enigma, the British machine that broke the German code. However, it was not until much later in the war that the German naval threat in the North Atlantic ceased.

The United States and Great Britain worked to formulate a strategy for the defeat of the Axis in Europe. The Americans wanted to launch an invasion in Western Europe to help drain German troops from the Soviet theatre of war. The Soviet Union had asked for the establishment of a second front for this very purpose. Great Britain, however, was more cautious perhaps unable to forget the slaughter on the Western Front during the First World War. Churchill and his advisors were able to persuade the Americans that the best place to launch a counteroffensive at this stage of the war was in North Africa. Most significantly, the allies did not have enough men and materiel to launch a full-scale invasion against a heavily armed and defended 'fortress Europe'. The North Africa invasion also offered the United States the opportunity to test its armed forces. It helped the allied cause when, in North Africa, Rommel's advance ran into problems as he reached the end of his supply and communication lines. At El Alamein in late October 1942 British Field Marshal Bernard Montgomery crushed Rommel's Army and broke through the lines on 4 November. Montgomery then proceeded to drive the Germans back to Tunisia. The allies quickly followed up on this triumph by launching the first invasion of occupied territory since the fall of France. On 8 November 1942 100,000 British and United States forces landed at Morocco and Algeria in Operation TORCH where Lieutenant General Dwight Eisenhower gained some valuable experience prior to being named overall allied commander in 1943 for the planned D-Day invasion of Normandy in 1944. By late 1942 Russia had held on against the German onslaught and Stalingrad and Leningrad remained in Soviet hands although the human toll was tremendous. The Russians died by the thousands in these sieges, but in 1943 they would begin to push the German's back.

The war in the Pacific took a different course. Rather than a land-based war with a clear battlefront, the conditions of the Pacific Theatre required different tactics. Battles in the Pacific involved the United States in an island hopping campaign in which commanders selected specific strategic Japanese-occupied islands for liberation while others were bypassed. The American Pacific campaign was two pronged with Admiral Chester Nimitz of the navy leading the Marine Corps up through the Solomon, Gilbert, Marshall and Mariana Islands while the army, under General Douglas MacArthur, attacked the Japanese through New Guinea, the Carolines and the Philippines. The overriding experience for troops in the Pacific revolved around the ferocity of the fighting and the fury of the battles, epitomized by legendary Japanese resistance.

While the allied position in the Pacific was as desperate as it was in Europe in early 1942, two major naval battles took place in May and June 1942. In the Coral Sea United States and Japanese forces met and Americans were able to halt the Japanese push towards Australia. At the Battle of Midway the United States and Japanese fleets converged including three aircraft carriers of the United States and four from the Japanese Navy. By the end of this battle the Japanese had lost all four while America had lost only one. These naval battles of the Second World War changed the face of war; from this point on aircraft carriers would determine the future of naval warfare.

In August 1942, just two months after the Battle of Midway, the United States launched its first amphibious assault in the Pacific at Guadalcanal in the Solomon Islands. By the end of the year American forces had secured the Guadalcanal area but only after a prolonged series of combat encounters and naval engagements. It took six months but it was, in the end, a US victory and the American people celebrated. By the end of 1942 Winston Churchill was able to give his now famous speech declaring that 'this is not the beginning of the end but the end of the beginning'.

Indeed, 1942 was the transition year. The tide not only turned in favour of the allies but the United States began to take more and more control of the overall allied command. The big question facing the allies in Europe for 1943 was where to go next. In March the last Italians and Germans in Tunisia had surrendered and the North African area was clearly in allied hands. Over a quarter of a million axis prisoners had been taken in the allied assault in North Africa. With this momentum behind them, the question of the second front took on some urgency. From the Soviet perspective a second front meant a second front in Western Europe. Stalin still needed Britain and the United States to attack Germany as soon as possible to take the pressure off the Russian people, but the issue of resources remained. In addition, Churchill, not only looking to the experience of the First World War but to the future of the British Empire in the Mediterranean, wanted to see the second front launched through Italy. Italy was indeed the weak link in the axis chain and Churchill reiterated this view by suggesting the allies would be better off attacking the 'soft underbelly' of Europe rather than the well-fortified coast of France.

The United States eventually agreed with Churchill's logic and on 10 July 1943 the allies launched an invasion of Sicily, securing the island by mid-August. Then, on 3 September, the allies launched another assault on mainland Italy, landing at Salerno. Mussolini, having stepped down in July, was no longer in charge and the Italian government surrendered to the allies, eventually joining the side of the allies on 8 September. However, German troops moved swiftly to occupy Italy and a long and extremely bloody fight up the Italian Peninsula ensued. By June 1944 the allies had reached Rome and taken only half of Italy from the German occupying forces. This laid the notion of Italy as a soft underbelly of Europe to rest.

While the ground war in North Africa and Italy raged in 1942 and 1943, the allies also took to the skies with their sustained and expanded bombing campaign of Germany. The Germans had been bombing Britain since 1940, but by 1943 the combined allied air forces were wreaking more destruction on Germany than Britain was receiving. The United States and United Kingdom shared responsibility for the bombing campaign with the Americans insisting on daylight, strategic bombing and the British utilising the night time, area bombing strategy. The year 1943 witnessed 1000 plane raids over Germany in which the Ruhr area, with its heavy industrial base, was the primary target. The effectiveness of the allied bombing campaign continues to be controversial. The British were well aware that bombing failed to break the morale of a determined people. In addition, the bombing did not stop or very much slow production in industry in part because strategic bombing did not exist or work. The bombing raids certainly did not weaken German resolve. Instead, the best news of 1943 came from the Eastern Front where the Russians continued pushing west, driving the Nazis back to Germany.

Meanwhile, major American operations in the Pacific occurred in November 1943 in the Gilbert Island chain. These battles came to symbolise all of the battles between US and Japanese forces. On the tiny island of Tarawa 5000 Japanese faced 18,000 US troops. Even though the Americans preceded the landing with a two-and-a-half hour bombardment, the Japanese, heavily dug in, managed to survive the battering. Of the initial landing force of 5000 US Marines, the Japanese hit approximately one-third on the beach. They made easy targets as they waded to shore through the coral reef. The battle raged from 6 to 22 November and by the end of the assault the United States had suffered 1000 dead and 2100 wounded while the Japanese military presence on the island had been virtually wiped out. The fierce Japanese resistance stayed in the minds of military strategists throughout the rest of the Pacific campaign. *Time* magazine published an article on the battle at Tarawa on 13 December 1943 and the American public were appalled at the sight of dead GIs. While numerous photographs of dead Japanese soldiers appeared throughout the article, the one photo showing dead US Marines, albeit face down and unidentifiable, outraged American sensibilities.

Finally, by 1944 in Europe, the allies were ready to launch the western offensive. With General Eisenhower in command, on 6 June 1944, the allies initiated Operation OVERLORD. In the early morning hours of D-Day allied troops landed on the beaches of the Normandy coast and paratroopers landed inland to secure towns and lines of communication. After the first uncertain 24 hours, the 150,000 strong allied force began to break out from the beaches and start the slow drive to push the Germans back to Berlin. The allied advance was relentless and each campaign yielded results, such as the liberation of Paris on 25 August, followed by sweeps across Belgium, the Netherlands and Norway. The push east was not without problems, however. In December 1944 the Germans launched their last major offensive in the Battle of the Bulge in the Ardennes where US troops were spread too thinly. Eventually the Americans were able to regroup and continue their assault on Germany but only after heavy losses. Still, the Germans continued to harass the British people with the use of the first rockets; the V1 launched in June 1944 and the V2 went into action in September that same year. The Soviet Red Army continued to push west, threatening Germany itself by the end of 1944. Meanwhile, the allies dominated the skies above the battlefield throughout the campaign on the Western Front with the noted fire bombing of Dresden taking place as late as February 1945.

By April 1945 the end of the war in Europe was in sight and major news stories toppled over one another. After over five-and-a-half years the end of the war was signalled by rapidly occurring events. Roosevelt, having won an unprecedented fourth term in office in November 1944, died on the 12th of April resulting in Harry Truman's inauguration as President. Allied and Russian troops met at the Elbe River on 27 April. Then, on the 30th, Hitler committed suicide. In early May German generals surrendered to Eisenhower and on 8 May 1945 the world was able to celebrate victory in Europe or VE-Day. However, the war in the Pacific looked set to continue for some time.

After the battle for Tarawa, the island campaigns did not get any easier. The war continued but the Americans made slow progress. In 1944 campaigns were launched in the Mariannas and Philippines. In June Saipan was taken and in July Americans attacked at Guam and Tinian. By October MacArthur was ready to return to the Philippines and Japanese naval power was virtually destroyed in the Battle of Leyte Gulf. Despite these reverses the Japanese continued to offer fierce resistance and their determination to persevere was evident in their introduction of the Kamikaze or 'divine wind' suicide pilots. These tactics not only inflicted damage on allied naval and army forces but also fed the growing legend of Japanese fanaticism and resistance.

In early 1945 the United States fought two major campaigns that would have a huge impact on military strategies with regard to the future assault of mainland Japan. From February to March a battle raged on the island of Iwo Jima. This battle produced the highest United States casualty rate of the war to date. The Japanese started the battle with a garrison of 23,000 and when the fighting was over the Americans had custody of 216 Japanese prisoners. The rest of the Japanese had either been killed or committed suicide. The United States sustained 26,000 casualties with 6000 killed, equating to a 25 per cent fatality rate. In April the three-month battle of Okinawa began and again the casualty rates of both sides were high. Over half a million men were involved on both sides. The Japanese lost 109,629 men killed and 7871 were taken prisoners. The United States lost 12,520 killed and 36,631 wounded. The high cost in men and materiel involved in taking these islands dominated discussions on the future invasion of mainland Japan. US strategists predicted 50 Okinawas should the allied invasion of mainland Japan proceed.

Historians and critics have hotly debated the events that followed the battle at Okinawa in July 1945 ever since. With the spectre of 50 Okinawas and with some casualty estimates for the planned invasion of mainland Japan as high as 1 million for the allies alone, Truman was faced with a series of momentous decisions. The Japanese were isolated on the main islands and the United States had launched a sustained and deadly bombing campaign against major cities. However, despite these efforts there was no suggestion of Japanese surrender. It looked as though the United States would have to lead an invasion force in late 1945. Then scientists in America working on the top-secret Manhattan Project presented Truman with a new weapon. They had tested the first atomic bomb on 16 July 1945 in New Mexico and relayed information on the success of the test to Truman while he attended the Potsdam Conference with Stalin and Churchill. Truman decided to use the bomb on mainland Japan in order to end the war quickly. On 6 August 1945

Colonel Paul Tibbets piloted his B-29 the *Enola Gay* from the small island of Tinian to the Japanese city of Hiroshima. On detonation, the bomb killed approximately 80,000 people, wounding another 80,000 and eventually inflicting radiation poisoning on thousands of others. There was no immediate sign from the Japanese regarding surrender so the second bomb was dropped on Nagasaki on 9 August with an estimated 40,000 killed. On 14 August Japan surrendered unconditionally and with this final victory the Second World War ended on VJ-Day, 2 September 1945.

By war's end there were 15 million Americans in uniform and another 1.5 million American civilians servicing the military. In total, a little over 290,000 Americans died fighting the Second World War. This was a small percentage of the total population and a small percentage when compared to the losses of other nations on either side of the conflict.

US HOME FRONT

The Second World War changed the United States both domestically and in terms of foreign policy. Immediately after the Japanese attack on Pearl Harbor, when FDR first declared war, the majority of Americans were behind the decision. Roosevelt understood, however, that the war would go on for years and the government would need to maintain public support over time. As had Wilson in the First World War, Roosevelt decided to use the power of the government to both control the flow of information and to sustain the support of the American people for the war effort. In the first step towards these goals FDR established the Office of Censorship in December 1941. At its peak this office employed over 14,000 people to read through and censor mail and control the flow of news. For example, the American people did not learn the full extent of the damage caused by the attack on Pearl Harbor until a year later. The Office of Censorship also controlled the release of photographs of the war to the public. In addition, the government established the Office of War Information (OWI) in 1942, which had certain parallels with the Committee on Public Information (CPI) of the First World War. The OWI began as an agency to help explain the war to the American people. It also, however, produced propaganda; most notably a series of films by Hollywood director Frank Capra titled 'Why We Fight', that demonised the enemy and played to an American patriotic spirit.

In other areas, problems arise when trying to make claims about the transformational nature of the Second World War on the United States home front. The 1930s was an unstable time in US history characterised by the Great Depression and the New Deal. Unfortunately, the Depression was by no means over when Pearl Harbor was bombed and the United States entered the war. Although the US economy was headed for recovery from the Depression by December 1941, when Roosevelt as Dr New Deal became Dr Win the War, it is clear that prosperity and the end of the Depression came about due of the war and not reform. It was the war that brought better economic times with the immediate post-war era becoming the most prosperous in United States history. However, the New Deal did contribute to America's wartime mobilisation. When the United States went to war the bureaucratic base of the New Deal provided an excellent foundation upon which to build. Roosevelt quickly established the War Resources Board and the Office of Production Management as ways in which to control mobilisation and the economy.

The government saw its role as more to do with keeping production organised rather than interfering directly in the economy. The administration established several agencies to oversee production in order to meet targets to outfit the military. These agencies echoed the proliferation of organisations witnessed during the New Deal. For example, FDR established the War Production Board (WPB) to oversee the organisation of production and control the distribution of resources for the manufacture of essential commodities. The War Manpower Commission (WMP) dealt with the important matter of guaranteeing sufficient workers in the right industries and locations to ensure continuous production while the National War Labor Board (NWLB) looked after issues of concern to the economy such as labour disputes and wage controls. Finally, the Office of Price Administration (OPA) looked to control inflation by the imposition of price controls. Eventually the Office of War Mobilization (OWM) oversaw all of these agencies. There was also no real armaments industry at the outbreak of the war. Instead, private contractors supplied necessary armaments and large vessels such as planes on a craft-shop basis. This situation swiftly changed once the United States went to war with a wide range of industrial manufacturers converting to the production of war materiel from tanks to uniforms. Manufacturers mass-produced ships and planes on a grand scale.

Labour benefited from this dramatic rise in production, most notably by the virtual end of unemployment. Conscription into military service helped to maintain the wartime labour shortage and eventually, approximately thirteen million Americans engaged in war-related work. While corporate profits rose so did general wage levels of workers especially notable in terms of their rise in standard of living. The government ensured stability by instituting a wartime wage and price freeze in 1942 in order to maintain the economy and ensure that no one segment would profit over another. The rush to work resulted in an increase in membership in labour unions. Organised labour thrived with union membership continuing to rise by 40 per cent to 15 million members by the end of the war. There were occasional strikes during the war but these were highly unpopular. As in the First World War, labour was generally supportive of the war with most labour leaders backing the general no-strike pledge given to FDR at the outbreak of war. There were a few exceptions, including the United Mine Workers (UMW), led by John L. Lewis, who went on strike several times in 1943. Rather than generate sympathy, these actions helped to encourage anti-labour legislation.

On 25 June 1943 Congress passed the Smith–Connally Anti-Strike Act which authorised the government to take over factories if strikes threatened to disrupt production of goods deemed to be necessary to the war effort. It was the invoking of this act that led to the railroads being run by the United States Army for a year from December 1943. For the most part, however, labour was happy with the wartime situation with most Americans enjoying economic benefits from United States entry into the war. For instance, with 15 million Americans in the armed forces, mainly men, and industries expanding to fill government contracts for munitions and material, there were many jobs available. The New Deal had played its part as well with unemployment reaching 9 million in 1940 but dropping to 3 million by the time war broke out. War mobilisation continued this trend. The surplus of employment opportunities meant that many previously hard hit segments of American society were now able to share in the benefits of a boom economy. Industries experienced a high turnover of employees as people went in search of the best jobs. Unlike Britain, the United States had no labour draft so people were free to move from one job to another. Hence, there was a huge migration of people all over the United States as they moved west and north in search of work in the war industries. On top of the 15 million Americans who left home and joined the armed services, approximately 15 million more Americans had moved by war's end, 4 million of these moves were long distance to new sections of the country. However, as the United States geared up to fight in this war against totalitarianism and aggression in the name of freedom, equality and democracy, and Americans moved about the country, some Americans noted the discrepancy between these wartime ideals and their own situation.

For many African Americans the prevailing attitudes towards race in the United States were fundamental to their decision to support the war and their hopes for post-war America. Blacks had been disappointed once already in the twentieth century when they participated in the First World War only to return to the United States and discover that their status had not changed despite their sacrifices to duty and honour. The Second World War brought a new challenge. At the outbreak of war the United States was a firmly racist and segregationist country. Even the Red Cross segregated blood according to the race of the donor. As the Second World War approached African American civil rights activists, most notably those working on the *Pittsburgh Courier*, claimed that blacks in the United States needed a double victory – both at home and abroad – and launched their 'Double V' campaign. Indeed, race relations were tested and pressed throughout the Second World War on both the battle and home fronts.

As early as 1941 A. Philip Randolph, President of the Brotherhood of Sleeping Car Porters, threatened to lead a march on Washington DC to protest the treatment of African Americans within the United States. Roosevelt, wanting to avoid both the march and the international publicity it would generate, moved to stop the march by addressing some of the issues raised by Randolph and his fellow activists. Roosevelt issued Executive Order 8802 on 25 June 1941 which banned racial discrimination in hiring in the national government and companies with war-related contracts, the fastest growing industries. The Executive Order also established the Fair Employment Practices Committee (FEPC) to oversee the treatment of African Americans in the work force and investigate complaints. The Order did not, however, address fundamental issues such as segregation in the armed forces and residential housing. In fact, the sheer demand for labour generated by the war production needs of the United States government and its allies did more to help African Americans than any official legislation. Any gains African Americans made in economic terms were due to the production demands of a wartime economy rather than a proactive move on the part of the government.

Sadly, many race problems continued unabated and even worsened during the war. War industries tended to be located in northern and western cities prompting, as was the case in the First World War, a large migration of African Americans out of the South. At the outbreak of the war 75 per cent of African Americans lived in the South. By war's end over 700,000 had migrated into wartime 'boom cities' creating problems of overcrowding in both housing and public facilities. In 1943 racial tensions finally exploded and there were incidents of racial violence in 47 cities in the United States. The worst event occurred in Detroit where 50,000 African Americans had arrived since 1940. On 20 June 1943 racial tensions exploded eventually encompassing 75 per cent of the city and requiring the services of 5000 army troops to quell. White gangs, estimated at 10,000 individuals, went on the rampage destroying property and beating African Americans. African Americans retaliated and when the riot ended there were 34 people dead, including 25 blacks and 9 whites, over 700 injured and millions of dollars of property damage incurred. Other incidents occurred in Harlem, Baltimore and Mobile. Although violence on this scale eventually ended, authorities never addressed the underlying problems and African Americans moving into cities continued to occupy overcrowded housing districts of inferior quality.

Yet the Second World War did provide the foundations for progress and change for African Americans. During the war years the membership of the National Association for the Advancement of Colored People (NAACP) increased dramatically from 50,000 in 1940 to 450,000 in 1946. In addition, the Congress of Racial Equality (CORE), established in 1942, worked to address issues of segregation and inequality holding a sit-in at a segregated Chicago restaurant in 1942. In 1943 the first African American was admitted to the American Bar Association and in 1944 the first black reporter attended Presidential press conferences. More importantly, as African Americans moved north they moved out of areas where they were disenfranchised into areas where they could vote. Once they could voice their political opinions the major political parties had to listen to their concerns. The Democratic coalition nurtured by Roosevelt depended, in part, on the African American vote. While the government did not address major issues of civil rights and desegregation during the war, African Americans made some gains and laid the foundations for future action, most notably with the increased membership of the NAACP, the establishment of the CORE and the demographic shift to the North.

By the end of the war the military had also increased access for African Americans. There were black combat troops in the army, some of whom served at the Battle of the Bulge. African Americans had moved out of the lower decks of the navy and there was an African American flying corps in the Army Air Force. At the same time African Americans serving overseas had experiences that broadened their understanding of what was possible in race relations and, at the same time, re-enforced their notion of what was wrong with America. But it was the wartime economy that did most to improve African Americans' situation. Over two million gained work in war industries and 200,000 found employment in the expanding federal government. African Americans also joined labour unions in unprecedented numbers reaching 1.25 million by the time the war had ended. Although still paid only a percentage of what white workers made, the average wage for African Americans increased fourfold by the end of the war.

Another group whose role in the work force also expanded during the war was women. Approximately 6.5 million women took jobs during the war, an increase of 57 per cent over pre-war levels resulting in 19 million women working for wages at some point during the war. Millions of other women did voluntary work throughout the war period including work with the Red Cross, United Service Organization (USO) or local charities. Before the outbreak of war 12 million women worked for wages, most of whom were confined to traditional job categories such as teaching, retail sales, clerical work and nursing or, in the case of many minority women, domestic service. Working women tended to be single, only 16 per cent of married women worked. By 1944 women made up 35 per cent of the work force in the United States and the biggest increase in female employment occurred among married women, which had risen to 26 per cent by 1944.

The overwhelming image of working women during the war remains that of Rosie the Riveter a woman working in the heavy war industries out of a patriotic sense of duty and obligation, who was doing a 'man's' job in order to ensure that a man was free to fight so America could win the war. Yet the reality and the myth were often at variance. There was no governmental labour draft of women during the war. Instead, the government relied on propaganda and persuasion to recruit women into the work force. Women responded to this call but, as some historians have suggested, not necessarily in large numbers. Only 2 million women in total worked in defence industries, which was equal to just 10 per cent of the total female work force. The others worked in offices, for the government, in service industries or in the professions. However, working women in a variety of jobs encountered similar problems. It was true that women had a higher rate of absenteeism than men but this was due to their dual roles as both wage earner and homemaker. It was difficult to balance outside work with the need to do the shopping, care for sick children and run the household. Childcare facilities were rarely available, with the notable exception of companies like the Kaiser Corporation, and were often available at the convenience of the employer or factory management rather than the female work force. Despite the numerous calls for childcare services the federal government did not step in, in any sustained or organised manner, to alleviate the burden this dual role placed on women. The War Manpower Commission created the Women's Advisory Committee in late 1942 to recommend policy but it never had much power or influence.

Two other issues were also to prove difficult to overcome for working women in wartime America. First, unions were not always happy to support the employment and organisation of female wage earners. Unsurprisingly, those unions that had been all male before the war were the most reluctant to include women during the war. Some men even went on strike when businesses hired women in order to make public their views. Some unions would support the renaming, reclassifying or dilution of jobs as a way of paying women less for their work. Just over 4 per cent of women workers during the Second World War held jobs that were classified by unions as skilled. However, some unions did accept and even recruit women, most notably the United Automobile Workers (UAW). Yet even these unions made different rules regarding classification of jobs or set up separate rankings of seniority of female employees. Equally important, while some unions did accept and recruit women they rarely addressed issues or concerns specific to women such as equal pay, the setting up of day care facilities or guaranteeing maternity leave.

In 1945, despite often doing the same job, women in manufacturing made less than their male counterparts. In fact, the gap between women and men's wages actually increased during the war. While it is true that both men and women were receiving much higher wages than ever before, women received approximately 55 per cent of what men made in 1945 compared to 1939 when they made 62 per cent. Some unions did join in the push for equal pay but usually only when the lower pay of women threatened to lower the pay scale for men doing the same job. Only the most liberal of the unions ever made a case for equality and, while the NWLB allowed employers to equalise pay in late 1942, it never prohibited the use of a pay differential based on gender. In addition, a Women's Equal Pay Act was introduced in Congress in 1945, having the backing of various groups and individuals, including the Women's Bureau, but a determined opposition defeated the act. Nonetheless, women did make gains in unionisation during the war. In 1941 approximately 800,000 women workers belonged to unions, equivalent to roughly 9 per cent of the unionised labour force. By 1944, 3 million women were union members, which equated to 22 per cent of overall union membership.

Some of the gains made by white women, in terms of employment, can be seen in the employment of women of colour. The first step up the employment ladder for black women occurred as white women abandoned their traditional jobs to go into defence or government work. Many African American women, especially in the South, moved into these vacancies. Approximately 20 per cent of black women previously classified as domestic servants fit this description. However, black women had to press harder to break into the more lucrative manufacturing jobs. While many manufacturers were reluctant to hire any women at the start of their expansion period, when labour shortages became acute they preferred to open their gates to white women rather than African American. Black women led protests and demonstrations against discriminatory hiring practices, most notably in Detroit, and gained the support of the UAW by 1943. The FEPC also moved to support the employment of African American women in the defence industry, although black women were often held back from the best-paid jobs in factories.

Estimates suggest that between 75 and 85 per cent of American women wanted to keep their jobs at the end of the war while fully 86 per cent of Americans believed that women should leave work and go back to the home. By 1945, as war production wound down, women began quitting their jobs or companies gradually laid them off. In fact, more women quit their jobs than were fired although those in the most highly paid positions were the most reluctant to quit. They also lost their jobs at a faster rate than male employees, especially in the heavy industries. Many women who left work were happy to do so for a range of reasons. Some agreed that returning veterans should have the first choice for jobs in the post-war economy. Others were anxious to return to homemaking, with the return of husbands and fiancés. At the end of the war the United States experienced a marriage and baby boom. All of this fed a national debate at the close of the war about whether or not women *should* work. In a survey by *Fortune* magazine in 1945 only 30 per cent of men and 40 per cent of women agreed they should.

Most scholarship about the impact of the Second World War on women suggests that there may have been a long-term gain for women because of their wartime work but that in the short term there was little change. In 1947 there were 2 million more women in the work force than there had been in 1940 although this number includes those who would naturally have gone into paid work anyway. Fully 90 per cent of black women who were working after the war had been in the work force in 1940 as well. The gains for women that did occur were slight. For example, the number of women in light manufacturing had increased somewhat. By 1947 the per cent of women in blue-collar work had decreased slightly and there were some increases in women's employment in white-collar jobs such as banking. African American women had moved, in some cases, into better-paid jobs. As a percentage of the work force, however, there had been only a small gain. Women were 26 per cent of the work force in 1940 and 28 per cent in 1947. Immediately after the war women were ahead of their pre-war pay levels as well, but only slightly. It must be remembered, however, that the Great Depression influenced pre-war figures.

What largely had not changed were attitudes towards women's place within society. As women had gone to work during the Second World War, into the male-dominated professions, they had faced sexual harassment and discrimination. They had faced pressure to remain feminine and attractive despite taking on new roles outside the home. Often the work they were asked to do in defence industries was compared to female occupations or skills in the home such as the often-repeated point that riveting or welding was comparable to sewing. All of this helped to re-enforce the notions of motherhood, femininity and a woman's role in raising a family. Hence, the country saw a rise in marriage rates and a lowering of the average age at time of marriage by the end of the war. In the years after the war, the number of women in the work force slowly rose but this was often due to rising expectations about the family income and rising costs of the post-war consumer society.

There were other indications that the war did not bring equality and freedom at home in America. Many observers, at the time and later, suggested there was a certain amount of social dislocation that reflected the negative impact of the war on American society. The great migration of labourers to the West and the North meant that there was an acute housing shortage that would not be relieved until many years after the war. The combination of military service and war work on the part of parents meant that many children spent the war years with less and less supervision. The media often commented on the new phenomenon of the 'latch key kid', children whose parents were so occupied with the war that they gave them keys to the front door and left them alone at home after school. A rise in juvenile delinquency rates during the war attests to the problems associated with decreased supervision. A Senate subcommittee on Education and Labor held hearings in 1943 on juvenile delinquency. Chroniclers of events could note that arrests of juveniles increased by 20 per cent in 1943 on average, although some localities had higher or lower figures. This statistic ran counter to the national, overall crime rate figure which had dropped during the war as the most obvious criminal 'type' (young, men) were drafted or enlisted into the military. The most frequent criminal acts perpetrated by young boys were vandalism and theft. For young girls the 'crime' tended to be sexual in nature, usually associated with promiscuous behaviour or prostitution, although these V-Girls were not professional prostitutes. Local authorities responded to this increase in anti-social behaviour by instituting curfews and trying to clamp down on unsupervised activities. Some neighbourhoods set up teen clubs to try to keep teenagers occupied in harmless pursuits such as dancing rather than breaking the law. Much of this pre-figured the teen culture that would emerge in the 1950s. Other social consequences of the war included the rise in marriage and divorce rates and an increase in the number of illegitimate births.

A few other social critics noted that, for a war being fought on the basis of ridding the world of evil, continued and pervasive racism marked the US home front. In June 1943 US sailors serving in Los Angeles attacked Mexican American youths in what came to be known as the Zoot Suit Riots. Southern California in general, and Los Angeles and San Diego in particular, had seen a tremendous population growth during the war. As with other cities, the influx of individuals included a wide range of ethnic and racial groups. These migrations were often cause for alarm to native-born white residents and reinforced long-established prejudices. There were also large populations of servicemen in these areas as government military bases in southern California expanded and military personnel multiplied. Prior to the riot there had been constant rumours of attacks on American servicemen. Minor conflicts between groups of servicemen and Hispanic males, known as Zoot Suiters because of their distinctive dress style, occurred occasionally. Then, in June 1943, a clash between these two groups escalated into a full-scale riot as thousands of sailors and white citizens attacked Hispanics throughout Los Angeles. At first the Military Police in the area were unmoved and stood by watching as the sailors and soldiers hounded the Mexican Americans. The riot went on for a full week and eventually city officials closed the city to men of the armed services and outlawed the wearing of the distinctive Zoot Suit.

This level of intolerance of groups seen as 'outsiders' was almost assured when Congress passed the Alien Registration Act of June 1940, otherwise known as the Smith Act. Under this act Congress required aliens to register with the government annually. In addition, the act strengthened the procedures necessary to deport undesirables. More ominously, and shadowing the repression of the First World War, this act made it illegal to advocate the violent overthrow of the US government or to organise any group with that aim. The Supreme Court upheld the act in *Dennis et al. v. United States* (1951), which followed the same general points of *Abrams v. United States* (1919), namely that freedom of speech could not be allowed if it had a 'bad tendency'. The Supreme Court later reversed this decision in 1957 but during the Second World War, as with the First, there was a decided government attack on the issue of freedom of speech.

Roosevelt claimed that he did not want to see the same level of repression or attack on civil liberties during the Second World War as the government had perpetrated during the First. However, he also felt there was a need to restrict the rights of groups and individuals with direct links to German or other enemy governments. He had enlisted the FBI in the 1930s to conduct domestic surveillance of potential enemies of the state and Congress established the Dies Committee in 1938 to investigate un-American activities in labour organisations and various federal projects. On the eve of the United States joining the war the government decided to re-enact the Espionage Act of the First World War and to institute the above-mentioned Smith Act. With both of these pieces of legislation the search was on for disloyal Americans. However, the Attorney General, Francis Biddle, did not support the essence of these acts and actively challenged them in court.

In *Hartzel v. United States* (1944) Elmer Hartzel was tried for distribution of pamphlets in 1940 that were anti-Semitic, anti-British and anti-Roosevelt. He appealed his conviction under the Espionage Act to the Supreme Court. This was the only case brought to the Supreme Court in the Second World War relating to the Espionage Act. The Court ruled, in a 5–4 decision, that the pamphlets themselves did not prove Hartzel tried to obstruct military recruitment or the military's operations. The ruling suggested that for any future prosecution the government would need to provide evidence beyond the written word of the defendant to prove they violated this act. In *Baumgartner v. United States*, decided on the same day, a case before the court involved a German American who had been denaturalised in 1942 for allegedly making statements suggesting he was still loyal to the German government and was clearly an admirer of the Nazi regime. However, the Supreme Court ruled in a unanimous decision that his statements in support of Germany did not mean that he had renounced his allegiance to the United States. Justice Felix Frankfurter's opinion clearly suggested that being a naturalised citizen of the United States did not mean that an individual had to give up their sense of affection for the land of their birth. Unlike the cases before the Court from the First World War I, these decisions worked against the government's attempts to repress freedom of speech of foreigners and naturalised citizens.

Although in these cases the Roosevelt administration managed to avoid some of the worst excesses of the Wilson era, FDR's government oversaw one of the largest single acts of wartime hysteria and prejudice that directly attacked civil liberties. Japanese had been immigrating to the United States since the late nineteenth century, settling mostly on the west coast. They initially took over many of the jobs previously done by the Chinese, once Congress excluded the Chinese from immigration in 1882. Eventually the Japanese began to move into areas of farming, especially in southern California. Although they prospered economically anti-Asian feelings in the late nineteenth and early twentieth centuries led the government to deny to Japanese immigrants the right to become American citizens. The first generation, or Issei, were victims of a sustained prejudice, which meant that no matter how successful they became they could never assimilate fully into American society. Furthermore, their children, the Nisei, who were American citizens by right of their birth in the United States, became victims of nativist sentiment as well. Although they were often highly educated, professional jobs were closed to them. Hence, Nisei tended to work in low paid jobs or on family farms. The Issei still managed to increase their share of production in the farming industry despite being denied the right to own land in some western states by law.

When war between the United States and Japan broke out in December 1941 there were many calls for something to be done about the Japanese American population on the west coast. Groups as diverse as the California Growers Association, military personnel and politicians called for the government to act against Japanese Americans before they could act against the country. Hence, on 19 February 1942 Roosevelt signed Executive Order 9066, which called for the evacuation of all persons of Japanese descent, both Issei as non-citizens and Nisei as citizens, to 10 relocation camps scattered throughout the interior western states. An estimated 120,000 persons were forcibly moved, at very short notice, and sent to these camps. Families were required to sell up quickly, which often meant they did not get the full value for their property. Estimates of the total amount of property value lost by the Japanese Americans run as high as 1 billion dollars.

More significant than lost property, however, was the violation of civil liberties that relocation signified. The government rounded up and interned Japanese Americans based on their race alone, not because they were guilty of any crime. There were never any charges brought against the Japanese Americans and no similar order targeted Italian Americans or German Americans. Even Earl Warren, then Attorney General for the State of California, worked to organise the evacuation. Although he would later go on to become one of the most liberal defenders of civil rights in the history of the United States Supreme Court as Chief Justice, in 1942 he was part of wartime hysteria. While there is no doubt that the evacuation took place in an atmosphere of fear and alarm occasioned by the Japanese surprise attack on Pearl Harbor, there is also no denying that this legitimate concern was exploited by those people who harboured anti-Japanese or anti-Asian feelings. Interestingly, the Japanese on Hawaii, where the surprise attack occurred, remained free. Had they been incarcerated, the whole economy of the island might have collapsed since Japanese Americans in Hawaii made a major contribution to the island's livelihood.

Some Japanese Americans challenged the constitutionality of their internment, as had victims of the civil liberties repression in the First World War. However, like those earlier cases, the Supreme Court ruled in favour of the government and against the victims. In 1943 the Supreme Court, in a case brought by Gordon Hirabayashi (*Hirabayashi v. United States*), ruled unanimously that the restrictions on Japanese American freedoms as stated in the demands for a curfew were constitutional despite the fact that Hirabayashi was an American citizen. In a second case, *Korematsu v. United States* (1944), the Supreme Court upheld the legality of the forced evacuation of United States citizens of Japanese ancestry. However, three justices dissented and declared the order unconstitutional. By this time, however, the government had begun to release some Japanese Americans from the camps. All of the Japanese Americans who experienced the conditions of the camps and the forced evacuation of their homes and neighbourhoods, felt the pain of the situation. In 1983 the US government admitted its mistake in instituting the policy of internment and in 1988 offered $20,000 compensation to each surviving victim of the incident. Despite the feelings of the Japanese Americans that they had been falsely accused and unlawfully interned, many Japanese American males volunteered for active military service. Some of these men formed the famous 442nd army unit, which served in Italy and became the most highly decorated unit in American history.

How then does one judge the impact of the war on the US home front? The Depression, massive unemployment and social dislocation ended with US involvement in the Second World War. More people were at work making a decent living. The level of employment and wages during the war directly led to the post-war economic boom of the late 1940s and the 1950s. The vast majority of Americans were far better off in 1945 than they had been in 1940. Added to this, there were some gains for some groups within American society. While African Americans still faced tremendous discrimination and segregation, the move north led to increased political participation; the war economy and demands meant that African Americans shared in the employment boom and participation in the war effort led many African Americans to believe in the need for change at home when the war was over, setting the stage for the post-war civil rights movement. For women the story was similar. They made tremendous economic gains during the war and in some cases after the war; for example, there were more married women in employment than there had been previously.

For the ex-servicemen as well there were post-war benefits. The US government passed a series of pieces of legislation to ensure benefits for veterans that became the Servicemen's Readjustment Act of 1944. These benefits were to be administered by the newly established Veterans' Administration and included grants for educational purposes either in higher education or for vocational training, loan guarantees for mortgages for home buyers and cash payments for servicemen who returned to the United States and could not immediately find work. Support for these provisions was widespread and included veterans' organisations such as the Veterans of Foreign Wars and the American Legion. Support was also forthcoming from those who were concerned that a large, demobilized military could cause havoc with the economy in terms of a return to the depression era level of unemployment. Between 1944 and 1949 over nine million veterans received $4 billion in benefits from this programme. The unemployment benefits helped avoid any problems of joblessness; the government guaranteed 3.5 million mortgages, which helped in the establishment of suburban areas throughout the United States, and over eight million returning veterans pursued further and higher education between 1945 and 1956. College enrolment increased by 70 per cent over pre-war levels and in 1947 half of the student body at American universities had been in the military. In total, 16 million veterans were eligible for benefits under this scheme and with the help of these benefits set up new homes and new businesses throughout post-war America.

THE CONSEQUENCES

As with the First World War, the Second World War produced far-reaching changes at home and abroad for the United States. The war in Europe ended on 8 May while the Pacific war continued until August. The terms of unconditional surrender, fashioned by the allies, led to the post-war occupation of Germany by the major allied powers, Great Britain, France, the Soviet Union and the United States. However, the United States alone controlled the occupation of Japan. With unconditional surrender and occupation came the move to prosecute and punish individuals who the allied governments considered responsible for starting the war as well as violating the moral standards laid out in the rules of war. Trials took place in the post-war years in Nuremberg and Tokyo, as well as in other locations in the Pacific Theatre of war where the Japanese occupiers had committed war crimes. However, the allies did not set out to prosecute all German and Japanese participants in the war. Instead, through programmes such as de-nazification in Germany, the allies worked to bring the citizens of the defeated countries back into a normal routine as quickly as possible.

The human impact of the war was tremendous. Although the United States lost relatively few of its citizens to the fighting, approximately 292,000, the total number of military and civilian dead in all theatres of war for all participants has been estimated as high as 50 million. As with the First World War, not all victims were soldiers. The most glaring example of this was the murder of approximately 6 million Jews, gypsies, homosexuals and disabled people by the Nazi leadership. The war also witnessed the fading of the line between soldier and civilian, home front and war front. Long-range bombers brought the war to the homes and work places of those not in uniform, on both sides of the conflict. Never again would civilian populations be able to feel safe from the hard hand of war. In the countries where the war had been fought the destruction of property was staggering. Virtually all of Europe and much of Asia would have to be rebuilt.

Unlike the post-First World War era, the United States did not retreat from its international role. As with the previous war the American home front was untouched and the United States' economy was clearly prosperous. However, rather than try to retreat into an isolationist position, the United States opted for working to direct the course of the post-war world. Whereas the United States had refused to join the League of Nations after the First World War, in the final year of the war the United

States was the driving force behind the establishment of the United Nations (UN), which was eventually located in New York. The establishment of the UN reflected a complete reversal of American attitudes towards entangling alliances; the United States not only acted as host of the UN it was its main financial backer.

The impact of the war on US foreign policy was also tremendous. In 1949 the United States signed the North Atlantic Treaty which, among other things, established the North Atlantic Treaty Organisation (NATO). Pledging to defend each other if attacked, NATO represented the first military alliance the United States had entered into since 1778. From the American point of view, no longer would the United States sit by and watch as other nations began conflicts then required Unites States intervention. The post-war division of the world into two opposing armed camps also reflected the impact of the war on US foreign policy. As early as 1946 Winston Churchill made his Iron Curtain speech in Fulton, Missouri, describing Europe as two opposing forces. The United States quickly moved from being a reluctant participant in the alliance system and wars of the early twentieth century into being at the centre of one side of the bi-polar alliance system and the first participant in the major wars of the second half of the twentieth century.

On the other hand, as the destruction of war occurred there were gains being made. For example, wars often prompt advances in medical care of the sick and wounded. The First World War had seen improvements in emergency medicine, the treatment of burns and the use of sulfa drugs for infections. The Second World War saw numerous medical advancing including improvements in plastic surgery techniques and the use of penicillin. If soldiers could get to the aid stations in the Second World War, then they stood a good chance of recovery. There were advances made technologically as well. While the atomic bomb was indicative of the destructive nature of human kind, the development of rocketry would go on to lead to many useful advances in satellite technology. Developments in sonar, radar and jet propulsion would work to shape the post-war world in ways never dreamed.

Of equal importance was the continued move to democracy that the war prompted in many regions. While the Soviet Union curtailed freedoms in its satellites, other areas of the world saw true democratic change. Germany and Japan, under the terms of occupation, laid the groundwork for democratically elected governments. Other areas of the world, previously dominated or ruled by the great powers began to exert their independence including India, the Philippines and Southeast Asia to name just three. The war and its aftermath planted the seeds for the eventual liberation of whole areas of the world in both Asia and Africa.

In military terms, throughout its history the United States had taken a brief role during times of war, fighting and then disbanding. After the First World War, and despite Wilson's proposal for a League of Nations, Americans rejected future US involvement in foreign affairs and quickly demobilised. Hence, in the years preceding the Second World War, there was no large standing army in the United States. The United States was anti-militarist for a number of reasons including a sense of security associated with the sheer isolation of the North American continent, a sense that a large standing army was a threat to democracy as outlined in the Declaration of Independence and the idea that a large standing army was not wise economically. All of this changed, however, in 1941 with the start of the Second World War for America. Never again would America's view of overseas wars return to that of pre-Second World War levels. The United States had been thrust upon the international stage and its preparedness, though occasionally hotly debated, would not fall to pre-war levels again.

Domestically as well, the war brought enormous change to the United States. As noted earlier, it is sometimes hard to calculate the extent of the influence of the Second World War on the United States because of the anomaly of the Great Depression which preceded it. Still, there were far-reaching changes linked to the war. The American economy boomed in the post-war period. Unlike the post-First World War boom, which was ephemeral, after the Second World War the American economy was at its most prosperous in history. While African Americans and women did not emerge from the war as equals to white middle- and upper-class men, echoing the post-First World War situation, they were continuing further along that road. Unions were strong and reflected the highly skilled work force in the United States and the government no longer shied from direct involvement in the economy. As with the First World War, big business was even bigger. The GI Bill insured that millions of Americans could participate in the prosperity by buying homes and setting up businesses.

Unfortunately, the war also reflected some of the same issues seen in the Great War. Japanese Americans, eventually released from internment camps, were left to re-build their lives without help or compensation. Although Japanese and Chinese immigrants could become citizens under the terms of the McCarren–Walter Act of 1952, racial prejudice had not disappeared. African Americans may have built a better foundation for launching the civil rights movement but they still faced a prolonged and uphill struggle. In addition, the concerns for loyalty brought about by war helped to feed a post-war conservative political climate. The bi-polar world was reflected in a need for conformity within the United States that would have long-range consequences for the issues of civil liberties.

4　The Korean War

THE INTERWAR PERIOD

A mere five years separated the close of the Second World War and the start of the Korean War. However, the five years between the two conflicts were incredibly eventful. By 1950, the Cold War had become pervasive both at home and abroad. In foreign policy terms the United States had asserted itself as the only major bulwark against communist expansion. In 1947 the Truman Doctrine and Marshall Plan confirmed the US commitment to keeping Europe free from communism. Then the United States signed the North Atlantic Treaty Organization (NATO) agreement in April 1949, the first military treaty since the American Revolution, confirming American willingness to go to war if necessary to protect democracy from communist challenges. The events of 1949, when the Chinese communists emerged victorious from their civil war and the Soviet Union detonated its first atomic bomb, seemed to confirm to the United States that communism was expansive and aggressive. The Berlin Blockade of 1948–1949 further suggested that the Soviet Union was interested in increasing its influence in a direct challenge to democracy. By 1950 old friends and allies, China and the Soviet Union had become enemies and old enemies, Japan and Germany, were now valued allies. In five short years the world had changed dramatically.

Domestically the United States also witnessed tremendous changes in those years. When Franklin Roosevelt died in April 1945 the mantle of the executive office passed to Harry S. Truman. He had only been Vice-President since January 1945 and had had very little time to settle into the office. While the burden of overseeing the end of the Second World War and the start of the peace fell on his shoulders, he quickly made his mark on the office of the President. He also quickly turned cold warrior and led his party to victory in a close election in 1948, beating the Republican nominee Thomas Dewey. In other domestic developments in the Truman years the returning veterans of the Second World War settled down to post-war circumstances. As noted earlier, the GI Bill of 1944 gave a wide range of benefits to millions of veterans. By 1950 ex-servicemen were integrated fully into the mainstream and the anticipated post-war slide back to depression had been avoided. The post-war economic boom was partly due to the fact that the economy had switched to the production of consumer goods relatively quickly, which heralded a record growth period. Automobile production skyrocketed, as did the manufacture of television sets and other consumer durables. Housing starts boomed as well and the ensuing suburban sprawl became ubiquitous.

Militarily the United States, though taking a lead in NATO and the United Nations (UN), had opted for rapid demobilisation after the Second World War. The size of the armed forces declined with many remaining troops stationed as occupying forces in both Japan and Germany. There was still a selective service in place until 1947 but Congress rejected Truman's suggestion of instituting a national service programme. Congress adopted a new draft law in 1948 requiring each draftee to give 21 months service, including training, with the power of selection still resting with local draft boards. The plan was to ensure that the post-war peacetime military would contain both volunteers and draftees. That same year Truman signed Executive Order 9981 calling for equality in the armed forces and creating the President's Committee on Equality of Treatment and Opportunity in the Armed Services leading to desegregation. Hence, the military, most especially the army, had been officially desegregated although it would take a war to implement it fully. By 1950 Harry Truman's priorities revolved around pushing through his Fair Deal reforms at home and focussing on security and economic recovery in Europe.

BEGINNINGS

The Korean Peninsula had been a target of imperialist desires of both the Japanese and the Russians for many years. It had been under Japanese rule since 1910 and, as a result, was part of the Japanese empire during the Second World War. During that war, the allied nations agreed that with the defeat of Japan, Korea would become an independent state. When the war was over, however, the Soviet Union occupied the northern part of Korea while the United States had troops in the South. From 1945 to 1948 the United States and the Soviet Union competed over influence and control in East Asia. Moscow wanted a friendly satellite nation on its border while the United States wanted to hold elections to unify North and South Korea. The Soviet Union rejected this proposal with the Korean Peninsula subsequently divided at the 38th parallel in 1945.

The South held elections in August 1948 and the newly established Republic of Korea elected Syngman Rhee as President; however, this supposedly democratic government became in fact a dictatorship. In September 1948 the Democratic People's Republic of Korea was formed in the North, headed by Premier Kim Il Sung, which was heavily influenced by and reliant on the Soviet Union. In late 1948 the Soviet occupation forces withdrew from North Korea leaving behind military advisors and a Soviet trained and equipped North Korean Army. The United States followed suit and withdrew from the South in June 1949, leaving just a small group of military advisors and a South Korean Army of small proportions because the United States was concerned that South Korea would start a war. The American withdrawal also reflected the fact that the United States' military budget was in the process of absorbing major reductions and few military or civilian advisors thought the Korean Peninsula was important strategically. Korea was not explicitly part of the United States sphere of interest, as outlined by Secretary of State Dean Acheson in a speech to the National Press Club in January 1950. It was only the idea of containment of communist expansion that worked to bring Korea into play in the concerns of the United States.

In the post-war era American policy makers saw the world as bi-polar with the ensuing Cold War becoming entrenched in the years 1946–1950. President Truman proclaimed that the United States should act as the leader of an international moral crusade against an evil and aggressive foe, meaning the Soviet Union. In a speech on 9 May 1950 Truman stated that 'communism denies freedom and liberty and human dignity. It denies God'. He called on the American people to 'demonstrate the moral and material superiority of the free world'. With the victory of the communists in China and the detonation of an atomic bomb by the Soviets in 1949, it appeared that the communist nations were making gains in the post-war world. Added to this were the Soviet Union's establishment of satellite states in the Baltic, as well as Poland, and the Berlin blockade of 1948. From the United States' perspective, these events gave evidence of an expansionist communist conspiracy. Truman, and the Democrats, were anxious to counter charges being levelled by their political enemies that they were soft on communism.

Yet America was not ready to go to war at this point to ensure a communist-free world. For example, National Security Council Report Number 68, developed in April 1950, sought to increase US military preparedness. In the wake of Soviet acquisition of nuclear weapons, the proposal called for an increase in annual defence spending from $13 to

$35 billion. The report predicted an atomic stalemate by 1954 and suggested that because of this the United States needed to invest in building up its conventional forces. As in previous eras, the United States' rapid demobilisation after the Second World War meant the army had reduced in size dramatically, especially in comparison to the Soviet Red Army. From a high of 12.4 million men in August 1945, the military now held 1.5 million or about one-sixth of its strength at the end of the war. NSC 68 also suggested that the United States needed to be ready to assist, anywhere in the world, where aggression threatened. Still, the United States saw Europe as the area of most importance while its view of Asia revolved around Japan. The government was due to reject the report when the Korean War broke out.

On 25 June 1950 (24 June in Washington DC) the Soviet sponsored regime in North Korea crossed the 38th parallel and invaded South Korea in an attempt to unify the country under communism. The western supported republic in the South offered weak resistance to this invasion. Although Truman was at home in Independence, Missouri when word reached him of the invasion, he, with his influential Secretary of State Acheson, reacted quickly. Truman pushed for a UN resolution from the Security Council calling for a ceasefire and immediate withdrawal of North Korean forces. The next day the UN passed a resolution condemning the attack and calling for withdrawal of North Korean forces back above the 38th parallel. The vote was unanimous (9–0) because the Soviet Union was boycotting the Security Council as protest against the UN refusal to recognise communist China and could not utilise its veto powers. A subsequent UN resolution on 27 June called for troops to be sent to help South Korea to 'repel the armed attack and to restore international peace and security' in the peninsula although the vote in this case was 7 to 1 with Yugoslavia abstaining. Truman initiated these resolutions without first consulting Congress or making a formal declaration of war; however, on 30 June the Senate passed a military assistance bill for Korea. On 7 July the UN passed another resolution, calling not only for military support to defend South Korea but also setting up a unified command under the leadership of the United States. The Joint Chiefs of Staff recommended that this job go to General Douglas MacArthur, who was currently in charge of the United States occupation forces in Japan.

President Truman was convinced that the Soviet Union incited the invasion as part of a worldwide offensive. Communism, in this scenario, was poised to become an aggressive ideology, much like National

Socialism under the Germans before the Second World War . This line of reasoning suggested that, since the Soviet Union had declared war on Japan so late during the Second World War, only days before the detonation of the second atomic bomb and the official surrender of the Japanese, the United States had been able to keep the Soviet Union out of the post-war occupation of Japan. Therefore, the Soviet Union was looking instead for influence in the North Pacific through Manchuria and Korea. In addition, this perspective of events meant that Truman was determined to stop the aggression as soon as possible rather than risk another appeasement fiasco, which many people believed had helped lead to the devastation of the Second World War .

On the battlefront, the invasion of the South by the North happened quickly. The North Koreans had begun a build up of forces along the border in the spring of 1950; however, observers were not alert to the possibility of invasion since there had been many invasion scares along the 38th parallel throughout the late 1940s. Then, on 25 June, the North invaded the South. The North Koreans expected a quick victory and gambled that the United States would not intervene. It appears that North Korea acted independently to reunify the country, certain of Soviet support if they did launch an invasion. The Soviet Union seems to have been taken by surprise although Moscow may well have known about the planned invasion but not been consulted on the timing of the event. Ultimately, if this move by the North Koreans proved successful, even without the active support of the Red Army, it would help to weaken US presence in the Far East to the benefit of both the Soviet Union and China.

Part of the confusion over who was behind the North Korean actions was due to the convictions of policy makers in Washington DC. Many people did not believe that North Korea was capable of deciding this action on its own. What was clear to the US government was that this invasion threatened the uneasy balance of power and the uneasy peace that had existed since 1945. In addition, the pre-Second World War policy of appeasement cast a long shadow in the post-war years. Would failure to stop aggression when it first began lead to another world war with more millions dead? As with most instances in war, decision makers often project situations from the last war on to the beginning of the next. Most senior officers and commanders at that time were veterans of the Second World War and used that war as the barometer of what needed to be done in Korea. Yet the circumstances were not at all similar – this was not total war, the full economy was not mobilised and, at this early stage, the goal was not unconditional surrender of the enemy. The circumstances and goals in the Korean War were less clear from the start than they had been at the outbreak of the Second World War. For one thing, it was altogether unclear who the enemy was exactly. In addition, the United States was not confronted with a clear foreign threat to its interests. Instead, it entered what was fundamentally a civil war between two sides of a recently divided country in the social context at home of a Cold War with any and all communists. American foreign policy decision makers believed, or expected, that this war on the Korean Peninsula was really about stopping the spread of communism by both the Soviets and the Chinese. Under these uncertain circumstances and conditions, the course of the ensuing war often took a different path than predicted back in Washington.

HOW THE WAR WAS FOUGHT

The North Korean invasion began at 4:30 a.m. 25 June and quickly pushed south in an amazingly successful military manoeuvre. On 26 June Truman approved American military operations below the 38th parallel but events moved rapidly. Between 25 and 30 June, as Truman met with numerous advisors and agreed to send troops to Korea, there was little chance to rally public support to the cause before taking action. On 30 June Truman met with congressional leaders to inform them of events and his decision to send US forces. In addition, 53 countries in the UN promised combat troops, with most of the support in men and materiel coming from Great Britain and the Commonwealth nations. In total, UN forces amounted to 19,000 troops working under US command. The Americans' initial response had been to use the air force and navy, both of which were approved for deployment as early as 26 June, but it was clear by the 30th that ground troops would be needed. MacArthur submitted the request for ground forces, which Truman approved on 30 June, and they were sent within 24 hours. Although the UN resolution allowed for a multinational move against the North Koreans, the subsequent action was very much an American-dominated affair. The United States and allied forces, led by General Douglas MacArthur, hero of the Philippine campaign of the Second World War , were first engaged to repel the North Korean attack below the 38th parallel. When the UN forces finally engaged in combat there was much doubt about the outcome.

The first American forces to see action in Korea were those transferred from MacArthur's Occupation Forces of Japan, consisting of mainly the

8th Army and 5th Air Force. There was a naval force of about 20 combat ships available. The problem with the troops was that they were serving in occupation duty and were not combat ready. They tended to be under trained and were not properly equipped for large-scale sustained warfare. Seoul fell to the North Koreans on 28/29 June when the United States had so far only committed air and naval forces. US ground forces were then deployed but were pushed south with the retreating South Koreans. Their continued retreat down the Korean Peninsula meant that there was little resistance offered to the invading North Korean Army. A term developed for the retreat – 'bug out fever', referring to the act of fleeing in the face of danger – and there was little that the UN command could do at this stage to rally resistance and improve morale. The problem was the lack of US/UN combat troops, less than 200,000, and that they were facing a determined and, at first, extremely successful army. By mid-September the American and allied forces, with the remaining South Korean troops, were holding off the North Koreans at the Pusan Perimeter. Not for the first or last time the United States clearly underestimated the strength and ability of enemy troops, in this case the North Korean People's Army (NKPA). What eventually worked to the advantage of the US was the general exhaustion of the North Koreans who, having pushed all the way south, had suffered many casualties.

The American and South Korean forces were eventually able to break out of North Korea's grip with a daring amphibious landing behind enemy lines at Inchon. This bold plan of MacArthur's entailed the landing of American and South Korean troops 150 miles behind North Korean forces. Launched on 15 September, the Inchon landing turned Korea into a two front war. The NKPA was cut off and by 23 September the allies broke out of Pusan. By 28 September they liberated Seoul and by 30 September the allied forces had reached the vicinity of the 38th parallel. In a mere 15 days the Americans and allies had managed to free the South from North Korean invasion forces. The rapid assault was stunning and, with what seems like certain inevitability, people were speaking of the war being over by Christmas.

If the United States had stuck to its original plan of stopping aggression the war would have indeed been over. But as with other wars, the reasons that leaders begin fighting are seldom the reasons that wars are continued. The Joint Chiefs of Staff argued to take the war north and Truman agreed. On 7 October the UN passed another resolution giving approval for action to liberate North Korea for the purpose of reunification. With the UN vote of 57 for, five against and seven abstaining, the United

States changed its wartime aims from liberation of the South and rein-
statement of the 38th parallel border to reunification of the peninsula
under South Korean rule. The plan was no longer to contain communism
in the Korean peninsula but rather to eradicate it. The United States and
the UN had widened the scope and aims of the war; they now wanted to
ensure stability throughout Korea. The goal was no longer a status quo
ante bellum but something much more aggressive.

The United States and UN based their decision to change the nature of
the Korean War on several factors. If the UN forces had stopped at the
38th parallel there was concern that the North Korean troops could
quickly regroup and continue to prove a threat to peace in the region. If
the UN troops stopped at the border there was no guarantee that the
North would not launch another attempt to take over the South. From this
point of view, the North and South needed to be unified in order to eliminate any future threat of a larger war. In addition, stopping at the
38th parallel would have given the military advantage back to the North.
To decision makers at the time a situation where the South was liberated
but the enemy was not defeated was unacceptable. Also, the UN forces
were clearly at an advantage in terms of material and morale. This push
into North Korea was justified at the time as a movement to restore international peace and security and there was little debate about this change
of goals. When UN troops crossed the 38th parallel on 8 October the war
broadened into a much larger conflict involving a push towards the Yalu
River and the boundary between Korea and the Manchurian province of
China. The rapid advance of the allied forces seemed to re-enforce the
notion that this would be an easy victory and that the UN forces would
be able to achieve their new war aims quickly.

The Chinese viewed the rapid advance of American and allied forces
with apprehension, voicing their worries about western aggression in the
region. Publicly the United States dismissed the threat of a Chinese entry
into the war although Truman did express some concern at his meeting
with MacArthur on Wake Island on 15 October. Despite the fact that the
Chinese Army was massing on the border with North Korea from 15 to
21 October, the United States military did not believe that China would
be drawn into the conflict. This proved to be a serious underestimation.
From the Chinese point of view the UN actions in Korea, led by the
United States, were quite clearly a threat to Asian security in general and
Chinese sovereignty in particular. The Chinese government warned of
potential consequences of aggressive behaviour on the part of the Allied
Powers but their warnings went unheeded.

As the UN forces crossed the 38th parallel in early October they made steady progress north against slowly decreasing resistance. On 19 October the North Korean capital Pyongyang fell.However, by then, and unbeknownst to the US/UN forces, a quarter million Chinese troops had moved south of the Yalu River. On 25 October North Korean troops, now including some Chinese volunteers, hit back. The fighting continued until 24 November, when MacArthur launched his big offensive that would, he predicted, 'for all practical purposes end the war' and bring the boys home for Christmas. However, the forces advancing toward the Yalu River and the Manchurian frontier were confronted on 25 November with a Chinese counteroffensive that shocked the Americans. Hundreds of thousands of Chinese troops, supported by Russian made jets, launched an attack against the UN forces. Over the next few weeks the communists proceeded to drive the allied forces south again in a long and costly retreat. By January 1951 the Chinese and North Korean forces had pushed south of the 38th parallel and retaken Seoul.

During the retreat, in December 1950, Truman met with British Prime Minister Clement Attlee and they agreed to change their war aims yet again by pursing a negotiated peace settlement. This reflected several important factors involved in the formulation of United States foreign policy in 1950. There was still very much a determination that America's top foreign policy priority was Europe. Policy advisers continued to express a great deal of concern over the Soviet Union and its threat to Europe, even in the midst of a war in Asia. This policy had the effect of putting limits on US involvement in Korea; unlike the situation during the world wars, unlimited resources to fight the war were not available. The US government made the decision not to increase troop strength, Opting instead, to replace troops as needed with the priority now of defending South Korea, not reunifying the peninsula.

While all of this change in policy and strategy was taking place at the executive level, at the front line MacArthur was displeased. By April 1951 the 8th Army had managed to push north back over the 38th parallel where they dug in and waited. MacArthur wanted more troops and the freedom to pursue the war into North Korea and beyond and he was willing to defy his own government if necessary. The ensuing controversy became one of the best-known episodes of the Korean War. Rather than bow to a civilian authority that advocated maintaining the UN position in the field and negotiating an end to the war, MacArthur went public with an ultimatum to the enemy commander. In addition, a congressman made public a letter, written by MacArthur, criticising the administration's policy in Korea. Ultimately General Douglas MacArthur's decision to pit himself against the President cost him his job. Truman's angry response was to relieve MacArthur of his command on 11 April 1951 and replace him with General Matthew Ridgway.

On the battlefield in late April the forces for the North had managed to push the US/UN troops back below the 38th parallel again. The United States counterattacked and took the Chinese by surprise, inflicting heavy casualties and making it back into North Korea by the end of May. By the middle of June the two sides faced each other just north of and along the length of the 38th parallel. The fluid nature of the Korean War battle-front, entailing rapid movement up and down the peninsula in the first year, works to disguise the nature of the battlefield itself. In combat terms the war reflected the short space of time between the end of the last war in 1945 and the start of this one, in the sense of an early reliance on tactics and strategies of the Second World War. However, some differences became more pronounced as the war progressed. Unlike the European theatre in the Second World War it was much more difficult to maintain a clear front in Korea. The terrain and extreme temperatures worked to increase the hardship the soldiers faced. Once the Chinese entered the war, the enemy often fought a war of attrition with massive charges and high casualty rates. And once the war had settled down to a stalemate along the border between the North and South, combat often entailed the tactic of taking small plots of land, usually hills or ridges, the result of which was hard fought gains of a limited nature.

The ebb and flow of battle also meant that civilians in both North and South Korea were caught up in the fighting. Those sympathetic to communist forces, and indeed those forces themselves wearing civilian clothes, were difficult for US/UN military personnel to identify. Unfortunately, like many wars before, the battlefront also produced its own share of atrocities like the killing of an unverified number of Korean civilians by US troops at No Gun Ri in July 1950. As with the Second World War , civilians could become targets, suggesting that modern wars continued to blur the boundaries between combatants and non-combatants, either accidentally or as deliberate strategy.

As for specific military branches, fighting a limited war had a direct impact on each. The navy never really faced a challenge and had control of the waters around the Korean Peninsula throughout the conflict. The most stunning achievement of the navy during the war was the amphibious landing at Inchon, which included the use of 230 ships transporting 70,000 soldiers. In addition, the navy contributed to evacuation procedures at various times throughout the war and aircraft carriers added their planes to the continuing air war. Equally, the air force dominated the skies above Korea. Mostly the air war from the US perspective included gaining supremacy of the air over the whole peninsula, a bombing campaign, air support of the ground troops and air transport. The most notable enemy action in the air involved the use of Russian MiG 15s with the Korean War producing the first jet-to-jet dog fights of the twentieth century with the US Air Force F-86 Sabres quickly countering the MiGs. With the American fighters dominating the air, the UN/US heavy bomber campaign took place in relative safety. Unlike the air war in the Second World War , there were only a few cities and industrial areas for the bombers to attack. Once these had been thoroughly hit the bombing campaigns turned to North Korean hydroelectric dams, irrigation dams, bridges and transport networks. However, daylight air campaigns were cancelled in 1951 due to heavy losses. Since the enemy was largely not an industrial country, the bombings had only a limited effect on Chinese and North Korean troop and materiel movements. Furthermore, the United States forbade fighters and bombers from venturing over Chinese territory, thus restricting the air war to Korean airspace. One innovation did make its debut in the Korean War. The helicopter, utilised for search and rescue missions as well as medical evacuation and reconnaissance, brought a new means of rapid transport to the battlefield. Despite or because of these battlefield conditions, the United States did not use nuclear or biological weapons; however, it did deploy napalm bombs on the Korean Peninsula. Often the fighting reflected the early decision to fight a limited war in terms of both means and goals.

As early as June 1951, one year into the war, it was clear that negotiations to end the war were not only a possibility but also a preferred course of action. On 10 July 1951 the North Korean and Chinese communists met with a UN delegation at Kaesong to discuss the armistice and by 26 July an agenda was agreed. A month earlier both sides had voiced their interest in a ceasefire; however, the talks were abandoned by the communists in August. In October both sides returned to the table in Panmunjom to resume the ceasefire talks. The major issues being discussed at the armistice talks entailed details of the location of the border between North and South Korea, how the truce could be overseen and assured, and the return of prisoners of war (POWs) from both sides. The fact that there was not a full and complete ceasefire while the negotiations continued added to the difficulty of reaching agreement. Skirmishes and battles occurred throughout the negotiating process. Fighting was especially heavy in the period August–October 1951 while the talks were on hold. By late 1951 the two sides were massed on either side of the front line and the military situation devolved into a stalemate with dug-in positions similar to the trench warfare of the First World War . The two enemies encountered each other in frequent, fierce attempts to gain a small advantage in the negotiations, at the cost of servicemen's lives.

One of the sticking points in the negotiated settlement was the repatriation of prisoners, which proved to be the hardest point to settle. There were two concerns regarding the issue of POWs. First, there was the issue of repatriation and second was the issue of the treatment of POWs by both sides. North Korean and communist prisoners had rioted in some of their South Korean prisons. On the other side there were accusations of brainwashing and mistreatment of US/UN prisoners by the communists. There were over 7000 US prisoners taken during the Korean War 2800 of whom died, mostly in the early stages of the war. There were approximately 125,000 North Korean and Chinese prisoners. From the UN perspective, the issue of prisoner exchange meant getting back all allied POWs while only returning those communist prisoners who volunteered to be repatriated to China or North Korea. Failure of both sides to come to an agreement on this issue prolonged the negotiations. Part of the reason the negotiations finally progressed was as a consequence of the presidential election of 1952. Truman chose not to run again and the Republicans nominated Dwight Eisenhower, the ex-general and the Second World War hero, to run against Democrat Adlai Stevenson. Eisenhower won the presidential contest, defeating Stevenson by 55 to 44 per cent of the popular vote. Eisenhower had used his authoritative standing during the campaign when the issue of Korea arose. He stated that, should he win the election, he would go to Korea to end the increasingly unpopular war. He fulfilled his pledge and visited Korea in November 1952, shortly after the election, although his presence there was mostly symbolic. In office, he continued the strategy of negotiating a settlement in Korea but he also decided to bring pressure to bear on the communists by increasing the bombing campaign against dams in the North and making it clear that he had not ruled out the use of nuclear weapons.

After Eisenhower's inauguration, by the spring of 1953, the negotiations reached the point where both sides agreed to exchange sick and wounded prisoners, which occurred in April 1953 at Panmunjom. The problem after this revolved around those prisoners who opted to remain in enemy hands rather than return to their national side. Both sides finally agreed that they would turn over any prisoners unwilling to be repatriated to a neutral commission for investigation and noted that after a waiting period any of those who refused to return home would be released and considered civilians. However, as the negotiations began to come together in June 1953, South Korean President Syngman Rhee, unhappy with a negotiated peace settlement, ordered the release of approximately 25,000 North Korean prisoners in order to disrupt the negotiations. Regardless, on 12 July 1953 both sides agreed terms and on 27 July the armistice itself was signed in Panmunjom. The negotiations had been going on for over two years and little territory or advantage had been gained by either side while soldiers died. In August both sides exchanged over 75,000 communist and 3500 American prisoners with approximately 22,000 communist and 359 UN troops refusing repatriation. Of the latter, 21 were Americans who opted to stay in Korea or China.

When war broke out the US armed forces numbered approximately 1.5 million in total. Since the 1948 draft law was in force, the government was able to call upon another 1.5 million men, between the ages of 18–25, as draftees. These men tended to enter into the ranks of the army while another 1.3 men who volunteered during the war often served in the navy or air force. During the Korean War period the military also included women. There were 22,000 on active duty when the war broke out with many serving as nurses. Unlike the Second World War, which saw men in uniform for the duration of the war, Korean War soldiers were able to rotate out of combat positions. A point system allowed soldiers to transfer from Korea with the accumulation of 36 points. These points were awarded for a variety of reasons and factors. In addition, soldiers' service was interrupted by the award of a period of rest and relaxation (R and R) behind the front, often in Japan, thus relieving men from the situation of continuous combat. Another contrast to the Second World War saw an increase in the percentage of draftees claiming conscientious objector (CO) status during the Korean War period. From 1950 to 1953, the government classified 1.5 per cent of those drafted for service, or approximately 28,000 men, as COs. The percentage of COs during the two world wars had been 0.15 per cent. Between 1951 and 1965 alternative, non-combat service was performed by an estimated 35,000 COs.

By the time the war was over 15 nations had been involved. The UN suffered 88,000 deaths, over 33,000 of which were American. There were over 100,000 American wounded. For Koreans, both North and

South, the toll of military dead, missing and wounded reached an estimated 2 million, about 1 million for each side, with another 1 million civilian casualties. The strategic outcome of the war was a return to status quo antebellum, a situation achieved in September 1950, three years before the war officially ended. Korea continued as a nation divided at the 38th parallel and China, the Soviet Union and North Korea rejected the proposal of popular elections as a means of settling the issue of re-unification. An uneasy truce was sustained at the demilitarised zone on the border with occasional small violations of territory occurring over the years. The west claimed that communist aggression had been contained and the communists and Asia claimed that it was the end of western imperialism in the east.

Many Asian countries branded the United States oppressive and exploitative. Seen with suspicion by the rest of Asia, the United States had shown itself capable of supporting a corrupt regime in order to maintain a front against communism. To the United States, the Korean War was a victory of sorts. The spread of communism was halted and the Korean War demonstrated that communism could and should be challenged whenever it was aggressive, as early as possible. The US sphere of influence expanded to include many areas of Asia previously seen as unimportant. The next American war would follow on from these developments.

US HOME FRONT

The American home front during the short period of the Korean War, 1950–1953, was dominated by the domestic struggle against communism. The war being fought on an Asian peninsula was only half of the story of confrontation with post-war communist expansion. Unlike earlier wars, the wartime targets of concern on the home front during this war depended less on racial factors or nationality and more on political affiliation. The Cold War phenomenon known as McCarthyism took its name from Senator Joseph McCarthy but actually predated his participation in the hunt for communists. There had been a previous Red Scare after the First World War in response to the Bolshevik Revolution. The Second Red Scare began as a response to post-Second World War tensions that developed between the United States and Stalinist controlled Soviet Union. However, the antecedents of the hunt for communist went as far back as the New Deal of Franklin Roosevelt when conservative forces attacked New Deal agencies, accusing them of being too liberal and anti-capitalist. In 1938, the same year the House of Representatives established the House Committee on Un-American Activities (HUAC), Congress passed the Hatch Act, which made Communist Party membership grounds for refusing employment in the federal government.

As noted in Chapter 3, the Smith Act of 1940 required aliens to register with the government and outlawed the teaching and advocating of the violent overthrowing of the US government. Already by 1950 several top officials of the Communist Party of the United States of America (CPUSA) had been convicted under this act and sent to prison. Later they appealed their convictions but these were upheld in the Supreme Court. Just two weeks after the Korean War began the appellate court suggested that there was a clear and present danger of these officers of the CPUSA working to overthrow the government. As noted earlier, in the Supreme Court case of *Dennis et al. v. United States* (1951) the court ruled by a vote of 6–2 that the Smith Act legitimately curbed the freedom of speech element of the First Amendment. In total, 126 members of the American Communist Party were indicted under the terms of the Smith Act with 93 convicted.

Anti-communist sentiment, with a long history in the United States, had been only temporarily suppressed during the Second World War while the United States was allied with the Soviet Union. By 1947 anti-communism was again on the march with many other acts that predated the appearance of Senator Joseph McCarthy. Executive Order 9835, issued by Truman in 1947, instituted what became known as the Loyalty Program requiring the investigation of all federal employees of the executive branch of the government. This 'act' called for a loyalty investigation of individuals based on a wide range of criteria including espionage or sabotage but also including actions serving the interests of another government or membership or affiliation with foreign or domestic organisations designated by the Attorney General as totalitarian, fascist, communist or subversive. This order was modified in 1951 to include the dismissal of any employee about whom there was reasonable doubt, rather than actual proof, of guilt. Much of the anti-communist rhetoric came from the top levels of the US government. Interestingly, perhaps because of the anti-communist push for conformity and support of all things American, the US government did not feel it necessary to establish propaganda organisations to rally support for the war. The Korean conflict did not see the rise of a Committee on Public Information (CPI) as in the First World War or an Office of War Information (OWI) as in the Second. It proved unnecessary to set up a separate agency to produce positive propaganda to rally support for US war efforts since there was already in place a well-established anti-foreign and anti-communist system.

It was during this period of a heightened loyalty and security scare that Senator Joseph McCarthy emerged to take advantage of anti-communist feelings and to whip the fear into hysteria. Having been elected to the Senate in 1946, Joseph McCarthy was searching for an issue to exploit to enhance his career and possibly provide a platform for his 1952 re-election campaign. He had decided to focus on the issue of communists in government when he delivered his famous speech on 9 February 1950 in Wheeling, West Virginia to the Ohio County Women's Republican Club. McCarthy claimed that there were 205 communists currently working in the State Department of the United States. His accusation generated considerable media attention and when, four months later, the Korean War broke out, McCarthy was well on the way to taking on the mantle of America's number one anti-communist. McCarthy had found his issue and after he won re-election he was catapulted onto the national scene by his presence on a series of Senate committee hearings into allegations of communists in government. Although McCarthy did not start the anti-communist hysteria, he came to symbolise an era when people's loyalty was an issue and the merest hint or whisper of disloyalty or suspicion could end careers and ruin lives. Over the next four years Senator McCarthy waged a domestic war on real and imagined communists within the United States.

At the same time that Joseph McCarthy was establishing his anti-communist credentials, the US Congress was broadening the legislative attack on communist influence in the United States. On 23 September 1950 Congress passed the Internal Security Act, otherwise known as the McCarran Act. This piece of legislation created a control board to investigate subversive activities and register members of the CPUSA. The act also outlawed the hiring of communists in the defence industry and barred anyone who had joined a totalitarian group from entering the United States. In addition, the Internal Security Act allowed for the detention of violators of the act and denied citizenship to people identified as suspect. Congress passed the act over the veto of Truman who described it as the biggest threat to First Amendment freedoms since the late eighteenth century. It was not until the 1960s that the act was successfully challenged in the Supreme Court. In fact the McCarran Act was further strengthened by the passage of the Communist Control Act in 1954. This act attempted to outlaw the CPUSA by denying it rights and re-enforced the restriction on the employment of communists in defence industries. Communist leadership of labour unions was also restricted further by amendment of the Subversive Activities Control Act of 1950. These anti-communist proceedings carried on regardless of the change of government after the 1952 election when Eisenhower became president. Despite the shift to a Republican in the White House and in control of the executive, Congress was reluctant to challenge trends of hunting for subversives until the Korean War had ended and McCarthy's influence had begun to wane.

Ironically, membership of the Communist Party dropped from around 80,000 in 1945 to an estimated 5000 by 1956, and most historians suggest that many of the few remaining members were actually FBI agents or informants. In total, between 1947 and 1956, an estimated 2700 people were dismissed from various branches of the government and armed forces for alleged communist links and another 12,000 had resigned. By 1953 an estimated 13.5 million employed people had gone through some sort of loyalty or security check, this equated to approximately 20 per cent of the work force in America.

The height of the anti-communist movement coincided with the outbreak and course of the Korean War. Probably nothing relates the Korean War to the McCarthy era anti-communist movement better than the case of Julius and Ethel Rosenberg. They were arrested in 1950, the year the Korean War began, for allegedly passing atomic bomb secrets to the Soviet Union in a 'conspiracy to commit wartime espionage' during the Second World War . They were charged with violation of the Espionage Act of 1917. After their conviction in 1951, they were executed in 1953, the year the Korean War ended. Significantly, the judge at their trial, Judge Irving Kaufman, noted the importance of US security against spies during the Cold War period by relating their alleged betrayal of the government to the ongoing Korean War. He suggested that their espionage had not only contributed directly to the outbreak of hostilities but had made them responsible for the casualties already suffered in that war. Under these circumstances very few people supported the right of an American to belong to the Communist Party. There had been, after all, other high profile spies who had confessed and/or been convicted including Klaus Fuchs and Alger Hiss.

But by 1954 some of the anti-communist hysteria began to ease. The man who had lent his name to the movement eventually overstepped his popular remit. In spring 1954 McCarthy accused the Secretary of the army of knowing about espionage within the army. The army retaliated by accusing McCarthy's aide Roy Cohn of seeking special privileged for a friend, David Shine, inducted into the army as a private. Congress decided to set up televised hearings to investigate these allegations and, although no charges were proven on either side, McCarthy's questionable tactics revealed he was a badgering prosecutor and often came across as a bully. The army–McCarthy hearings worked to repudiate the system of accusations used previously. McCarthy's reputation never recovered and the Senate voted to condemn him in December 1954. By that time the Korean War was over and the immediate concerns that had fed America's stance against communism had eased. With the Democrats retaking control of Congress in the November elections and the increasing criticism in the media against the pursuit of domestic enemies, 1954 marked a turning point in the anti-communist crusade.

Although anti-communism did not cease to exist with the debacle of the army–McCarthy hearings, it did begin to decline in its level of hysteria. For one thing, Eisenhower had begun to transform the movement by issuing Executive Order 10450 in April 1953, which made being a security risk rather than loyalty the reason for dismissal from government employment – a small but significant distinction. By 1957 the Supreme Court had also shifted its position when its stance on the Smith Act was modified in *Yates v. United States* where it declared that any defendant charged under the act had to have been proven to have committed overt acts rather than simply advocating them. Future court decisions restricted other pieces of legislation that had been passed at the height of hysteria such as the rulings in *Aptheker v. Secretary of State* (1964) and *Albertson v. Subversive Activities Control Board* (1965) which declared segments of the McCarran Act unconstitutional.

The result of the hysteria about communists in the United States had been a clear assault on the basic civil liberties of the American people. Freedom itself had been attacked – freedom of speech, freedom of thought, freedom of action. An American citizen's civil liberties are guaranteed under the Constitution of the United States, yet during the anti-communist scare of the early 1950s civil liberties were sacrificed to the idea of loyalty to the state. The anti-communist hysteria meant that there was very little in the way of compassion for or restraint towards anyone seen as different or suspicious. Although only a minority of US citizens were ever investigated or called before a committee, the atmosphere in which this took place tended to stifle debate among the majority. There was a call for consensus on some issues such as the fight against communism in terms of foreign policy, while there was a push for conformity in other areas on the domestic front. Yet the view of America in the 1950s as a static society, wracked by hysteria and devoid of individualism does not present a true picture. We now know that American society in the 1950s was nowhere near as conformist and conventional as some social commentators and historians have suggested.

A Gallup poll in the early 1950s asked Americans who they thought was a communist. The answers included atheists, employees of the UN and those who worked for world peace. The latter two categories quite clearly indicated that anyone who suggested that anti-communist concern was unfounded or that people should learn to get along in the world could be branded as an enemy of the state. Who was not a communist according to this poll?: home owners. Home ownership was clearly an indication of a belief in capitalism. The establishment of a post-Second World War domestic ideal was well underway by 1950 and the outbreak of the Korean War. The Second World War veterans contributed to a marriage boom and these post-war couples launched the much-discussed baby boom of the 1950s and 1960s. It is this picture of domestic life of a young couple with two to four children living in a recently constructed home in the suburbs that suffuses the image of the 1950s home front.

Young adults in the years after the Second World War did get married in increased numbers. The median age at marriage was lower by the 1950s and by 1953 one-third of brides were married by the age of 19. The birth rate also increased from under 20 births per 1000 women in 1940 to over 25 per 1000 in 1957. Couples began having three or four children, increasing family size, rather than having fewer children as might be expected with the increase in economic status of the family. Children were being born sooner in marriages and were spaced close together. The birth rate peaked in the mid 1950s and from 1946 to 1950 there was an average of 3.6 million births per year which continued to rise in the 1950s to 4 million in 1954 with a high of 4.3 million in 1957. The divorce rate also dropped during the period.

This increase in marriage and birth rates contributed further to the housing shortage in post-Second World War America. The construction of new homes had slowed or halted during the Depression and the Second World War; however, once the economy came off the wartime footing a housing boom began. The stereotype of the 1950s flight to the suburbs of young couples, moving into newly built homes holds true for those moving up the economic ladder. There were 13 million housing units built in the United States between 1948 and 1958. Two million homes were built in 1950 alone with an average of 1.5 million a year after that. Of the

13 million new homes built in this ten-year period, 11 million were located in the suburbs. The suburban population, estimated at over twenty million in 1950, had grown to 36 million by 1960. Equally relevant to the stereotype of 1950s America, the vast majority of these suburban dwellers were white, with fewer than 2 million non-whites participating in this shift to the outskirts of towns and cities. Probably less recognised as part of this demographic shift is the fact that some people were also moving into the cities. Inner city populations increased although not at the rate of the flight to the suburbs. Hence, the post-Second World War period and the 1950s saw a relocation of people across the United States. Consequently, the farm population dropped and certain regions within America witnessed an influx of new residents. California, for instance, became the fastest growing state in the 1950s.

But there were trends within 1950s America that did not necessarily conform to the stereotype of a model family with consensus views on American society. While Betty Friedan later reported in her 1963 book *The Feminine Mystique* that many women in these suburban homes did not feel fulfilled or happy, neither were women in 1950s America the stereotypical housewife and mother. By the 1950s over 16 million women worked outside the home and by 1955 this figure had risen to 22 million, which equated to one-third of the total work force. Of significance is the fact that by 1950 married women made up 50 percent of the female work force, with this percentage increasing every year. This also meant that more women with young children worked. While only 25 per cent of women with children between the ages of 6 and 17 were employed in 1948 this figure rose to 40 per cent by 1960. Admittedly, most were working part-time, but by 1960, three times as many women were working as in 1940.

Why were they working? What prompted this shift of more married women with children entering paid employment? For many it was the opportunity to contribute financially to the ever-increasing consumerism of the 1950s. The post-Second World War economic boom was in full swing by 1950 and, despite some economic fluctuations because of the Korean War, during the war years American spending on consumer goods and leisure activity increased. Polls suggested that 75 per cent of Americans saw themselves as middle class and belonging to the middle class entailed a level of consumerism to acquire the goods and trappings associated with that life. Television sales are only one example. By the 1950s over five million television sets were being sold each year. The new suburban houses needed to be fitted with the latest appliances and devices; hence, women went out to work to generate the extra income. Clearly, the stereotype of the suburban family of the 1950s was not the whole picture for white men and women in the era, and other segments of society, such as the large African American population, rarely fit the stereotype at all.

The African American population in the United States seemed to be facing huge changes to their circumstances, not least in terms of segregation. When Truman initiated his Executive Order 9981 in 1948, calling for desegregation of the military and equality of opportunity and treatment for African Americans in the armed forces, it seemed that at last the federal government was taking a lead in tackling racial discrimination in America. Unfortunately, the various branches of the military took it upon themselves to delay the implementation of this order, for instance the army continued to maintain its 10 per cent quota for African Americans. However, with the outbreak of the Korean War the desegregation of the military went forward. The previous organisation of African American troops into their own segregated units was eventually abandoned in both Korea and Europe by 1952 and the army's last all black unit was integrated by late 1954. While both training and service facilities were fully integrated, blacks were still underrepresented in the upper ranks although they constituted 12 per cent of army personnel.

As with African Americans during the Second World War, some gains were made on the home front as well during the Korean conflict. While these gains were limited in many ways they did lay the groundwork for future expansion of civil rights in the post-war period. In some areas local governments were spending more money on schooling and there was a slow increase in the number of registered African American voters. By 1952 there were 1.2 million blacks registered to vote. But for most African Americans the system of discrimination and segregation known as Jim Crow was firmly in place. The biggest changes in black Americans' lives during the 1950s came about because of the booming economy. The migration to urban centres continued, including in the South. The decline of agriculture transformed the lives of many southern blacks and increased the move to cities. While some manufacturing jobs were still out of reach of many African Americans in the South, blacks could get unskilled and low paid jobs and take advantage of the anonymity that the urban environment provided. They still faced segregation and racist authorities but they were able to live closer to black controlled establishments such as local businesses, newspapers and churches.

By 1950 African Americans were earning a median of 50 per cent of white wages, up from 41 percent in 1939. The black middle class grew, with African Americans' income rising 80 per cent faster than white income between 1937 and 1952. There were more African Americans in white-collar employment and an increase in the number of high school graduates, as well as an increase in the number of blacks going on to college. Yet a higher percentage of blacks than whites suffered unemployment, 6.9 per cent compared to 4 per cent from 1947–1952, up to 9.3 per cent by 1954. All of this took place in the face of racial discrimination in everything from jobs to housing to education. Clearly there was still much to be done regarding civil rights in the Korean War era for the African American citizens of the United States. However, the rise of an effective African American civil rights movement in the early 1950s had to play out in the shadow of the Cold War.

The anti-communist crusade did not bypass the black population. In fact, there had been a long heritage of accusing civil rights groups of being influenced or even controlled by communists and by the late 1940s, as noted earlier, the longstanding anti-communist views of much of America had crystallised into the Red Scare. The Cold War atmosphere of McCarthyism resulted in many liberal or left leaning organisations being accused of communist influences. Issues of race relations were especially tricky. It was argued by many that outside enemies, such as the Soviet Union, could seize upon the treatment of African Americans and other minorities to illustrate that the United States did not really uphold the principles of democracy and freedom at home. American attitudes towards African Americans was even criticised in the United Nations. On the other hand, a much larger group countered this argument by claiming that groups and organisations calling for reform or indeed even a shift in policy towards minority groups in the United States was an indication of the spread of communist influence. HUAC launched an investigation in 1949 titled Hearings Regarding Communist Infiltration of Minority Groups, which heard from various African Americans, including Jackie Robinson, who denounced the communist party. As it happened, there were never many African Americans in the Communist Party; they comprised an estimated 7.2 per cent of the party membership in 1931, rising to a high of 14 per cent by 1946. Their numbers declined after this although the accusations against blacks continued. Still, other witnesses appeared before HUAC who supported the role of the party in the civil rights movement. The hearings ended in 1950 but the hunt for communists in the civil rights movement did not and it was in this anti-communist atmosphere that African Americans hoping for change or progress in civil rights found themselves.

In this conservative atmosphere it was unlikely that the Congress of the United States was going to launch legislation that would transform the lives of African Americans. In the late 1940s some headway was made in civil rights but systematic discrimination was not attacked directly. For instance, the issue of civil rights for African Americans came up during the presidential race of 1948. Differences within the Democratic Party ultimately led to a split, which resulted in the establishment of the Dixiecrats or States' Rights Party on the right and the Progressive Party on the left. Strom Thurmond, presidential candidate for the Dixiecrats, even campaigned against what he called 'Black Bolshevism'. The middle ground of the party, represented by Harry S. Truman, won for the Democrats, partly by receiving two-thirds of the black vote. The year 1948 also witnessed the establishment of executive orders barring discrimination in federal employment (EO 9980) and establishing a committee to guarantee equal opportunities in the military (EO 9981). These were small, often symbolic victories for African Americans while the real issue of overthrowing racial discrimination was not addressed directly. Still, the foundations for a campaign for civil rights were laid in the 1940s. Eventually, in the early Cold War era, a push for civil rights did come from the government, in the executive and judicial branches. However, these advances were spurred on by the work of African American organisations and individuals.

The largest and best-known civil rights organisation at the time was the National Association for the Advancement of Colored People (NAACP). After the surge in membership during and shortly after the Second World War, the organisation had to confront the anti-communist mood of the Cold War era. The late 1940s and early 1950s was not the first time the NAACP had to address the issue of communism. Most notably the influence of communists had taken front-page headlines during the trial of the Scottsboro boys in 1931 when the CPUSA had stepped in to mount their defence in the appeals process. In this particular case the NAACP initially spoke out against the CPUSA's defence of the convicted young black men but eventually agreed to a reluctant alliance with the communists in the appeals process. Part of the attitude of the NAACP towards communists came from the head of the organisation. Walter White had been elected executive secretary in 1931. He was personally responsible for helping to turn the NAACP away from any leftist or liberal leanings. White went so far as to denounce W. E. B. Du Bois, one of the founding fathers of the NAACP, as too radical and had feuded with Du Bois in the 1930s. When the anti-communist hysteria arose in the Cold War period White supported the search for communists in government and even went so far as to have the NAACP declare at its 1950 convention in Boston that it was officially anti-communist. In 1950–1951 Du Bois, along with another prominent black Paul Robeson, was accused of being communist. The government denied passports to both men at one stage and W. E. B. Du Bois was even jailed briefly at the age of 82. Although White's influence was challenged in 1950 when the NAACP Board put Roy Wilkins in charge of internal affairs, the organisation proceeded throughout the era to reflect its basic middle-class, conservative tendencies in pursuit of civil rights. However, the one area where the NAACP did go forward in challenging segregation, racism and Jim Crow was through the arena it had traditionally used – the court system.

Civil rights litigation began in the Korean War era with a series of decisions about segregation in 1950 and culminated in 1954 with the *Brown v. Board of Education* decision that helped to launch the modern civil rights movement. The NAACP had managed to bring numerous civil rights cases to the Supreme Court throughout the 1940s and three of these cases led to a series of decisions that gave hope to the black community that they could attack the racist and segregationist system of Jim Crow. The Supreme Court announced decisions on these three cases on 5 June 1950, just weeks before the outbreak of the Korean War. The Supreme Court and the NAACP were both walking a fine line. The NAACP did not want to challenge directly the *Plessy v. Ferguson* (1896) decision of the court, which had set up the formula of separate but equal, for fear that the court would rule against them. On the other hand, the Supreme Court did not want to overrule the *Plessy* decision if it could avoid it. So in June 1950 a unanimous court ruled on issues of segregation in a brief and limited way. In *Sweatt v. Painter* the court ruled that a separate law school, set up hastily by the University of Texas, did not provide an education equal to that provided to white students at the long established law school. In *McLaurin v. Oklahoma State Regents* the court ruled that the seating of a black graduate student in a segregated section of classrooms, the cafeteria and the library at Oklahoma State University denied the African American student an opportunity to enhance his education by interacting with other students. Finally, in *Henderson v. the United States* the court ruled that setting up a separate, segregated and curtained off area of the dining car by a railway company went against the Interstate Commerce Act because it denied the traveller a seat that he would have been allowed to occupy had he been white, which was clearly a case of discrimination.

While the Supreme Court had tried to limit these decisions to the specific cases in point, the NAACP took heart from the decisions and decided to switch tactics from showing that separate facilities were rarely if ever equal, to attacking the notion of separate but equal directly and proclaiming that by its nature separate was unequal. They decided to do this by bringing together several suits under an umbrella title of *Brown v. Board of Education of Topeka Kansas*. This would be their attempt to overthrow *Plessy* directly. The case was filed in 1952 and the Supreme Court rendered their unanimous decision on 17 May 1954, ruling that, indeed, separate but equal did not exist. The seeds of this landmark decision, often seen as the first major victory against the Jim Crow system, which eventually led to its demise, were sown during the late 1940s and early 1950s.

Despite achieving these successes, the NAACP had changed from its high point during the Second World War . By 1950 the organisation was smaller and somewhat weaker than it had been and was also even more conservative than it had been at the time of its foundation. Other civil rights organisations also fell under the spell of anti-communism. The CORE, a biracial organisation established during the Second World War, struggled through the 1950s. CORE had attempted, in the years since its foundation, to bring about change for African Americans in the United States. It had attacked segregation in public and private facilities, the use of housing covenants and discrimination in education. But CORE was a loose confederation of local affiliates and hence lacked the ability to launch national campaigns effectively. From the high point in 1947 when CORE ran its Journey of Reconciliation to test the Supreme Court ruling against segregation on interstate transport, CORE had slowly declined. Like the NAACP it too pronounced itself anti-communist, proclaiming in 1952 that it was a civil rights not a civil liberties group. However, like the NAACP, CORE was unable to completely throw off the taint of communist influence. It was not strong enough at a national level to maintain a concerted attack on racial discrimination. The number of chapters declined in the early 1950s as part of the anti-reform spirit of the McCarthy era.

Nevertheless, during the early 1950s some progress was made in the attack upon segregation in areas outside the courtroom. Washington DC was desegregated, as Eisenhower had pledged in the 1952 campaign, partly because the president was concerned about the perception of

America that visitors to the Capitol gained from seeing Jim Crow at work. The number of lynchings decreased, although no anti-lynching bill was passed. More local areas began to desegregate both public and private facilities such as lunch counters, restaurants and libraries. However, these advances tended to be in the northern or border states. The Deep South was least affected. But by the end of the Korean War more African Americans were attending public universities at both the graduate and post-graduate level. There were also responses to the issue of desegregation at the primary and secondary school level with some attempts to increase spending on African American schools, although in the South it was often the case of local school boards trying to improve separate facilities in order to avoid desegregation being forced upon them by the federal government.

Despite the limited nature of these few concessions to African American civil rights, a backlash movement developed. For instance, many acts of violence continued to take place. In 1951 a bomb exploded in Florida killing Harry Moore and his wife. Moore had been running a successful voter registration drive and was active in the state NAACP. When the *Brown* decision was announced in 1954 many whites throughout the South and elsewhere decried the decision and vowed to fight its implementation. And, despite Truman's initial 'support' of civil rights and the eventual desegregation of the military, by 1950 attempts to make the Fair Employment Practices Committee (established on the eve of the Second World War) permanent had failed. What some historians consider being the start of the modern civil rights movement, the *Brown* decision and the Montgomery Bus Boycott, would not take place until after the Korean War. The war itself seemed to have less of an impact on the home front for progress in the struggle for equality of African Americans than previous wars. There were also other areas of the home front that were not heavily affected by the war.

Unlike the Second World War, Korea was not a total war, meaning the government attempted to mobilise for war on a limited basis. In addition, organised labour was not willing to give up its demands for higher wages and better conditions as part of a patriotic act. Truman had created the Office of Defense Mobilization in late 1950 when he also declared that the war in Korea had created a national emergency. This declaration sparked some panic buying and led to a rise in inflation. This in turn prompted Truman, in January 1951, to institute a wage and price freeze. Meanwhile, labour had been refusing to join in mobilisation talks that were being held by the federal government for fear that the war emergency would result in a cut back of their wages and curtail any future demands. When labour organisations finally did join the talks, in May 1951, it did not help to ease the concerns of the labour movement. Subsequently, a series of labour strikes throughout 1951 hit many major industries such as copper and aluminium. This led ultimately to the steel crisis of December that year. Eventually, there were an estimated 3.5 million workers on strike in numerous sectors by the start of 1952.

Truman tried to engage in the issue of mobilisation, most directly when it came to the steel strike in April 1952. Steel workers announced that a strike would begin on April 9 and Truman, declaring that steel production was vital to the war effort and mobilisation, announced that the federal government would seize the steel mills at midnight on the April 8. The government ran the mills for two months until the Supreme Court, on 2 June 1952, declared the seizure to be unconstitutional in its decision in *Youngstown Sheet and Tube Co. v. Sawyer*. A 53-day strike of all 600,000 steel workers followed the Supreme Court decision. Other industries, especially those industries that were consumers of steel such as the railroads and manufacturing sector, subsequently witnessed problems. The knock-on effect led to layoffs and ultimately the intervention of Truman again only this time to try to negotiate a settlement. This eventually took place in July and things shortly began to return to normal in the steel and related industries.

The use of strikes by unions and workers did not, however, stop here. For example, in September 1952 the United Mine Workers (UMW) under John L. Lewis instituted a three-month strike which, once again, eventually led to Truman's intervention in the negotiations. This time Truman backed the miners in their demands for an increase in wages that went against the wage/price controls put in place by his government. The Republicans had already realised the political nature of wage/price controls and had come out against them in the party platform in 1952. Although there was poll information suggesting that 61 per cent of the public supported economic controls, Eisenhower announced the end of this government policy early in his tenure in office, in February 1953.

With governmental steps to control both the economy and mobilisation, and the labour movement's decision not to succumb to wartime patriotic impulses to restrict demands, the American economy was transformed during the Korean War years. The production of military goods had increased tremendously and, when the war ended, this production did not return to pre-war levels. The military-industrial complex resulted and became an integral part of the US economy. By the end of the war incomes were up and the economy was on a much stronger footing than it had been previously. New industries appeared and boomed in areas of the United States outside the traditional industrial centres of the Northeast. The west coast and the South gained new industries, often dependent on the defence industry.

The returning veterans of the Korean War faced a very different America than had the veterans of the two world wars. The nature of the limited war meant that, proportionate to the population, a far smaller percentage of draft age men had been involved in the war effort. Approximately six million men served in the military through the course of the Korean War, not all of whom served in Korea itself. However, as the war was not universally popular, and the government opted to fight it on a limited basis, the veterans were often overlooked upon their return. The civilian population had been able to go about their business without sacrificing anything to the war effort. The war itself was quickly 'forgotten' by the wider population. Although the US government did institute a Veterans Readjustment Assistance Act in 1952, which gave some benefits to veterans along the lines of the GI Bill after the Second World War, these benefits were not as broad. There was a sense that, after the peace negotiations ended, Americans wanted to forget the war and get on with the ideal of a peacetime existence. It was easier to ignore the veterans and the war itself than perhaps it was to confront directly the issues it raised. Part of the way to do that was to focus on the domestic agenda rather than issues of foreign policy.

What had become clear by the end of the Korean War was that the United States had become a much more conservative country than it had been in the 1930s and, even to some extent, the 1940s. Dwight Eisenhower's election marked the beginning of eight years of Republican rule in the White House. And while the oppression of McCarthyism had eased, the generally conservative nature of the era remained. Yet the Korean War period had seen the development of liberal ideas by some groups within America such as women and African Americans. However the seeds that were sown in the 1950s did not grow into large-scale social movements until the 1960s.

THE CONSEQUENCES

At the end of the Korean War, with a new president in the White House, it was time to reassess the future of US preparedness. The National

Security Council produced report NSC 162/3 for the Eisenhower administration. This proposal launched plans for the future defence of the
United States, later called the New Look defence. It called for a scaling
down of the size of the armed forces from those proposed in NSC 68 and,
instead, suggested it would be better to rely on more powerful weapons
in what became known as the concept of 'more bang for the buck' or
massive retaliation. This policy limited military spending and reduced
the size of the armed forces while incorporating the potential use of
nuclear weapons into future foreign policy and military strategies. In
1953 defence spending costs reached the sum of $50 billion per year and
these costs were reduced under Eisenhower so that by 1956 the costs
were just under $36 billion. The military strength of the United States
also reduced from the peak of 3.6 million in 1953 to 2.8 million by 1956.
However, the idea of preparedness became permanent; it was clear the
United States needed to be ready to fight its enemies at any time and any
place.

The Korean War helped to formalise a relationship between the
government and the manufacturing sector that became known as the
military–industrial complex. With the decision to fight a limited war but
also be prepared to respond to future technological developments by
potential enemy nations, the US government forged a relationship with
the civilian defence industry. Previously, when war threatened the government had gone through the lengthy process of converting industries to
production of military materiel. In the Cold War it was possible that war
could happen at any time. Hence, it made more sense for the government
to rely on the private sector to develop new technologies and produce new
hardware continually. This could be done with the financial backing of the
federal government in the form of defence contracts. While Eisenhower
would go on to issue his famous warning against the military–industrial
complex in his farewell address, that complex was already well in place in
part due to his policies and the way in which America's preparations for
defence had been organised since the outbreak of the Korean War. The
increase in military spending advocated by NSC 68, while curbed a little,
did not reduce to pre-war levels after the fighting stopped. The United
States also did not retreat from overseas commitments after Korea, so
there was a need to maintain high levels of military materiel.

Of equal importance to the institutionalisation of the military–industrial
complex was the escalation of the Cold War arms race, again influenced
by America's involvement in the Korean War. When the Soviet Union
detonated its first atomic bomb in 1949 the American government was

caught off guard. Officials had estimated that it would take much longer for the Soviets to acquire nuclear knowledge and reach parity with the United States. This development prompted Truman to authorise the development of the more powerful hydrogen bomb in January 1950. The outbreak of the war in Korea seemed to lend credence to United States' concerns about an aggressive communism armed with nuclear weapons. The United States tested the first hydrogen bomb on 1 November 1952, while the Korean War persisted. The Soviet Union responded with its own hydrogen bomb detonation in November 1955. This escalation of the development and production of more powerful bombs led to an arms race that continued well into the next two decades.

Politically, the Korean War era witnessed the defeat of the Democratic Party in 1952. The Democrats had managed to dominate American politics since the first election of Franklin Roosevelt in 1932 through to Truman's decision not to run for re-election in 1952. The rise of McCarthyism, the taint of the Democrats as being soft on communism, as well as the increasingly drawn-out and unpopular war in Korea and fissures within the Democratic Party, helped to ensure the election of Eisenhower in 1952. At the same time as Eisenhower's elevation to the White House the Republican Party gained control of both Houses of Congress. Although the Democrats regained congressional dominance in 1954, the executive branch remained in the hands of the Republican Party's Eisenhower until his retirement in 1961. The events and the climate of the 1950s led to a more conservative political atmosphere that was the forerunner of the resurgent New Right in the late 1960s.

The most obvious conservative feature of the early 1950s was the anti-communist movement. Although concern about communist influence and the search for communist party members predated the outbreak of the Korean War and occurred under the leadership of a Democrat, the war itself helped to intensify these anxieties. There was no doubt that communists were behind the war effort in North Korea and this confirmed to the American government and the American people that the underlying premise of the Cold War was accurate. Communism itself seemed to be aggressive and the United States foreign policy of containment was the only obvious response. Crossing the 38th parallel and trying to reunite North and South Korea had not worked but holding the line had.

Of equal importance was the lesson learned about the nature of war itself. While not everyone was happy about the resultant status quo ante-bellum that resulted from the negotiated end of the Korean War, most people were glad to know that wars after the development of nuclear weapons did not mean certain Armageddon. Whether or not this was because the war was fought by proxy rather than directly between the United States and Soviet Russia or Communist China was of some interest but the vital lesson learned was that wars could be fought on a limited basis, with minimal disruption to the daily lives of the people back home. Hence, it was possible to stand up to local communist governments, that may or may not be backed by one or more large communist nations, in a limited fight in an area remote from mainland America. What may not have been so easily understood was that fighting a limited war often gave the advantage to the opposing side who could take their time and wait things out, since they had the advantage of fighting on their home field. It helped as well that the enemy knew that the war itself was increasingly unpopular at home in the United States. These factors would come into play again in the next war.

5   The Vietnam War

THE INTERWAR PERIOD

The exact dates of the interwar period between Korea and Vietnam are difficult to define since the United States was involved in Vietnam at different levels, at different times. Although the Vietnam War dominated American foreign policy and domestic affairs after 1964, before that time American interests abroad were wide ranging. For example, US foreign policy was still dominated by concern over the relationship with the Soviet Union. From 1953 to 1964, under both Eisenhower and Kennedy, the US government continued to wage a Cold War with the other major superpower. While Eisenhower was responsible for getting the Central Intelligence Agency (CIA) involved in far-flung regions such as Iran and Guatemala, his major focus was on the Soviet Union. The continuing arms race throughout the 1950s and specific incidents like the shooting down of an American U2 spy plane while over the Soviet Union in 1960, kept the White House focussed on the communist threat. This focus continued under Kennedy, after his election in 1960, with major encounters with the Soviets taking place at both Berlin and Cuba. The construction of the Berlin Wall and the Bay of Pigs fiasco in Cuba in 1961 did little to enhance Kennedy's reputation or to remove the tarnish from the Democratic Party that they were soft on communism. In 1962 however Kennedy was able to show his determination to stand up to the Soviet Union when he managed to stop the construction of Soviet missile launch sites in Cuba. The Cuban Missile Crisis was resolved and Kennedy's credibility as a Cold Warrior was confirmed. The US involvement in Vietnam deepened during this time as well, under both presidents. By the time the Korean War ended in 1953 the US government was firmly committed to the Cold War policy of containment and had expanded its commitment to Asia. Direct American involvement in Southeast Asia, however, developed slowly, over many years and took many forms.

While the US participation in the internal affairs of Vietnam only began in earnest once the French were no longer involved, before the French gave up their claims a long, drawn-out conflict occurred. The

Vietnam region had been the target of foreign imperialism for a long time first by the Chinese and later by the French. In 1893 the French formed a union of Vietnam, Cambodia and Laos, although there was some native resistance to this union, especially in the central area of Vietnam. This imperialist history left the Vietnam region with a strange mix of cultures. The Chinese had left their mark as the Mandarin class which was overlain by French colonial bureaucracy with French rule carried out by local agents who were French-speaking, Roman Catholic Vietnamese elite in competition with the Mandarins. Simultaneously, a nationalist and long-established independence movement began working against these imperialist constraints whose goal was Vietnam's independence. France worked to consolidate its control over Vietnam making French the official language and renaming the area French Indochina. They tore down many Buddhist pagodas, replacing them with Roman Catholic churches and changed the land policies of the Vietnamese, previously based on family inheritance and ancestry, to accommodate French monopolies.

During Japanese expansion in the 1930s and 1940s Vietnam was occupied by yet another foreign force. Ho Chi Minh returned to Vietnam in 1941 after a 30-year absence and launched a guerrilla war of nationalism to throw off the oppressive Japanese occupiers and establish an independent Vietnam. He established the Vietminh or League of Vietnamese Independence in 1941 made up of urban intellectuals and peasants. He went to China to seek help from Chiang Kai-shek but was thrown in prison, only to be released in 1943. During the Second World War the situation in Vietnam was dire with estimates of between one half to two million Vietnamese dying from starvation because the Japanese took the rice harvests. Ho eventually turned to the Office of Strategic Services (OSS), the United States wartime forerunner of the CIA, for help in overthrowing the Japanese; the OSS agreed to supply the help.

When the war was over Ho Chi Minh tried to consolidate the gains of the nationalists. In September 1945 he announced the creation of the Democratic Republic of Vietnam using the United States Declaration of Independence as the template for the foundation of this new government. Unfortunately, the post-Second World War world quickly became one of two opposing camps, one communist and one capitalist, and any moves to change governments in Southeast Asia was viewed as either a loss or a gain for one side or the other. The United States applied its policy of containment to the gains of communists and American policy makers viewed Ho Chi Minh's attempts to overthrow the French as the thin wedge of communist expansion.

In addition, the United States wanted to gain French aid in other areas. After the Second World War, Truman agreed to remain silent in the face of the resurgence of French rule in Indochina in return for French support of US efforts in Europe. A growing communist party movement in Europe, especially in France, worried American policy makers. Simultaneously, France was in desperate need of money to wage its war in Indochina. The French effort in Asia was backed not only by the United States but also by Britain and China and some Japanese in the area were even re-armed in an effort to hold back Ho's success. However, in the post-Second World War era, old empires began to crumble despite western countries' desperate attempts to hold on to their overseas assets. By the end of 1946, as Britain and other countries withdrew from Vietnam, the French were left on their own, with the only remaining support for France coming in the form of American money.

The First Indochina War, from 1946 to 1954, was waged by the French against the nationalist Vietnamese. French General LeClerc, realising the problems the French faced by trying to wage war against a native, nationalist movement, suggested that 'fighting the Vietminh would be like ridding a dog of its fleas. We can pick them, drown them, and poison them, but they will be back in a few days'. On 6 March 1946 the French and North Vietnamese signed the Franco Vietminh Accords, which was a truce of sorts. Under the terms of the Accords the French agreed to recognise Ho and his government in the North; however, it was not long before the French reneged on this agreement, and it quickly became clear that the French had no intention of relinquishing control. Ho wanted unification of the North and South not least because the South was incredibly rich in resources. The two sides failed to reach agreement and fighting broke out between the French and the Vietminh in November 1946.

The French military found itself fighting a guerrilla war against nationalism in Southeast Asia. To begin with the French decided to utilise the strategy of 'hedgehogs' to wage war in Vietnam. Hedgehogs were isolated outposts housing expert French troops from which the French could conduct forays into the countryside to destroy the Vietminh. The Vietminh, trained by General Vo Nguyen Giap in the use of guerrilla warfare, worked to wear down the French forces. In the South the French created the Vietnam State led by a puppet government which could be controlled easily and, while the South was allegedly independent, the

French controlled the defensive, financial and diplomatic arms of the government with the South Vietnamese establishing the Vietnamese National Army.

The post-Second World War communist scare in the United States, along with the policy of containment, helped to encourage the American government's belief that there were no unimportant areas of the world in terms of national security. Worse yet, from the American perspective, when Ho Chi Minh proclaimed the establishment of the Democratic Republic of Vietnam in 1950, the Soviet Union and China both recognised Hanoi as the legitimate capitol of the North and Ho Chi Minh as the legitimate ruler of the Vietnamese. At this point Truman agreed to give the French $15 million to assist them in their fight against the Vietminh. In addition, 1950 witnessed the start of the Korean War, seeming to prove to America that the Soviet Union and China were looking to expand in Asia leading to the United States' increased commitment to the French government in Vietnam.

Throughout the years 1946–1954 the French Army met the Vietminh on numerous occasions while the French public grew increasingly sceptical about the French presence in Southeast Asia. At the same time the United States took on more and more of the costs of waging the war against the Vietnamese. By 1954 the United States was supplying 75 per cent of the annual war budget and there was very little progress being made in the war. Then in March 1954 the most famous fight between the French and Vietnamese took place at Dien Bien Phu. In this instance the French had picked a particularly bad location for one of their hedgehog emplacements and had seriously underestimated the Vietminh presence in the area. The French military situation was fundamentally unsound as the French continued to try to fight a guerrilla war by conventional means and on 12 March 1954 the Vietminh attacked the French position. By 17 March the French were cut off and had to be supplied by air with the help of the United States although the US response was somewhat mixed. By 1954 Eisenhower was in the White House, the Korean War had just finished and the government was reluctant to become involved militarily in another overseas conflict. On the other hand, during the siege at Dien Bien Phu, Eisenhower voiced his concerns about the possibility of a domino effect should communists win, suggesting that there was a pressing need to keep any country from 'falling' to communism because once one went the neighbouring countries were sure to fall. The Domino Theory in Southeast Asia implied that if Vietnam fell to the communist forces of Ho Chi Minh then Cambodia, Laos, Thailand,

Burma, Pakistan and India itself were not safe. Secretary of State John Foster Dulles flew to Europe to get North Atlantic Treaty Organization (NATO) support for the war in Vietnam but the French did not want to give up control and the British were not interested in getting involved.

Meanwhile, an international conference took place in Geneva where attendees included representatives from the Vietminh (Pham van Dong), the French backed leader in South Vietnam (Bao Dai), representatives from Cambodia and Laos, the French representative Georges-Augustin Bidault, the United States representative Dulles and Anthony Eden for Britain. The main issue in Vietnam would not easily be resolved since the two sides were so diametrically opposed, the Vietminh wanted independence while the French were in search of a simple ceasefire. Then, on 6 May, just as the Geneva talks turned to the issue of Indochina, the Vietminh took Dien Bien Phu, resulting in one of the biggest defeats in French history and nearly toppling the French government. This victory for the Vietminh and Ho Chi Minh reinforced the legitimacy of the Vietnamese government. The delegates at Geneva agreed there would be a temporary partitioning of Vietnam at the 17th parallel, to be followed by reunification elections. The agreement allowed for an immediate ceasefire, withdrawal of forces on both sides, freedom for Vietnamese citizens to move across the border and a withdrawal of forces from Cambodia and Laos with free elections to take place in 1956. These Geneva Accords were signed by France, Great Britain, China and the Soviet Union but not by the United States. Although not completely satisfied with the arrangements, the Vietminh signed the Accords in order to uphold the Democratic Republic of Vietnam while Ngo Dinh Diem, recently appointed Premier of the South refused to sign.

BEGINNINGS

It is difficult to determine just when the war in Vietnam truly began for the United States. Its involvement deepened over time from a financial commitment to back French imperialist claims to the sending of American troops to protect an American backed puppet government. It is perhaps easiest to put the beginning of the fighting for Americans at the arrival of the first troops in 1965. However, how the war began, in an American sense, goes back much earlier. From 1954 to 1960 the governments of both the North and South tried to consolidate their positions while the United States moved slowly into escalating involvement in the conflict. In the North Ho was harsh as he exerted his authority over the country while, in the South, a number of conflicting factions vied for control. The majority of the Vietnamese in the South were happy to see the French go but recognised that the French departure left a leadership vacuum. The South's economy was unstable and numerous groups wanted to exert influence including the Roman Catholics, Buddhists, various cults, the criminal mafia, the Vietminh and ethnic minorities such as the Chinese, Khmer and Mountain People. The Roman Catholic elite tended to have the power and to be resented by the others. The eventual leader who emerged from this contest, Diem, had grown up in the Catholic Church, isolated from other ethnic Vietnamese, but the United States approved of him because he was anti-communist, although he was also anti-French and anti-democratic. Although he was Premier, his political backing from the people was limited. In 1955 he declared the South the Republic of Vietnam and named himself its president while simultaneously establishing the Army of the Republic of Vietnam (ARVN). As early as 1954 the United States contributed military advisors to South Vietnam who were attached to the US Army and to the CIA, while the last of the French troops withdrew in 1956.

In 1955, in a move backed by the US government which was supplying money to prop up the government in the South, Diem cancelled the scheduled reunification elections as called for in the Geneva Accords. From 1955–1960 Diem attacked the remaining Vietminh in the South, otherwise known as Viet Cong or Vietnamese communists. He had somewhere between 20,000 and 75,000 individuals killed outright, without trial or charges, and another 100,000 put in re-education camps. The Viet Cong retaliated by killing local officials in small villages, who were unpopular with the peasantry anyway. In 1959 Ho reacted to Diem's actions by sending more Vietminh south, establishing the National Liberation Front (NLF) whose primary goal was to construct a supply route to the South, later known as the Ho Chi Minh Trail. Ho also threw his backing behind the communist guerrillas in Laos. The United States reacted to these developments by building up its military advisors to the ARVN to around 900 in anticipation of an invasion by the northern communists.

In 1959–1960 the situation deteriorated even further with the Viet Cong infiltrating US bases, killing two Americans in 1959 and, in November 1960, in the same month Americans elected John F. Kennedy to the presidency, there was an attempted coup against Diem. At a time when the Cold War situation was tense, Kennedy was keen to see the post-Second World War consensus that he inherited continue. The domestic anti-communist hysteria of the McCarthy era was gone but anti-communism still dominated American foreign policy with most of Kennedy's foreign policy advisors tending to be hardliners on this issue. Furthermore, in January of 1961 Prime Minister Nikita Khrushchev announced that the Soviet Union would support wars of national liberation, which clearly applied to Vietnam. Not wanting to appear weak, and with the charge of being soft on communism frequently levelled at the Democratic Party, Kennedy wanted to maintain the United States' firm commitment to containing the communist threat.

From 1955 to 1961 the United States had spent approximately 1.5 billion dollars in Vietnam to support the South, and ARVN troops were still not ready to deal with the threat from the North. In May 1961 Kennedy took the decision to send an additional 500 advisors, bringing the total number of United States advisors to 1400, which was a breach of the Geneva Accord limit. Kennedy's advisors suggested that American troops were needed in Vietnam until the ARVN was ready to shoulder the burden of defence of the country but Kennedy vetoed the idea. Kennedy was trying to maintain a middle-of-the-road response to the situation in Vietnam, somewhere between sending troops and withdrawing all support. Fundamentally, while the benign term 'advisor' suggested the United States was barely involved, this approach to the situation in Vietnam translated into a slow escalation of involvement. By the end of 1961 there were 3200 American advisors in Vietnam. To Kennedy and the foreign policy establishment the Domino Theory looked real; Laos was already figuring in the conflict in Southeast Asia and with the establishment of the Ho Chi Minh Trail it seemed just a matter of time before the situation worsened. Hence, the CIA, under the guise of Air America, worked to supply the Hmong tribesmen with materiel to fight against communism.

By the end of 1962 there were approximately 11,300 American personnel in South Vietnam and US spending levels in Vietnam had reached $500 million a year. Most of the personnel were army although there was also continued American air support for the ARVN. By mid-1963 there were 15,000 US personnel in South Vietnam yet, technically, the United States was not at war. Estimates of the size of the main force of the Viet Cong suggested 3000 in 1960 but this number increased to 35,000 by 1963. Most of the Vietminh were native southerners, hence the communist-inspired movement that the American government believed was foreign controlled was actually a nationalist movement under the umbrella of communism.

Meanwhile, Diem continued to attack dissidents; they were tortured, jailed and killed. In addition, elections were corrupt and Diem instituted strict censorship of news. In the summer of 1963 the Buddhist crisis erupted and Diem's government came under even more scrutiny. The Buddhists turned political in an attempt to break away from the Roman Catholic dominance of the government leadership. Diem reacted by attacking Buddhist protesters in May and the Buddhist protesters responded with hunger strikes. Diem declared martial law and on 11 June 1963 a 73-year-old monk set himself on fire in front of television cameras as a means of protest against Diem's harsh rule. The situation in Vietnam was clearly reaching breaking point. The majority of Kennedy's advisors suggested that America's response should be to increase its involvement; any lone voices of dissent from this majority view were unheeded. In one example, Paul Kattenberg, a State Department official, voiced opposition to this view and Dean Rusk had him posted to Guyana. In an attempt to get an accurate picture of the problem Kennedy sent two men to Vietnam to assess the situation. One returned to report that the war was being won and the other reported that the Viet Cong were getting stronger. Kennedy asked them if they had visited the same country. All of these problems within South Vietnam led to plots to oust Diem some of which the US government backed.

At the time of Kennedy's assassination in November 1963 there were 16,000 US advisors in South Vietnam and 108 Americans had been killed. The Viet Cong presence in the South was growing and there was a successful coup against Diem. Although Kennedy had plans to review the situation in Vietnam and possibly offer a new approach, he was killed before this could happen and the problems of Vietnam remained for Lyndon Johnson to address. Clearly, when Johnson came to office the consensus within the foreign policy establishment still existed. Policy makers were convinced that the United States needed to take a stand against communism in Vietnam. There was no debate on the morality of US involvement in Southeast Asia; the debate that did ensue was one of tactics rather than strategy. The problem was determining who, exactly, the United States was fighting. The Soviet-Sino split of the era seemed real so the question was who was backing the North Vietnamese? There was great concern that, as with Korean and the 38th parallel, if the United States ventured north of the 17th parallel American actions might bring in either Soviet or Chinese forces. Johnson, like Kennedy before him, sought a middle-of-the-road approach to the problems of Vietnam and, as with the Kennedy era, US involvement in Southeast Asia slowly and inexorably escalated so that by the summer of 1964 there were 20,000 US personnel in Vietnam.

HOW THE WAR WAS FOUGHT

As noted earlier, it is difficult, given the circumstances of slow escalation, to pinpoint an exact date when the US war in Vietnam began. This is made even more difficult by the fact that even before the US government passed the resolution authorising the sending of troops to Vietnam, US military personnel were already there fighting and dying. Adding to the complexity was the problem that the fighting that was taking place was unconventional. Much of the flavour of the war in Vietnam revolved around the question of how to fight against a native guerrilla force, which created problems for the United States from the beginning of American involvement under Eisenhower and later Kennedy. US strategy was twofold: first, America felt it was necessary to win the hearts and minds of the South Vietnamese people, which included a propaganda campaign against the Viet Cong and North Vietnamese; second, in order to fight the guerrilla war effectively, in 1961 Kennedy authorised the use of a special counterinsurgency force, the Green Beret. In the belief that progress against the Viet Cong could be achieved if villages could be isolated from Viet Cong influence, in 1962 the Americans helped to establish the strategic hamlet programme whereby villages were surrounded by barbed wire and mine fields. The Viet Cong, however, used this programme to illustrate to the Vietnamese civilians that the Americans were little different from previous colonial powers and promised that once the Americans left everyone's homes could be restored. Meanwhile, with more and more North Vietnamese infiltrators arriving in the South via the Ho Chi Minh Trail, the United States instituted a bombing campaign, which turned many more Vietnamese against them. By mid-1963 the United States was flying 1500 sorties a month using napalm, rockets and bombs as well as strafing targets on the ground. As early as this phase of the conflict the American policy in Vietnam revolved around the idea of attrition, of wearing down the opposition. It was also early on that the United States government implemented a scheme of counting dead enemy bodies as a means of measuring 'success'.

Yet as late as November 1963 when Kennedy was assassinated, the United States was not officially at war with North Vietnam. Unfortunately, Johnson could find no other solution to the problem of the expansion of communism in Southeast Asia than to continue the slow escalation of hostilities against the North. On 1 February 1964 Johnson authorised secret missions on North Vietnamese coastal installations, which Kennedy had approved before his death. Operation Ranch Hand, started under Kennedy and continued with Johnson's approval, was the code name for the use of Agent Orange and other defoliants as a technological solution to the problem of jungle warfare. The plan was to overcome the difficulties of fighting in heavy ground vegetation by the use of chemicals to eliminate the jungle and make fighting easier. Despite these military manoeuvres, General William Westmoreland, recently appointed commander of Military Assistance Command Vietnam (MACV), believed that there was no substitute for ground forces and lobbied the White House to approve the use of troops. The ARVN had experienced huge desertion rates after Diem was killed in a coup in November 1963 and the Viet Cong presence in the South was increasing. Estimates suggested that the Viet Cong had control of 40 per cent of the territory in the South and 50 per cent of the people supported the Viet Cong efforts.

US decision makers saw the need to take the war to the North, to Hanoi, through the use of strategic bombing. Johnson wanted a clear consensus on this decision so he had a resolution drafted for joint congressional approval of policies in Southeast Asia. Much like the publication of the NSC 68 before the outbreak of hostilities in Korea, the resolution was ready when an incident occurred which allowed the president to put it into operation. On 1 August 1964 the *USS Maddox*, an American destroyer, was patrolling off the coast of North Vietnam in the Tonkin Gulf, collecting data on North Vietnamese movements. There were also four South Vietnamese gunboats as well as North Vietnamese patrol boats in the area. As the North Vietnamese boats approached the *Maddox* it opened fire on the boats and the North Vietnamese responded by launching torpedoes. American jets then responded by attacking and damaging all the patrol boats. The following day the *Maddox* was joined by the *USS C. Turner Joy* and they continued to patrol off the North Vietnam coast. On 4 August, when tensions were high, men on both ships reported seeing radar blips but only the *Maddox* reported incoming torpedoes. The ship took evasive action and fired into the night, although no visual sightings were made. Several hours later the Captain of the *Maddox* concluded that there probably had not been an attack, however his revised judgement came too late. The first reports of the attack had reached Washington DC where both the Pentagon and White House went into action.

The government ordered retaliatory air strikes on torpedo boat bases in the North and President Johnson went live on television to outline the events. The next day Johnson met with congressional leaders to discuss the situation and on 7 August the administration submitted its resolution to Congress. Congress supported the Tonkin Gulf Resolution and gave the President authority to 'take all necessary measures' to repel armed attack. The House of Representatives passed the resolution by voice vote (414–0) and the Senate debated the measure but passed it with only two votes opposed, Senators Ernst Gruening of Alaska and Wayne Morse of Oregon (88 for, 2 against). Hence, a confused incident off the coast of North Vietnam led to the Gulf of Tonkin Resolution, which finally escalated US involvement in Vietnam to the point of official war.

In America the president's popularity soared; he was seen as taking decisive action against a military challenge despite the fact he continued to advocate moderation. His domestic policies, collectively grouped under the term the Great Society, still occupied much of his time. His expansion of Social Security and Medicare, commitment to job training and civil rights and his war on poverty were the basis of his presidential campaign in 1964. He ran on the platform of expanding the welfare state and keeping the United States out of a land war in Asia while at the same time reiterating that the United States would not run away from a challenge. In any event, Johnson's rhetoric appeared moderate when compared to his Republican opponent Barry Goldwater who advocated the use of nuclear weapons if necessary. Johnson won the 1964 election by a landslide, gaining 61 per cent of the popular vote and instilling a sense of popular mandate for his policies, both domestic and foreign.

Meanwhile, the situation in South Vietnam continued to deteriorate. The government of the South was increasingly unstable; there had been various coalition governments since the coup which ousted Diem in November 1963. In the 14 months after Diem's death, South Vietnam had seven different governments, prompting Johnson to state 'I'm sick and tired of this coup shit'. In the fighting US tactics underwent continuous evolution. The strategic hamlet programme meant that America maintained a defensive position against the enemy. The Viet Cong responded by increasing their aggressive campaign in the South and stepping up attacks on American personnel with the use of urban and jungle guerrilla tactics to taunt the Americans, sometimes infiltrating US military installations and leaving graffiti. After America began bombing the North the Viet Cong became even more aggressive. Their tactics changed from direct attacks on American personnel to car bombs and other forms of terrorist activity, which meant that more Americans were being killed. In an escalation of the air war, in February 1965 the United States initiated Operation Rolling Thunder, the sustained bombing of the North, which continued, off and on, until late 1968. There was also an escalation of the movement of North Vietnamese troops to the South and by 1964 the North Vietnamese were shipping Soviet and Chinese weapons down the Ho Chi Minh Trail at an increasing rate. The North also sent weapons specialists and Northern troops to bolster the ranks of the Viet Cong in the South.

Finally, in February 1965, when Johnson approved Westmoreland's request for marine troops, the United States participation rate in the conflict began to soar. The Americans were joined by other troops from allied countries such as Australia, New Zealand and the Philippines. Johnson did suggest negotiation with the North, off and on at various points, but neither side was willing to budge on the fundamental issue of the status of South Vietnam. The United States insisted the North must withdraw from the South and the North Vietnamese insisted that the United States should get out of Vietnam altogether. By the end of May 1965 there were 50,000 US troops in Vietnam, although Westmoreland continually asked for more and more troops to resolve the situation. By the summer of 1965 it was clear that Johnson needed to make a decision about the direction of United States involvement in Vietnam and he decided to send in more troops, switching from a defensive to an offensive war. In the process of increasing American involvement LBJ hoped to balance the provision of both guns and butter to the America people under the terms of the Great Society; however, increasingly the war in Vietnam came to dominate the US agenda.

The Vietnam War was at the forefront of American minds partly due to the images that emerged and were caught on film or published in the media. As the first war to be reported on the television nightly news and without official military censorship, the war in Vietnam produced many strong images. One example is the now famous photograph of the naked, young girl fleeing from a napalm attack. In terms of fighting the war, the combat coverage that the media carried to the American people involved three main images. The use of air cavalry is probably one of the most enduring. The helicopter was to the Vietnam conflict what the tank or airplane was to the Second World War . While the helicopter made its debut in the Korean War, it seemed to dominate in Vietnam. It functioned as a method of getting troops in and out of remote areas quickly and acted as an air ambulance for the wounded, helping to save numerous lives.

Another 'image' of the war was a regular feature of the nightly news. The increasingly numbing reports of the daily body count, with the ever present row of body bags, brought a new dimension to war reporting. The images of dead bodies and the reliance on the body count applied to the enemy as well. Since the Viet Cong often hid from view, even in skirmishes with American troops, enemy soldiers could go unseen. Equally, because gains could not be measured in terms of territory, the body count became one way of measuring which side was winning. If Americans killed more Viet Cong than the Viet Cong killed Americans then the United States must be ahead. Vietnam became a war of mathematics and every night the American people were able to hear who was winning according to the recorded statistics. Unfortunately, the data used to calculate body count was not always accurate and, as one statistician explained, if the figures were right then the United States won the war in 1965.

The third enduring image revolved around the search and destroy tactic. The search and destroy mission was an attempt, on the part of the United States military, to take the offensive in the war in Vietnam. Small units would go out into the jungle to villages in search of Viet Cong and for Vietminh sympathisers. Often, if troops felt the villagers were uncooperative or not telling the truth, the villages would be destroyed. The image of the American soldier setting the Vietnamese huts alight with his Zippo lighter was captured on film, both still and moving. One of the most famous quotes of the war was the Major who allegedly noted that 'It became necessary to destroy the town in order to save it'. As in Korea, but on a grander scale, it was not always possible to tell who the enemy was. Even when there was a battle in a more classic sense of the word, the outcome was not straightforward. For example, the US military met the North Vietnamese at a major battle in Ia Drang Valley in November 1965. Technically the US military emerged victorious, despite the heavy losses on both sides, and the North Vietnamese withdrew. However, the United States also withdrew from the area. Clearly the United States was not going to fight a war for territory as such, hence the search and destroy tactic became the alternative.

Yet with all of the efforts on the part of the United States, there was very little progress being made. Despite American money and training the South Vietnamese did not appear capable of their own defence. Even with the continuous build up of American troops, the United States was still fighting a limited and not a total war. In any limited war the advantage goes to the native population who can patiently outwait the foreign troops. Yet American troop numbers increased dramatically over the next few years. By the end of 1965 there were 184,300 American troops in Vietnam with another 200,000 en route. Government officials kept insisting that the United States was winning but more and more newspaper reporters and journalists in Vietnam were taking pictures and telling stories that seemed to contradict that assertion. A credibility gap developed between what the American government was saying and what journalists and observers were reporting. April 1965 witnessed the first Students for a Democratic Society (SDS) anti-war march in Washington DC. Talk of the immorality of the war grew while protests at home increased and still there was no progress.

Despite being a limited war the United States used massive amounts of high-tech weaponry. The United States dropped an estimated 1 million tons of explosives on North Vietnam and another 1.5 million tons on the Ho Chi Minh Trail but these bombings had little impact. An estimated 3.5 million pounds of explosives were dropped in the South by the United States each day of the war. Some areas were declared free fire zones, which meant that pilots could carpet bomb whole areas with impunity under the assumption that only the enemy remained in these areas. The reality was that women and children were caught up in the air war. Ultimately the bombings failed to bring about the end of the war although they did achieve the creation of a huge homeless population and hundreds of thousands of civilian deaths. In addition, the bombing campaigns meant that more and more US pilots were shot down over Vietnam until there were an estimated 900 pilots missing or captured as prisoners of war (POWs). The United States also continued and increased its use of defoliants in the South. An estimated 19 million gallons were dropped over 6 million acres of land which meant that over 20 per cent of the land area of the South was hit, although this too had little impact on the war. But the war did play havoc with South Vietnamese society. The major employment opportunity in the South was working for the Americans and the economy suffered from inflation and corruption. The original goal of winning the hearts and minds of the Vietnamese people failed.

Newly elected President of South Vietnam, Nguyen Van Thieu took over in late 1967. By the end of that year there were 485,000 American troops in Vietnam and the consensus in the American government on the correct policy towards Vietnam was finally breaking. Robert McNamara left office as Secretary of Defense and in April 1967 approximately 100,000 anti-war protesters gathered in New York. Campuses erupted and Johnson was forced to begin re-examining the American strategy in

Vietnam. As the year wore on, by late 1967 American military commanders in Vietnam were anticipating an attack of some sort although most believed it would be a direct assault on American and South Vietnamese troops. Instead, the Viet Cong infiltrated the cities of the South and on 31 January 1968, during the Tet New Year, they launched an attack on 36 of the 44 provincial capitals and five of the six major cities in the South. The most spectacular achievement of the Viet Cong was the storming of the American Embassy in Saigon.

The United States quickly counterattacked and pushed the Viet Cong back. In all it was a tactical defeat for the Viet Cong, since they did not manage to achieve permanently any of their goals. However, it was a political defeat for the United States. Images of the Viet Cong within the Embassy compound in Saigon flashed across the television screens of America. Even more horrific was the public execution of a Viet Cong commander by a South Vietnamese general at point blank range, captured on camera. In total 40,000 Viet Cong died during the offensive while casualties for America were 1100, for South Vietnamese soldiers 2300 and for South Vietnamese civilians 45,000. Over one million South Vietnamese were homeless as a result of the offensive. This state of affairs, which seemed to be in direct contradiction to government reports of the situation, prompted television anchorman Walter Cronkite to utter the famous line 'What the hell is going on?' Johnson noted that once he had lost the trust of Walter Cronkite he had lost the trust of America.

While the Tet offensive was not a battlefield victory for the Viet Cong it did signal the beginning of a shift in American policy in Vietnam. Johnson decided that it was time to turn the fighting of the war in Southeast Asia over to the people of Southeast Asia. Since 1968 was an election year Johnson was well aware of the political ramifications of any policy change. He had already received challenges to his presidential nomination from members of his own party. A public opinion poll in mid-March had indicated that only 25 per cent of the American people were in favour of continued United States involvement in Vietnam. In March 1968, just two months after Tet, Johnson went on television to announce a change in policy towards the war in Vietnam. He told the American people that it was time to begin to negotiate for a peaceful solution to the conflict, to pursue peace with honour. He also shocked the nation by announcing his withdrawal from the presidential race.

As a direct result of Johnson's actions peace negotiations began in Paris in May 1968. Unfortunately the process quickly bogged down in haggling over insignificant issues much as it had in Korea. By the end of

1968, the bloodiest year of the war, there were 536,000 US troops in Vietnam while over 30,000 Americans had died to date. In November 1968 Richard Nixon won the presidency for the Republican Party having campaigned on his 'secret plan' to win the war. When Nixon came to office he wanted to achieve an end to the war in Vietnam but without loss of face. He carried on from Johnson's announced policy of gradual withdrawal from the conflict in Vietnam with the peak of US troop presence in Vietnam occurring in April 1969 when there were 543,000 Americans serving in the area. In June 1969 the first troop withdrawals took place as part of the policy of Vietnamization – or turning the war over to the South Vietnamese to fight – suggested by Johnson and instituted by Nixon. The peace talks in Paris had stalled and there was very little progress in negotiating an end to the fighting.

In March 1969 Nixon authorised increased B52 bombing raids of the North in an attempt to bring pressure on the negotiations. In May the *New York Times* exposed these secret bombings and a series of protests took place in the United States. In September Ho Chi Minh died, but any hope that the United States had that the North Vietnamese might be more willing to negotiate with Ho gone was quickly quashed. Also in 1969, in November, the murder of over 500 Vietnamese civilians in the village of My Lai was revealed to the American public. The incident occurred in March 1968 but was covered up by army officials. When the story was revealed to the American public there was much debate over the nature of the war in Vietnam and the American fighting men. By late 1969 the morale of US troops in Vietnam was at an all time low. The number of troops going absent without official leave (AWOL) increased as did the incidents of drug abuse and fragging (the killing of non-commissioned and commissioned officers by their own troops). While troops were deserting in record numbers, those who were eligible for the draft were fleeing to Canada and elsewhere to avoid military service in Vietnam.

In February 1970 the US bombings of Laos was revealed to a disillusioned American public and in May 1970, when the use of US troops in Cambodia was made public, protests took place on numerous college campuses, most famously at Kent State, Ohio. During this time troop withdrawals continued and the peace negotiations seemed to be dragging on. In June 1971 the Pentagon Papers were published which outlined US policy towards Vietnam and substantiated most Americans' concerns about the reality of the credibility gap between what the government said was happening in Vietnam and what was really happening. By January 1972 there were only 157,000 American troops left in Vietnam.

The government in the South, run by Thieu, was as corrupt as its predecessors. As the problems of corruption and repression in the South became more widely known, the morality and ethics of US involvement was increasingly being called into question. Also in the early 1970s Henry Kissinger, close personal friend and advisor to Nixon, had become Secretary of State and the Nixon administration adopted its policy of détente, or morality free diplomacy resulting in Nixon's visits to China and the Soviet Union in 1972. This coincided with the Nixon administration's adoption of the madman strategy of foreign policy, which suggested that the best way to make your enemies negotiate was to keep them guessing about your next move. With Nixon's welcome in Moscow and Beijing, the North Vietnamese were left to wonder if they would be able to get outside help should the situation warrant it.

In addition, the Nixon administration initiated a massive bombing campaign to try to bring a decisive conclusion to the peace negotiations. In April 1972 the bombing campaign was meant to counter an invasion from the North. By August only one American combat battalion remained in South Vietnam. As the United States left South Vietnam it left behind materiel that, by 1972, meant the South Vietnamese had the fourth largest army, fifth largest navy and fourth largest air force in the world.

Nixon campaigned for re-election in 1972 with the promise that an end to the war in Vietnam was near to hand. Previously stalled peace talks resumed on 27 January 1973 at which time there were only 24,000 United States troops left in Vietnam. The final peace negotiations resulted in an agreement that the United States would withdraw all remaining troops but that any North Vietnamese troops already there could remain in the South. In addition, Thieu would remain in office while there would be an immediate ceasefire and an exchange of prisoners. Both sides agreed to work together to create a council of reconciliation. The North and South of Vietnam were more or less forced to sign the agreement due to a combination of United States pressure and the silence or lack of protest from the Soviet Union and China. Shortly after the negotiated settlement was signed the Watergate scandal began to unfold in the pages of American newspapers and the American public quickly turned from concern about the war in Vietnam to concern about the exploits of the head of state. Eventually Nixon was forced to resign in August 1974 and the American people closed the book on Vietnam by turning inward.

In late 1974 North Vietnam attacked the South and the ARVN collapsed. From 29 to 30 April 1975 television cameras showed the world the spectacular helicopter evacuation of 7100 American and South Vietnamese personnel from the roof of the United States Embassy. Soon afterward the South surrendered unconditionally and North and South Vietnam were finally reunified. Twenty-one years after the Geneva Accords were signed in 1954, Indochina finally 'fell' to communism.

The results of the American phase of the war in Southeast Asia were devastating. There were approximately two million dead Vietnamese (900,000 North Vietnamese and the rest in the South). Approximately 58,000–60,000 Americans were dead with an additional 150,000 wounded with over half of the American casualties occurring after 1968. There were approximately 10.5 million refugees in Vietnam and a legacy of an estimated 21 million bomb craters in the South alone. The cost of the war ran into the billions, as much as 900 billion dollars. After Vietnam was unified under communism Laos and Cambodia both 'fell' to communism as well, but that was as far as the dominoes went. For the American military the outcome of the Vietnam War would cast a long shadow, so long that it was not until the United States led the first war in the Gulf in 1992 that observers began to suggest that the ghost of Vietnam had been laid to rest for the US military.

US HOME FRONT

In the immediate post-Second World War years, when American involvement in Vietnam remained a mainly economic one, the conflict had little impact on American society at home. The economy was booming and American foreign aid flowed to numerous countries, including the French government in Indochina. The Korean War had come but it had been limited in nature and Americans were glad to put it and the Red Scare behind them. Little attention was paid to United States Cold War foreign policy manoeuvres outside Europe. It was not until the 1960s, as the American military presence increased in Vietnam, that the conflict had a significant impact on the home front.

Issues of foreign policy often dominated Kennedy's presidency from January 1961 to November 1963. Despite this, by the time of his assassination Kennedy had voiced his concerns about and tried to address other subjects such as poverty and civil rights. Yet while his nearly three years in office witnessed an increased involvement of American personnel in Vietnam, it was under Johnson's administration that the massive build up of United States military presence and the beginnings of an official shooting war began. Johnson's administration not only authorised and oversaw the war, it also made a serious commitment to improvements on the domestic front. Johnson's plan was to build a Great Society, to extend the benefits of the welfare state, started under Franklin Roosevelt, to less fortunate segments of American society. Critics of America's involvement in Vietnam have suggested that the eventual failure of Johnson's Great Society can be traced to the United States' involvement in the war in Vietnam; the American economy could not sustain an effort to supply both guns and butter.

Johnson's plans revolved around his belief in the need to reform aspects of American society by using the abundance and prosperity of the era to fix various remaining problems such as inequality and poverty. Johnson's Great Society was a serious attempt at social reform involving legislation on tax reform, education from kindergarten to university, Medicare, food stamps, housing subsidies, job training, transportation, the environment and, not least, civil rights. His 1964 landslide victory, coupled with election of the most active Congress in history, caused many reformers to believe that poverty could be ended and injustice addressed. Part of this liberal agenda included the extension of rights to areas of society that had been previously denied them, such as African Americans. The early days of Johnson's presidency were a high watermark for American liberalism with many of the ideas being extensions of goals outlined by liberals earlier in the Progressive Era and the New Deal, as well as under Kennedy.

The 1960s witnessed the doubling of America's gross national product (GNP) and the creation of a total of 10 million new jobs. The median family income doubled and the number of families living below the poverty line fell. However, there were still many problems and, like Roosevelt and the New Deal, Johnson and his Great Society faced critics from both the left and the right of the political spectrum. Critics on the left argued that the Johnson administration was not doing enough. The total amount of money allocated to run the Great Society and to wage his proposed war on poverty was only $2 billion annually. This was less that one-fourth of one per cent of the GNP. Liberal critics also claimed that the problems of equality could not be overcome without the redistribution of wealth which the Great Society programmes did not address. In addition, there was no commitment on the part of the government to guaranteeing jobs.

Yet the Great Society went far beyond any previous attempts at social reform; it expanded government involvement as never before. Of equal importance, the Great Society was limited because the Johnson administration could not ignore critics on the right. Although Johnson defeated Goldwater in 1964 by what was termed a landslide, Goldwater spoke to a hard core of conservative Americans. Tellingly, Goldwater's area of greatest support was in the Deep South, an area that had been part of the Democratic Party since the Civil War era. Hence, Johnson's victory did not mean that the conservative forces disappeared; in fact they were very evident and vocal in their criticism of Johnson's extension of government into American lives and the economy. These 1960s conservatives formed the foundation of the conservative upsurge of the 1970s and 1980s which came about as a direct result of the backlash to many aspects of the Great Society and the failure of the Democrats to deliver on their promises. Indeed, the Great Society did not achieve all of its goals, for example the war on poverty reduced overall privation but made little or no impact on the black urban ghetto. Unfortunately, the Great Society and the social reforms of the 1960s were undermined by the war, just as had been the Progressive Era in the First World War, the New Deal in the Second World War and the Fair Deal in the Korean War. The urban unrest, riots and violence of the period had many direct links to the war in Vietnam. A sense of alienation pervaded American society among many of the young and old, whites and blacks, males and females. Rapid changes in American society since the Second World War often increased concern about society's future. This concern was articulated in the 1960s by the blossoming youth, civil rights and feminist movements.

The New Left captured the imagination of many of America's alienated youth. The New Left was a grassroots liberalism based on the rejection of both the old left or Marxism and old style liberalism. Those in the New Left movement admitted that Marxism was clearly not working; the worker's revolt was not imminent and the working class did not appear to be on the verge of revolt; in fact, the working class was doing pretty well. In addition, Marxism had failed to alter or remedy inequities in society. Old style liberalism, on the other hand, had not worked either. Any reforms in society that occurred as a result of liberal campaigns took place in a piecemeal fashion. This slow approach did not represent real change in society, instead it acted to delude people into thinking that change for the better was occurring. Liberalism, in this sense, undercut the forces of discontent in society and meant the real push for change was stifled. The New Left claimed to offer a new perspective on long-standing problems in society.

The first appearance of the proponents of a New Left philosophy in the 1960s occurred on college campuses. The number of people attending college had risen dramatically since the early part of the century. Between 1960 and 1972 approximately 45 million Americans turned 18. While only about 4 per cent of the population went on to college in 1900, by 1940 this percentage was 15 per cent and rising. By 1965 fully 44 per cent of Americans went on to higher education and this figure rose to 50 per cent by 1970. In numbers that meant that there were 8 million students enrolled in college or university in 1970 compared to 2 million in 1940. These were middle-class kids whose parents had experienced the Depression and World War II. The adult generation was devoted to working hard, fighting just wars and putting their faith in the system. Eventually, all of this hard work, sacrifice and faith would pay off in the form of a good job, good income and financial security. The children of this affluent society, however, appeared to be rejecting this vision. Getting ahead was no longer good enough, the goals had changed and students began to voice their opinions on an ever-expanding national stage.

Although its roots went back to the student branch of the League for Industrial Democracy, the SDS was founded in 1960, at the University of Michigan where Al Haber was elected President. Then, in 1962, Tom Hayden, another founding member of the SDS, drafted the Port Huron Statement which became the manifesto for the New Left. The Statement was critical of American life and its pervasive racism, imperialism and poverty. The SDS predicted that it would be the students, and not the workers, who would bring about the necessary changes to society. According to the New Left, the power structure in the United States rested with a corporate power elite who did not have the interests of the individual at heart. The statement called for a decentralised society run with 'participatory democracy' so that the real power within America would rest with the people.

In another manifestation of the essence of New Left ideas, Mario Savio helped to launch the Free Speech Movement in Berkeley, California in 1964. University of California at Berkeley students had been active in previous protests, most notably against the meetings of the House Committee on Un-American Activities (HUAC) in 1960, as well as working on African American civil rights. Partly because of this, the university authorities at Berkeley announced a new rule whereby no political information could be disseminated on or near campus. On 1 October some activists challenged the administration's restrictions and Jack Weinberg, a campaigner for CORE, was arrested. Before police could leave the area with Weinberg in the patrol car, students surrounded the car blocking it for over 30 hours. Eventually Weinberg was released but this incident launched the Free Speech Movement. Tensions continued and over the next few months students and administrators clashed, culminating in the December occupation of Spoul Hall by over 1000 students, resulting eventually in over 800 arrests. Mario Savio, who had worked within the Civil Rights Movement and been influenced by the tactics of direct action, gave his famous speech about the need for student activism to guarantee the basic rights of Americans in the face of official, arbitrary acts. According to students, the administrations of universities were restrictive, impersonal bureaucracies. Eventually the Berkeley University President backed down and allowed the Free Speech Movement to continue unmolested. Meanwhile, the American press was full of reports of the behaviour of the students at Berkeley because their actions surprised most Americans. These young people were part of a privileged group within society who had access to higher education and their discontent and hostility seemed ungrateful. But the protest spoke to a core of students who were not happy with the status quo and the publicity of the movement at Berkeley spurred action on other campuses.

Much of the student movement, from 1965 onwards, was linked to Johnson's decision to escalate the war in Vietnam, which the SDS had opposed from the outset. Increased United States participation in the war brought more and more people onto campuses to protest. As the United States commitment to the war grew the SDS denounced the war in Vietnam as an American imperialist war. Eventually the New Left shifted its stance from wanting to reform society to proposing a revolution. There was an emphasis now on the need to radicalise people; nonviolence had not worked so direct confrontation was required. The existing political system was no longer viable, according to the New Left, because there was very little difference between the Democratic and Republican parties. A new approach was necessary.

According to this philosophy, the Vietnam War was not just Johnson's mistake; it was illustrative of a society made sick by its Cold War mentality. The universities were the focus of numerous attacks because of their direct or indirect participation in the war. Many university administrations allowed recruiters on campus including the CIA, an organisation which many students felt was symbolic of American overseas blunders. The chemical firm Dow was responsible for making war materiel such as napalm and became the target of student protests as well. Equally significant and symbolic were the Reserve Officer Training Corps (ROTC) offices on campuses which recruited and trained the next generation of military officers. Hence, ROTC offices were often the targets of protest and, as violence escalated, of bombing campaigns. The university system attracted protests by students for the above reasons but also because they were an easy target. Campus protests became more widespread throughout 1966, increasing substantially in 1967.

Yet it was 1968 that came to be seen as the watershed year of the decade. The Great Society was in serious trouble with budgetary cutbacks on domestic programmes going to help finance the increased cost of the war in Vietnam. After years of prosperity the economy finally began to sputter. The reforms had not ended, however, and future legislation would include the Housing and Urban Development Act, rent subsidies and the establishment of the work study programme for college students, along with insured student loans. In fact, spending on welfare and social legislation continued, even increasing during Nixon's terms in office. However, after 1968 the idea of the Great Society was dead. By the early 1970s the American economy was hit with inflation, decreased productivity and declining competitiveness in the world economy. The economic growth rate had been holding steady at 4 per cent from 1947 to 1967. After this, until 1979, the growth rate was less than 3 per cent so that by 1980 many more Americans were worse off than they had been in 1968.

While the year 1968 witnessed a major event of the war, the Tet offensive, it also saw significant events occurring within the youth movement. The SDS, as the New Left's largest organisation, continued to lead protests against the Vietnam War and the inequalities within American society. The SDS provided the bodies for numerous protests including the 100,000 strong 1967 Pentagon march, the Dow Chemical protest at the University of Wisconsin and the protest at the Oakland induction centre as part of the Stop the Draft Week. In 1968 some SDS alumni were moving into politics and forming a new party, New Politics, and SDS estimated its membership at over 100,000 students in 350 chapters on campuses across the United States. In the academic year 1967–1968 almost three quarters of all American campuses witnessed some kind of student-led protest activity and it was in 1968 that one of the most spectacular campus revolts occurred which changed the course of the protest movement and serves as an example of the escalation of protest by the late 1960s.

Columbia University was situated close to Harlem in New York City, and in 1968 the university authorities, intending to expand the campus, issued eviction notices to people living in the area to make way for the construction of a new gymnasium. Black students on campus organised to protest the move claiming that the gym was symbolic of Columbia's racism and indifference to the plight of its African American neighbours. Columbia University also happened to belong to the Institute for Defense Analysis which worked to evaluate weapons for the Defense Department. Coincidentally, the SDS chapter at Columbia was one of the most militant in the United States and it organised a protest in early 1968. On 23 April the SDS led a rally against the Institute for Defense Analysis and took over a hall with three professors inside. The professors were released 24 hours later but not until after the SDS had called in the media. They occupied four other halls on campus with the protest lasting about a week. The police eventually moved in and violence erupted with over 100 students injured and 700 arrested. The police actions radicalised the campus even more and the police brutality, as captured by the news cameras, threw public sympathy behind the protesters. The students then initiated a strike and boycott of the university.

The Columbia University protest was one of the most televised of all campus protests. Equally important, the Columbia action took place at the same time that students were protesting in Germany and France where the actions of French students nearly toppled the government. The possibility of a real revolution occurring no longer seemed so remote. In 1967–1968 only 2 per cent of all college students in the United States claimed affiliation with the SDS but a full 13 per cent called themselves radicals or revolutionaries, and by the fall of 1968, 20 per cent of students surveyed supported the idea of revolutionary change. This move towards revolution, however, was the harbinger of a split within the movement as radicals who advocated more violent action disagreed with more moderate elements. By the 1968–1969 academic year more violence was occurring on American campuses. Sit-ins, arsons and bombings, especially of ROTC offices, occurred in Berkeley, Delaware, Oregon and Seattle.

The last public meeting of the national SDS organisation occurred in late 1969. The hard core of the movement, turning to terrorism as their frustration grew, set up a new organisation, the Weatherman. The Weatherman took the movement underground, adopting revolutionary tactics, and briefly aligning with the Black Panthers. The Weathermen tried to counter the attitude that white people did not count in the serious struggles for equality and called for Third Worldism or revolution. It was no longer a youth movement; it had become an armed struggle, as they saw it, requiring a small band of committed revolutionaries working in secret rather than a national organisation with branches across America. The last major public act notice of the Weatherman occurred in March 1970 when one of their bomb factories exploded in New York's Greenwich Village killing several members.

Although the SDS eventually disbanded, it did manage to achieve several major milestones in the 1960s. SDS protests against the war in Vietnam brought the issue, through their use of the media, to the attention of the American public. University administrations began to listen to student concerns and issues as a result of the organisation of student groups. The SDS also helped to spawn other grassroots movements such as the environmental movement and the anti-nuclear movement. Without the war in Vietnam, however, it is hard to imagine the SDS growing as powerful and influential as it did. Yet it is important to remember that the SDS was always a minority organisation and although it rallied thousands at various protests there were still many hundreds of thousands of students who did not participate. And when students outside SDS did participate, it was often because they were against a specific issue such as the Vietnam War, and not because they believed in the Manifesto. Hence, further student protests occurred as events unfolded in the war. Most notoriously, in 1970 students at Kent State University, Ohio, launched a protest against the expansion of the Vietnam War into Cambodia. After incidents on campus including a suspected arson attack, the Ohio National Guard came under direct attack from stone-throwing students and opened fire on the crowd killing four. This set off further demonstrations on campuses across the United States involving thousands of Americans.

Ultimately, the campus protests were not just about the fairness or unfairness of the draft, or even about the problems of the credibility gap where some Americans believed the information about the progress of the war coming from both military and civilian authorities was untrue. The morality of the war itself came under attack. Whereas in previous wars the just or unjust nature of the conflict may have been discussed or debated after the war, or by small numbers of people during the war, in the Vietnam era and by the time Johnson sent troops in 1965, there was a growing nucleus of people and organisations that questioned United States presence in Vietnam and its motivations. The protests eventually covered many aspects of the war including the justifiability of committing men and materiel to prop up a corrupt government just because it was anti-communist to the methods used to fight the war itself. Hence, campus protests could target universities with defence contracts as well as those who let corporations such as Dow Chemicals, manufacturer of napalm, recruit from the student body. Also of concern to many protestors was the obvious connection between expending millions of dollars in a far off war while it was becoming increasingly clear through a variety of means such as the urban riots, that there were areas of poverty and privation within the United States itself that could benefit from the application of that money to social reform projects.

There are some obvious points to be made about the protests and their effects. First, the protests began and were sustained by a minority of Americans, just 5 per cent of the United States population, or approximately 6 million people, participated in anti-war or civil rights protests. Sometimes, in fact, a counter demonstration in support of the US government's policies in Vietnam occurred such as the 1967 march of members of the Young Americans for Freedom (YAF) organisation, founded in 1960, that espoused their belief in the future of a conservative America. However, as the war continued, and by late 1967, over half of those polled about the Vietnam War believed that US involvement in the war was wrong. Second, protests relied upon the ability of protestors to exercise their constitutional right of freedom of speech, a right curtailed in previous wars. Unlike during previous wars, the Supreme Court safeguarded freedom of speech in the Vietnam era. For example, in *United States v. Seeger* (1965) it upheld the fundamental right of conscientious objectors (COs) and expanded the definition of the term to go beyond simple religious belief to include secular concerns of a philosophical and moral nature. In *New York Times v. United States* (1971) the court upheld the right of the newspaper to publish excerpts from a governmental document (the Pentagon Papers) over the objections of the government. Furthermore, in *Brandenburg v. Ohio* (1969) the court made it clear that before the US government could restrict freedom of speech of an individual it had to prove that there was an immediate and real threat that the speech was aimed at inciting lawlessness; gone was the nebulous criteria of a 'clear and present danger'. But the anti-war and student protests were only part of the story of dissent of the Vietnam War era.

The Vietnam War had a direct and immediate impact on the status and experiences of African Americans. A series of events after the Second World War and during the Korean War brought the push for civil rights to the forefront of American society. Most notably the 1954 Supreme Court *Brown v. Board of Education of Topeka Kansas* decision, which ruled that school segregation was unconstitutional, led the way in bringing real change to the status of African Americans within the United States. Combined with events such as the Montgomery Bus Boycott of 1955 and the desegregation of Little Rock High School in Arkansas in 1957, the push for change in race relations and the struggle for equality gained momentum. The Civil Rights Movement's activities of the late 1950s continued into the 1960s. African Americans who wanted to take more direct action in pushing for their civil rights, however, were challenging the non-violent work of Martin Luther King Jr and the Southern Christian Leadership Conference (SCLC) by 1960.

While the United States was sending more military advisors to Vietnam under the Kennedy administration, blacks were challenging the status quo at home. In 1960 African American students led a sit-in at the Woolworth's lunch counter in Greensboro, South Carolina to push for desegregation. They eventually founded a new organization called Student Non-Violent Co-Ordinating Committee (SNCC), initially embracing the methods of King while also challenging the leadership of the established civil rights organisations like the NAACP and SCLC. African American activists' actions and methods acted as a model for other protest groups such as the SDS, many of whose members had worked for African American civil rights in their first forays into protesting. In 1961 civil rights activists from SNCC and CORE, both black and white, launched the Freedom Ride campaign in the South in an attempt to challenge illegal discriminatory practices on interstate buses. In 1962 James Meredith attempted to enrol at the University of Mississippi only to be barred at the door by the Governor, Ross Barnett. In 1963 protesters, led by Martin Luther King Jr, were attacked by dogs and faced fire hoses in Birmingham in front of national television, and then the nation witnessed a quarter-of-a-million people marching on Washington DC to protest the treatment of blacks within American society. Martin Luther King's famous 'I have a dream' speech on the steps of the Lincoln Memorial, however, failed to move the government. Kennedy, who had only reluctantly come out in favour of changes in race relations, faced resistance in Congress to his suggestion of civil rights legislation.

With Johnson's arrival in office, however, civil rights moved up on the government's agenda. The Johnson administration oversaw the passage of more and better civil rights legislation than any previous government. Unfortunately, the problems of African Americans and their status within American society were not going to be easily solved. Despite the government's best intentions, the problems of black Americans were endemic and needed more than legislation to correct. For instance, in July 1964 Congress passed the Civil Rights Act, originally proposed by Kennedy but finessed through into law by Johnson. This act prohibited discrimination in places of public accommodation such as hotels and called for the equal treatment of people in all public facilities. The act also forbade government money from going to institutions that practised discrimination such as universities or hospitals. The act also provided protection of some, but not all, voting rights. While the act suggested the government was serious about redressing the problems of discrimination in public facilities, just two weeks after its passage Harlem erupted in a three-day riot. From 18 to 20 July 1964 Harlem was engulfed in a display of violence that shocked the nation. Approximately one year later, on 6 August 1965, Congress passed the Voting Rights Act. This act made age, residence and citizenship the only requirements for voting. It was a direct attack on the Jim Crow institutions, mainly of the South, that had kept African Americans from exercising their right to vote. The act was given enforcement capabilities with the commitment of federal agents to register voters and it seemed to work because voter registration among southern blacks increased by almost 50 per cent within three years. Within a decade southern politics shifted with recognition of the need to court the African American vote. Yet one week after the passage of this act, on 11 August 1965, the Watts area of Los Angeles erupted in a violent riot.

While these pieces of legislation were securing political and social rights of African Americans everywhere, the inner cities of the nation continued to erupt in violence. Watts was a relatively less poverty stricken black neighbourhood than those in Harlem, Chicago or Detroit. There were numerous African Americans who owned their own homes in Watts. However, the adult unemployment rate was a staggering 30 per cent while the overall US unemployment rate was only five per cent. The Watts area was patrolled by a mostly all-white police force. The new civil rights laws promised much by way of political and social change but it was hard to see any immediate economic benefit. In addition, even the aspects of the Great Society that might have relieved chronic problems such as unemployment were under funded. This under funding of government programmes to help the poor grew worse as the Vietnam War progressed and more and more money went into the war effort.

The immediate effect of the variance between the promises of society and the reality for African Americans was to create a sense of frustration. Many blacks felt that there was no way out of the poverty trap they found themselves in. The Watts riot, like many others, was triggered by the arrest of a black by white police officers. By the end of the riot 34 people had been killed, $35 million dollars of property damage was incurred and 856 people were injured. The police eventually arrested over 3000 people. A commission was set up to look into the violence of Watts and the commission's report warned that there was a racial breach in America. Watts, it stated, 'would only be the beginning'. This statement turned prophetic when, from 1964 to 1967, hundreds of violent protests took place in American cities in both the North and the South. Often these violent episodes were spontaneous, unorganised acts directed at symbols of authority such as the police. A pattern of summer violence developed which, when coupled with the campus protests, stunned middle America.

Most of the violent riots of the late 1960s were not directly about black people attacking or being attacked by whites. It was most often directed at property and was characterised by looting. It was only when police or firemen, persons of authority, entered the riot area that attacks on humans occurred. In 1966 dozens of cities experienced violent episodes including Chicago, Milwaukee, Dayton, San Francisco and Cleveland. In 1967 the riots continued with over 150 separate incidents being reported but the worst riot occurred in Detroit as it had during the Second World War . The Detroit riot of 1967 remained the worst riot on record until 1992 when the Rodney King trial set off an even more deadly riot in South Central Los Angeles. In Detroit in 1967, 43 people died and thousands were injured. Over 7000 people were eventually arrested and property damage was estimated at $50 million. Eventually the Kerner Commission reviewed the causes of the urban violence witnessed in America in the latter half of the decade. The commission report, published in 1968, described the riots as 'riots of rising expectations'. While African American families earned an average of 48 per cent of what white families earned in 1960, by 1970 this had only increased to 61 per cent. There was improvement but there was no equality and all the discussions of civil rights and giving power to the people had only served to make people more frustrated when they could not improve their circumstances.

While these acts of violence and spontaneous expressions of frustration were occurring, the Civil Rights Movement was experiencing difficulties. There was a split among the leaders of the movement as early as the 1963 March on Washington and the ensuing fragmentation of the leadership took its toll on the movement itself. White, liberal support slowly eroded with the rise of black militancy and the use of confrontational tactics within the movement. Martin Luther King's SCLC, the NAACP and CORE were seen by some African Americans as being too slow to react to the inequality and violence directed at civil rights workers. It is true that with each new protest African Americans, and other civil rights workers, were greeted with increased violence. In 1964 during the Mississippi Summer Project three civil rights workers, two white and one black, were killed. Each step forward seemed to bring about even more determination on the part of white racists to halt the progress of black Americans. This confrontational atmosphere helped to foster the split within the movement.

The charismatic Malcolm X had espoused the idea of Black Nationalism, even black separatism, earlier in the decade. He spoke for the Black Muslim community and encouraged African Americans to be proud of their heritage and African backgrounds. Although he had split with the Nation of Islam and was revising his view toward separatism when he was assassinated in 1965, many blacks in America embraced the core of his earlier statements. For instance, the Black Panther party, founded in October 1966 by Bobby Seale and Huey Newton, grew out of the Civil Rights Movement and moved toward the theme of Black Power as advocated by Stokely Carmichael of SNCC.

SCLC was also changing and Martin Luther King Jr was moving towards a more direct action approach by the late 1960s. King came out against the Vietnam War in 1967, proclaiming that the United States government's decision to continue fighting the war took food from the mouths of the nation's poor. He was also beginning to bring his influence to bear on the plight of blacks in northern cities and on his Poor People's Campaign. Then, on 4 April 1968, King was assassinated. His murder triggered a series of riots in 110 different cities across America, with the worst riot occurring in Washington DC. The SCLC's power among African Americans had already been on the wane and it never fully recovered from the death of Martin Luther King. It limped along through the 1970s but with reduced funding. In 1977 there was a power struggle within the organisation but by 1979 there was talk of disbanding.

SNCC, established in 1960, had grown increasingly radical in the early 1960s. By the latter part of the decade, however, the more moderate elements within the organisation prevailed. They expelled Stokely Carmichael for his alliance with the Black Panthers and by 1970 there were only two active chapters of SNCC remaining. CORE, established during the Second World War as a biracial organisation working for African American civil rights, had ejected whites as well and lost most of its influence by the late 1960s. It toyed with black separatist rhetoric but eventually faded from view.

By 1968 the radicalism of the Black Panthers had gained national attention with their militant rhetoric in direct opposition to the more middle-of-the-road organisations such as SCLC and CORE. Eldridge Cleaver was eventually indicted by the police and fled to Algeria to avoid arrest and prosecution. Perhaps the most symbolic act of the Black Panther or Black Power Movement occurred at the 1968 Olympics in Mexico City when several black athletes bowed their heads and raised their gloved fists into the air during the playing of the American national anthem. The Black Panthers were highly visible and their tactics achieved one goal, which was to awaken white America to the potential for revolution that African Americans possessed. However, they were never an effective force for change. The government sanctioned a series of raids on their headquarters and harassment of their membership and by the 1970s the Black Panthers were a spent force in the Civil Rights Movement.

The one civil rights organisation to survive the turmoil of the 1960s was the NAACP. The most conservative of the black organisations, the NAACP, along with the Urban League, worked to bring about change in civil rights through the legal system. However, after 1968 the NAACP did more to act as a watchdog over the gains that had already been made than to act as the instigator of new and more radical changes. The NAACP did move on to press for affirmative action in the 1970s but the conservative backlash of the 1970s and 1980s meant that any progress they made was slow. The focus of the Civil Rights Movement moved on to the issue of jobs; however, the endemic problems outlined by the commissions which investigated black violence of the 1960s still existed.

Part of what fuelled both the Civil Rights Movement and the student movement was an issue directly related to the Vietnam War – the draft. As the number of troops in Vietnam increased so too did the number of young men inducted into the military. From 1964 to 1966 the number of men drafted into the military each year rose from 100,000 to 400,000. While all men aged 18 had to register for the draft, a potential inductee could obtain a deferment for college attendance. Clearly this type of deferment favoured the middle and upper classes. As the war continued more and more draftees were from poor backgrounds, often members of minority groups. In the late 1960s African Americans, for example, made up a disproportionate number of men drafted into the military and serving in Vietnam. From 1965 to 1969 the black population in the United States was roughly 11 per cent of the total but African Americans constituted over 12 per cent of the military in Vietnam while their proportion of the fatalities was nearly 15 per cent. There were also incidents of racial confrontation between black and white troops in both Vietnam and on military bases in the United States. Protests against the draft ensued with young men publicly burning their draft cards. Eventually even veterans of the war itself came out against the war in Vietnam. Figures for the number of men who avoided the draft range as high as 570,000. Of these the US government indicted 25,000 and approximately 4000 served jail time. It was during the Vietnam War era that the level of conscientious objection (CO) rose as well with an estimated 87,000 men being granted CO status upon being drafted and, by 1972, more men were receiving CO status than were being admitted to the military by the draft. A sizeable number of American men, estimated between 30,000 and 50,000, fled the country rather than serve in the Vietnam War, some of whom were pardoned years later under Presidents Gerald Ford and Jimmy Carter.

Participating in both the civil rights and anti-war protest movements, but never under threat of the draft, more and more women became politically active during the decade. The women's movement of the 1960s grew from these women's experience. By 1960 one-third of American marriages were ending in divorce and this, coupled with growing inflation and consumerism, meant that more and more women were going in search of jobs and careers. Unfortunately, the historical problems of unequal pay and inequality in the labour force were still very much in evidence. Approximately 50 per cent of American women were working in 1960 but at lower salaries than men with little change in the rhetoric that suggested that women's place was in the home. In 1963 Betty Freidan attacked the prevailing view of a woman's place when she wrote her book *The Feminine Mystique*. Freidan suggested, while America prided itself on its rising middle class and affluent society, there were many women who were part of that society who felt unfulfilled and uninvolved. Young women working for the civil rights and student movements discovered that even in these organisations, allegedly devoted to changing the status quo and bringing about genuine equality in America, women were often seen as second-class citizens. Women then began forming their own organisations and in 1966 the National Organization of Women (NOW) was founded. NOW published its bill of rights which called for an Equal Rights Amendment to the Constitution of the United States. More and more women challenged the social constructs of respectability that kept them in second-class status and re-enforced a double standard in sexual behaviour. With the introduction of the birth control pill in 1960 women could take control of their reproductive rights. Women also wanted equal employment opportunities, guaranteed maternity leave, community child care facilities, tax deductions for child care, equal educational opportunities and the right to an abortion.

The tactics employed by the women's movement emulated the other protest movements in some ways, but the main thrust was not a call for revolution as much as it was an attempt to raise consciousness of the American population, both male and female, to the current situation for women in the United States. Women publicly burned bras as a symbol of freeing their bodies and invaded all male clubs and bars. They protested institutions such as the Miss America pageant and sponsored mass marches to rally support for their cause. The 1964 Civil Rights Act gave them one of their most powerful legal weapons in the Title VII clause which stated that discrimination based on sex as well as race was illegal. The woman's movement, however, developed relatively late in the 1960s and by the early 1970s the conservative backlash was beginning to take its toll on the feminist agenda as well as other social movements. While the Supreme Court upheld a woman's right to an abortion on the basis of a right to privacy in the historic *Roe v. Wade* (1973) case, the Equal Rights Amendment was held back in many states by conservative forces which were becoming alarmed by the number and scope of minority rights campaigns being waged across America. Many other minority movements had developed along the same line as those outlined above. Mexican Americans pushed the Chicano movement forward and Native Americans protested their treatment, often with violent outcomes such as the occupation of Alcatraz Island in 1969 by American Indian Movement (AIM) and the confrontation at Wounded Knee Reservation in 1973. However, these movements, in some cases, spurred legislation that was more liberal. For instance, in 1971 the states ratified the 26th Amendment to the Constitution, which lowered the voting age from 21 to 18 as a direct result of the Vietnam War and the 'old enough to fight, old enough to vote' campaign. Other liberal interpretations of the law came from the courts.

The United States Supreme Court played a major role in shaping 1960s American society. Chief Justice Earl Warren, the same man who as Attorney General of California had pushed for the internment of Japanese Americans, hence violating their constitutional rights, led the Court in the 1960s through a series of decisions expanding civil rights and civil liberties for all Americans. The Supreme Court ruled on a variety of issues touching a wide range of topics in American society. As noted earlier, the Court made several rulings in the area of freedom of speech, which widen the application of this right including broadening the definition of obscenity along a more permissive line, voiding federal laws which required subversive organisations to register with the government and broadened the first amendment as it applied to libel and public figures. The Court ruled to bar school prayer requirements in recognition of minority religions within the United States. In a series of decisions the Court strengthened the rights of the accused in criminal cases by deciding that the accused had the right to an attorney in *Gideon v. Wainwright* (1963) and the right to remain silent and be informed of these rights at the time of arrest in *Miranda v. Arizona* (1966). In *Loving v. Virginia* (1967) the court overturned a Virginia law outlawing interracial marriage. The Warren Court so outraged conservatives within America that there was a campaign to impeach Earl Warren as Chief Justice of the Supreme Court.

By the end of the decade the protest marches, riots, liberal congress and court, legislation of the Great Society and the proliferation of the counterculture combined to help produce a conservative backlash. Although the counterculture was really only a small minority movement within American society, its impact was tremendous. The vision of free love and communal living by young people in jeans and long hair gained widespread publicity. Hippies and Haight Asbury pervaded the fashion, music and literary scene. The prescription to turn-on, tune-in and drop out, with drugs, sex and rock and roll, left many conservatives feeling that American society was crumbling at all levels.

As with other wartime and post-war periods in America in the twentieth century, the conservative agenda began to reassert itself in politics towards the end of the war after a last ditch effort by liberals to continue the reform spirit. Even before Lyndon Johnson decided to pull out of the presidential race in 1968, he was being challenged for the nomination from within his own party. Eugene McCarthy of Minnesota was campaigning for the Democratic Party nomination on an anti-war platform. Once again the war had a tremendous impact on the domestic front. Anti-war forces had been building in politics since 1965 and were strong by 1968. Despite government attempts to stop grassroots anti-war protests by the use of wire taps, false papers, spying and smear campaigns, the anti-war movement took on legitimacy as it was adopted by politicians. Congress eventually became a contesting ground for both hawk and dove (pro and anti-war) forces. In the earliest primary of 1968, in New Hampshire on 12 March, McCarthy made a strong showing against Johnson. This successful challenge eventually led to Robert

Kennedy's decision to run against the presidential incumbent in upcoming primaries.

The Democratic Party was beginning to split, a process that had been ongoing since 1948. A backlash element was growing within the party itself; Southern Democrats, a traditionally strong segment of the party, were beginning to turn more conservative. The Civil Rights Movement directly challenged the status quo of the South vis-à-vis race relations and federal interference in state prerogatives. Racism was still rampant within certain segments of the party. In addition, crime rates began to rise in the mid-1960s at an alarming rate. Violent crime increased as incidences of muggings, armed robberies, rapes and murder grew. While this might be explained by the natural increase in the number of young men who fit the age profile of the criminal class as the baby boomers grew older, the end result was a call for law and order from both the conservative elements within the Democratic Party and among the Republicans.

Concerns over what many people saw as social chaos were growing. Law and order politicians were not only responding to increases in crime rates but also to worries manifest by changes in American society. The student protest movement, use of drugs, increase in illegitimate births, growth in pornography and rising divorce rate all seemed to indicate a decaying society. Many people blamed the courts for being too liberal but also began to criticise liberals and intellectuals within American society. Professors, writers, artists and journalists were blamed for encouraging unsociable behaviour among American youth. As a consequence, Johnson signed the Omnibus Crime Act in June 1968 which made wiretaps easier to obtain for the purpose of collecting evidence and also allowed previously inadmissible evidence to be submitted in court. The civil rights and civil liberties of Americans were expanding and contracting at the same time.

No better symbol of this conservative backlash within Democratic Party quarters exists than George Wallace. In January 1963 Wallace was sworn in as Governor of Alabama. In his inaugural speech he promised 'segregation now, segregation tomorrow and segregation forever' in Alabama. He stood at the door of the University of Alabama to defy the desegregation order being enforced by federal troops. Wallace ran in the Democratic Primaries of 1964 in Wisconsin, Maryland and Indiana where he won approximately 30 per cent of the vote. Lyndon Johnson recognised that Wallace spoke to a group of people within the Democratic Party who were keen to preserve certain conservative values in America. These people represented what Johnson called the 'white backlash'. In 1968 Wallace decided to run for President on a third party ticket for the American Independent Party.

Faced with the negative publicity surrounding the Tet offensive and challenges to his authority within his own party, Johnson announced his decision not to run on 31 March 1968. The Democratic candidates proceeded to pursue their party's nomination through the primary system. Politics continued to witness its share of the violence of the decade when Robert Kennedy was assassinated after winning the California primary on 6 June 1968. Eventually the Democratic convention took place in Chicago and many of the symbols of the decade came together during that week in August. Various elements of the protest movements decided to confront the politicians at Chicago over the major issues of the moment. Tom Hayden and Rennie Davis of the SDS worked with the National Mobilization Committee (MOBE) against the Vietnam War, to launch protests at the convention. Abbie Hoffman and Jerry Rubin took the more anarchic route and suggested that Chicago should host a Festival of Life to counteract the Convention of Death, in obvious reference to the Vietnam War. Hoffman and Rubin supported the idea of total anarchy with drugs, sex and rock and roll ruling the day. Their Yippie (Youth International Party) movement nominated a pig for President and set about trying to disrupt one of American politics' most sacred rituals, the nominating convention.

Waiting for the arrival of anti-war protesters and other members of youth movements as well as the official Democratic Party delegates, was the Democratic Mayor of Chicago, Richard Daley. In total only about 5000 people appeared in Chicago to protest the convention and American participation in the Vietnam War, yet the atmosphere in Chicago was one of an armed camp. Daley was determined that 'outside agitators' should not be allowed to disrupt the proceedings of the convention or the peace of Chicago. There were small clashes between the various members of the protest movements and the police on the days preceding the convention but the real trouble began on Wednesday, 28 August, when violence erupted. Mayor Daley's hard-line, law and order stance meant that student protesters were met with baton wielding police officers whose response to the gathering crowd was to strike out first. As the convention convened inside, what was later termed a police riot took place outside, protesters were beaten and abused by the police, all of which was captured on television cameras and shown inside the convention hall. No group's reputation went unscathed by the end of the convention. The Democratic nomination went to Johnson's Vice

President, Hubert Humphrey, and the leaders of the various movements were arrested and charged with conspiracy to cross state lines with intent to incite riot, a charge issued under the Civil Rights Act of 1968. Their subsequent trial in September 1969 was a four-month affair which received widespread television coverage. The defendants became known as the Chicago 7. Originally there had been eight but Bobby Seale of the Black Panthers was separated from the others and his part declared a mistrial when the presiding Judge, Julius Hoffman, decided not to allow Seale to represent himself, charged Seale with 16 counts of contempt and eventually had Seale chained to his metal chair and gagged during the proceedings. The other seven, however, went on trial together. The news coverage of the trial showed much of the legal foundations of the trial to be a farce and after a lengthy appeals process the defendants were spared from serving time in prison. Yet in the end, to many Americans, the defendants in this trial represented all of what was wrong with America.

The Republican convention, on the other hand, was relatively quiet. At the end of the nomination process the Republicans had backed the ticket of Richard Nixon for president with Spiro Agnew his vice-presidential running mate. The ensuing election campaign pitted Humphrey who represented the liberal forces of the Johnson administration at home and the costly war abroad, against Nixon who campaigned on a return to law and order. Nixon claimed that it was time for the silent majority to be heard. Protesters and activists were the most vocal Americans but they were not the majority of Americans, according to Nixon. He cashed in on what has been called the 'cultural politics of resentment'. By 1968 the economy was beginning to feel the strains of trying to sustain spending on both state welfare programmes and the war in Vietnam. The New Left was in decline due to factionalism and government harassment, the Civil Rights Movement had given way to race riots and a growing black militancy and America seemed to be pulling apart. Nixon was able to bring together the conservative elements of American politics, whose seeds had been evident in Barry Goldwater's 1964 campaign, and combine it with the white backlash identified by Johnson as a result of the liberal agenda of the early part of the decade. With Nixon in office the country began to retrench. Though Nixon was not able to undo the Great Society, its expansion was slowed and, while Nixon's administration initiated tax reform and consumer protection legislation, it also moved to promote a more conservative Supreme Court as well as worked actively against the Civil Rights Movement. Helped by the demise of the left, Nixon was able to gain re-election in 1972 by a large majority which spelt the end of the Democratic coalition originally brokered by Roosevelt. A year later the United States ended its presence in Vietnam.

THE CONSEQUENCES

From 1960 to 1972 the United States underwent an upheaval in both foreign and domestic spheres. In foreign policy, the United States began a retreat from overseas involvement that remained part of American foreign policy up until the 1990s. Domestically, social change and social reform had occurred on an unprecedented scale. Women had made gains in work and in establishing the right to an abortion but they were still paid less than men and a new phenomenon, the feminisation of poverty, was developing as an economic trend. For African Americans civil rights legislation now guaranteed them the vote, equal access to public institutions and facilities, and the desegregation of public transport and education. However, the underlying economic realities for African Americans had not changed; blacks were consistently kept on the lower rungs of the economic ladder and the inner city ghetto continued to remain an almost exclusively black realm. In addition, a backlash against affirmative action ensued and was supported by the Supreme Court in the *Regents of the University of California v. Bakke* case of 1978, which curtailed affirmative action by suggesting it denied equality of opportunity. Other minority and ethnic groups made some strides forward by gaining recognition of their concerns and problems but they too continued to have to struggle against the conservative backlash of the era and its legacy.

Still, the United States government was not able to manipulate the American public completely. As during the Korean War period, the government in the 1960s during the conflict in Vietnam did not set up agencies comparable to the Committee on Public Information (CPI) and Office of War Information (OWI) in the First World War I and Second World War, respectively. In one sense this was not necessary since for the most part, in the early days at least, the flow of information about the situation in Vietnam was controlled by the government itself. For instance, military authorities invited journalists in Saigon to a daily briefing about the day's events and the ongoing war effort. Known as the '5 o'clock follies' these briefings gave only the establishment's views. Slowly journalists and observers began to question and then challenge the information being provided to the American people. From this beginning a belief developed that the media had a large role in helping to bring an end to the war in Vietnam. This would have consequences for the amount of access the US government would give journalists in future wars.

Despite Nixon's humiliation and disgrace at being forced to resign from office, the Republican Party and the conservative coalition kept a tight rein on the leadership of American politics. Jimmy Carter, a Democrat, won election in 1976 but he campaigned as an outsider of both the Democratic Party and Washington DC. His reign was brief and he was soon replaced by arch conservative Ronald Reagan who not only testified against his fellow actors as President of the Screen Actors Guild during the McCarthy Era but, as Governor of California, supported Samuel Hayakawa's draconian treatment of student protesters at San Francisco State University. The New Right was triumphant from 1968–1992. Yet the number of Americans who truly believed in the message of the New Right is hard to gauge since the real victim of the turmoil of the 1960s and early 1970s appears to have been voter turnout. Disillusionment with the government over issues such as the credibility gap in reporting the Vietnam War, combined with disenchantment with politicians after the illegal activities of the Nixon administration involved in Watergate, led many Americans to abandon politics altogether. Whereas the voter turn out rate was 62.8 per cent in 1960, by 1972, the first year that 18 year olds could vote, the turn out rate was a mere 55 per cent. By 1988 the turn out rate had been reduced even further to just 50 per cent. Only half of all eligible Americans bothered to participate in the election of their president.

The post-Vietnam war apathy had long ranging consequences. Social reform became an uphill battle. The Supreme Court, through appointments by Nixon and Reagan, took on a conservative mantle. Americans shied away from any overseas foreign policy interests, at least those that would require a major commitment of troops. Much later, debate ensued about the nature of limited warfare and whether or not the United States military would have been victorious if it had been allowed to fight a total war. In more immediate terms, Congress passed the War Powers Resolution in 1973 that limited the president's ability to wage war. Under the terms of this act the president had to inform Congress of any decision to send troops within 48 hours and Congress had to approve the use of troops within 60 days. This could be seen as a counterpoint to the Tonkin Gulf Resolution but in the time since Vietnam American presidents have been able to exercise their role as Commander in Chief in numerous conflicts without hindrance. Still the United States' longest war had long-term effects that the American people felt far into the twenty-first century.

6 Conclusions

HOW THE WARS BEGAN – JUSTICE OF WAR

Since just war theory suggests that the side fighting against aggression is the just side, in the First World War the United States could argue that they were fighting on the side of justice. In fact, that is exactly what Wilson claimed in his declaration of war. When the Germans implemented their Schlieffen Plan, invading neutral Belgium, they committed an act of aggression. While other countries had mobilised they had not opened fire. The same could be said for the outbreak of the Second World War. In this case, aggression began long before the war. In 1931 Japan began its expansionist campaign in Manchuria and in 1935 Mussolini did the same in North Africa. In fact, Hitler was the last of the aggressors to begin his campaign of conquest when he entered Austria in 1938, although he claimed he was only re-uniting German peoples. None of these early acts of aggression brought a wider war although under just war theory they could, even maybe should, have. The League of Nations, however, was weak and offered no meaningful response even though leaders such as Hailie Selassie asked for assistance. At any stage countries willing to stand up to this aggression would have been able to claim that they were fighting a just war, but it was not until Hitler invaded Poland in 1939 that other countries attempted to stop further aggression by resort to declarations of war. Although no country resisted the aggression in North Africa, Europe or Asia until 1939, the United States waited longer than others. Even in this just war circumstance, the United States held back until, finally, in 1941 with the Japanese attack on Pearl Harbor the Americans came into the Second World War claiming their just response had been provoked by intolerable acts of aggression.

While the United States' initial reluctance to enter the war and its claims of neutrality were permitted under international law, several points can be raised in a just war theory analysis. First, is it justifiable to sit back and allow aggression to prevail while people are dying in the name of resistance, especially when the United States had the capacity to make a meaningful contribution to the fight for justice? Second, was the United

States truly neutral? In both wars the United States was able to gain financially from the war before it entered into the conflict. In the First World War American manufacturers and farmers gained by working to supply the warring nations, at first including the Central Powers. Eventually, however, this trade benefited the Entente Powers more. From 1939 to 1941 US businesses also made money out of supplying the nations resisting aggression. As most scholars agree it was the war that pulled America out of the Depression, not the government's New Deal programmes. Moreover, despite the passing of several Neutrality Acts, the United States was anything but neutral.

But the United States did eventually enter both wars when its interests were attacked directly, in the First World War by the German return to unrestricted submarine warfare and, in the Second World War, by the Japanese attack on Pearl Harbor. Hence, America laid claim to its place on the list of nations fighting a just war. The US commitment to the concept of only fighting a just war was re-enforced in these wars. Despite the complaints by Americans in the 1930s interwar period that the United States had no business getting involved in overseas conflicts (outside the western hemisphere of course), the surprise attack on Pearl Harbor in 1941 left an impressionable memory of the consequences of failing to face up to aggression when it first occurs. While the United States had learned this lesson by the end of the Second World War, it did not apply it faithfully until the outbreak of the next war.

The immediate post-war years witnessed the expansion of the Soviet Union into areas of Eastern Europe that did not prompt any resistance from the United States or other ex-allies of the Second World War. Instead, the west watched as Stalin moved to ensure the safety of the Soviet Union from future aggression by gaining control of the satellite nations bordering his country. The existence of his massive Red Army acted as a disincentive to a military response on the part of the United States. By 1950 the United States had learned to live with Soviet control of Eastern Europe and was beginning to adjust to the victory of the communists in China. The official foreign policy of the United States became containment; keeping communism where it was, not letting it expand.

Then, when the North Koreans invaded South Korea in June 1950, the United States felt that it could, and in fact should, react swiftly to this naked aggression. Truman told the American people that the United States needed to uphold the rule of law. The situation in Korea suggested that aggressive communism was threatening weak and vulnerable areas and that the United States needed to help protect fledgling democracies such as the one in South Korea when it could. The US government had more trouble justifying its decision to extend the fighting, once it had pushed the North Koreans back, by crossing the 38th parallel. The policy of containment had somehow transformed to one of eradication and there was little in just war theory that could be utilised to explain this act of aggression on America's part. But the act of pursuing the North Korean communists above the 38th parallel did not need justifying at home in the United States, because it was in the grip of an anti-communist hysteria that generated its own justification for questionable acts. Since communism was perceived to be waging an aggressive campaign within the United States, military actions against communism outside of the United States could be justified. In the black and white world of the Cold War any country that was not democratic was the enemy and you did not need any further justification than that. So, American participation in the Korean War, unlike the two previous wars, began immediately after the North Koreans made the first move south.

The moral justification for United States involvement in the Vietnam War presented a more complex problem. After the Second World War the Cold War was raging and while the Vietnamese people tried to stop a resurgence of French colonial rule, the anti-communist agenda was being set in Washington DC. US participation in the immediate post-war period entailed financial support to the French, justified as necessary to hold back the aggressive forces of communism. With the defeat of the French at Dien Bien Phu in 1954 the United States had to determine how far it would go to hold off the growth of communism in yet another Asian country, and just war theory played little part in the decision. It was not the first time that the United States decided to back a corrupt regime; that had happened in South Korea. What was different this time was that there was, crucially, no clear invasion or pinpointed moment of aggression. Furthermore, when the South Vietnamese government, without protest from the United States, decided to ignore the reunification elections agreed at the Geneva conference, any possibility of justifying subsequent actions in Vietnam was lost. And while the United States was not technically fighting in Vietnam until troops arrived in 1965, American 'advisors' had been waging war in all but name. What transpired was a slow escalation of US involvement from 1945 up to the point where troops were called in. The Gulf of Tonkin incident, however, was used by Lyndon Johnson to justify and explain this rise in the level of US involvement. The rhetoric was much the same as it had been when Wilson discussed German U-Boats, Roosevelt spoke of Pearl

Harbor and Truman commented on the actions of North Korea. Aggression was presented as being at the root of the problem and the United States had no choice but to fight.

HOW THE WARS WERE FOUGHT – JUSTICE IN WAR

When just war theory meets twentieth century wars philosophical problems ensue, especially with regard to how the wars were fought.It is easy to agree with the theory that there is a right way and a wrong way to fight, and that there are legitimate and illegitimate targets of that fight. As any person who has participated in combat will tell you, however, the theory is difficult to sustain during the waging of war. In the First World War the machine gun and ever-larger artillery made the subsequent trench warfare deadly. Battle after battle, as men poured over the tops of trenches and ran toward the enemy lines, astronomical casualty figures resulted. Even the newly introduced planes and tanks, which would change the nature of future wars, were devices meant ultimately to spare lives by breaking the stalemate and ending the war quickly. The fact that all of these tactics and innovations sat firmly within the realms of the battlefront and were directed squarely at enemy soldiers, however, makes them legitimate, if deadly, acts of war.

The problems of justifying the killing in the First World War arose with the introduction of technologies and techniques that endangered the lives of civilians. The most obvious example of this is the use of the U-boat or submarine by the German Navy. From the outset the Germans targeted shipping indiscriminately and the result was the loss of innocent civilians as in the sinking of the *Lusitania* in May 1915. What people often fail to acknowledge, however, is that Germany was reacting to the institution of a blockade by the British that was a violation of international law and also targeted civilians. Countries at war that are denied supplies usually give what supplies remain to the military, to sustain the fight. Hence, the civilian population suffers. In these cases, both sides of the conflict expanded the nature of the battlefield as both countries struggled to adjust to twentieth century warfare. Modern, total war required the participation of not just large numbers of troops but also substantial industrial production on the home front. Techniques were deployed that were meant to take advantage of this at home and nullify a similar advantage for the enemy. US President Wilson protested against both actions, the blockade and the use of the U-boat, because they were seen to be widening the targets and victims of war.

Interestingly there were also protests against the deployment of gas as a weapon when it was introduced in the First World War. When the Germans first used gas the intention was, again, to break the stalemate in the trenches and get the war moving toward a conclusion. Theoretically, an earlier end or conclusion to the war would save lives, both allied and enemy. But somehow gas seemed wrong despite the fact that it was a military weapon used against the armed forces of the enemy. The slow, agonising death that ensued from inhalation of poisonous gas did much to feed the protest against this technology. However, if you could legiti- mately kill the enemy with bullets, bombs, torpedoes and artillery why was it wrong to kill them with chemical weapons? The nature of this new weapon brought it into the debate about justice in war. Justice in war recognises that combatants will die during war but also suggests that there should be rules about how that death occurs. Subsequently, there were many international agreements that banned the use of poisonous gas although the United States did not sign the Geneva Protocol of 1925 until 1975. By the end of the First World War much of these concerns became subsumed under one banner – the horrors of war itself. Yet somehow the vast numbers of killed and wounded produced in modern combat made discussions of justice in war ring hollow.

By the time of the outbreak of the Second World War the ways of fighting wars changed again. Soldiers faced the usual array of weaponry; bullets, artillery, torpedoes and bombs, sent from one belligerent against another, which were the normal methods of waging war by this time. Poisonous gas was not used, perhaps in part due to the Geneva Protocol, which suggested not only that using poisonous gas was wrong but also that should one side use it the other side would be free, in a moral sense, to use it as well. Another problem with the deployment of gas in the Second World War was the fact that the battlefield was fluid, compared to the trenches of the First World War, and enemy soldiers fought each other across ever shifting battle fronts. This situation was due to the fur- ther development of military hardware that had begun in the First World War. The tank played a large role in the Second World War and, as utilised by the Germans for example, kept the war moving at a lightning pace. While the tank, the artillery, the torpedoes and the guns, as utilised on the battle front, were aimed at enemy soldiers during the Second World War, the civilian population also came increasingly under attack.

The development of bomber aircraft by the outbreak of the Second World War moved the combat of war into a new realm – the home front. While battlefield aviation had occurred during the First World War, it was not until the Second World War that the strategic use of bomber aircraft systematically targeted enemy positions behind the lines of battle on a grand scale. Bombing of civilians had taken place in the First World War by both the British and German military. Air warfare that included aerial dog fights, the first in history, also included indiscriminate bombing of towns and cities, as well as bridges, communication lines and factories. However, these early forays into targeting civilians pale in comparison to the level of deliberate destruction and death reached by the belligerents of the Second World War. It is estimated that 5 per cent of deaths due to wartime combat were civilian in the First World War I but that this number rose to 50 per cent during the Second World War II.[1]

What was different about the Second World War and the evolving bombing campaign was the deliberate targeting of non-combatants, on a massive scale, to try to weaken the resolve of the enemy. Whether referred to as terror bombing, indiscriminate bombing or carpet bombing, the main targets of these bombing campaigns were not specific buildings or factories, but rather the whole population of a town or city. The American air force tried to limit its involvement in indiscriminate bombing early in the war in Europe by insisting on conducting daytime, precision bombing raids. The question was a moral one, with the United States insisting that its use of bombing to conduct offensive war was legitimate as long as care was taken to avoid any direct targeting of civilian populations. It was acknowledged that some civilian casualties were to be expected due to the compact nature of cities and the location of legitimate targets such as arms factories, in proximity to homes and businesses, but these casualties needed to be kept at a minimum. Hence, American pilots flew daylight missions at first. Eventually, however, the United States succumbed to the widening of bombing targets and abandoned its full commitment to precision bombing.

---

[1] The statistics for civilian death rates vary in the literature, as do most statistics. Civilian casualties for the First World War have been variously stated as 5 and/or 15 per cent. For the Second World War the rate has been suggested as 48, 50 and as high as 65 per cent. The same is true for Korea (84 per cent) and Vietnam (from 60 or 70 to as high as 98 per cent). None of these statistics, however, are civilian death rates solely from the air war; they also include deliberate massacres and attacks as well as civilian deaths from starvation. They also include statistics for both sides of each war.

Part of the problem with the bombing campaign was that by bombing in daylight the bomber aircraft were more exposed and hence the rate of loss of aircraft and their crews was high. The British had recognised this much earlier and proceeded to conduct their air war against Germany with the use of nighttime raids. By the time the tactic of daylight bombing was abandoned, the bombing of enemy cities by the allies had progressed to the point of saturation bombing. Any resistance in the sky from Germany had been eliminated as was the case in the Pacific war as the American military approached the Japanese home islands. Subsequently, the firebombing of Dresden in February 1945 by the British and American air forces and the firebombing of Tokyo in March 1945 by the United States meant that any pretext of debate about the morality of bombing civilians had disappeared. Instead, it was replaced with the concept of trying to bring the enemy to the point of surrender using any means while simultaneously sparing the lives of United States and allied soldiers.

It was in this atmosphere that the ultimate bombing campaign of the war took place. The use of atomic weapons on the Japanese mainland in August of 1945 has been variously applauded and condemned. The controversy over the use of atomic weapons in the Second World War is fuelled by speculation and theories about the 'real' reason the United States decided to drop the bombs. Some commentators have claimed that the United States used the atomic weapons because they wanted to force the Japanese surrender before the Soviet Union could become involved in the Pacific War. Indeed the Soviets declared war on Japan in the days between the first and second bombing. Others have argued, less convincingly, that the American use of the atomic bomb was a racist attack and that the device would not have been used on European peoples, despite the obvious point that the bomb was not ready until after the war in Europe had ended. Still others have suggested that the United States used the bombs in order to prepare the way for a more dominant position in the post-war world. The fact was the United States was clearly untouched by the hard hand of war, the America home front was relatively unscathed and the United States was already in a position to dominate the post-war world. Other critics point out that the Japanese had been sending out peace feelers and hence the need to drop the bomb had been reduced because a negotiated peace could have occurred.

Most defenders of the decision point to the estimates of casualties had the United States invaded the mainland of Japan. Rarely is the decision to drop the atomic bombs discussed in relation to the fire bombings of

Tokyo or Dresden, where more civilian casualties were suffered or the siege of Leningrad where, as Walzer has pointed out, more innocent people died than in the bombings of Hamburg, Dresden, Tokyo, Hiroshima and Nagasaki combined. Equally important to any discussion of the decision is recognition of, not only US strategic policy and post-war plans, but also how the decision was viewed by the men on the way to the fighting in the Pacific. Few Second World War soldiers, on the way to the front line in Japan, criticised Truman's actions. Indeed, Truman stated that he never lost any sleep worrying about his decision to use the atomic bombs.

How did the belligerents in the Second World War get to the point of indiscriminate bombing, the use of V1 and V2 rockets by the Germans, the fire bombings of major urban centres and the use of nuclear weapons on whole populations? In part, the bombing deaths of the civilian populations during the war occurred because precision bombing had rarely been precise in the first place. The technology was not developed enough during the Second World War to produce a guaranteed hit on a specific location without incurring collateral damage. Surveys of bombing raids by the allies suggested that a bomb was considered to have been precise if it hit within five miles of the target. Under these circumstances commanders were willing to sacrifice the unfortunate deaths within the civilian population in the belief that these deaths were necessary in order for military goals to be achieved. Of equal importance was the deliberate targeting of civilian populations in the hope that the subsequent deaths and destruction would prove unsustainable for the enemy. Decision makers spoke of 'de-housing' people and breaking public morale. Then there was the argument that the civilian population during the large-scale, modern world war was, after all, a legitimate target in itself because the people within the country, once considered civilians and hence non-combatants, were working in a military capacity when they worked and contributed to the manufacture of bombs, planes, ships and other war materiel. It was not a large leap to make from the use of conventional bombs to the use of the atomic bomb under these circumstances.

But the discussion of the morality of these tactics did not completely disappear. Some of the very scientists who helped to develop the atomic bomb lobbied to keep it from being used. After Dresden too there was an eerie sense of having gone a step too far. The combat immunity of the civilian population had been overridden in the heat of conducting a total war but once the war was over, and people began to count the number of dead, the need to somehow contain future wars became a topic of discussion. Unfortunately, post-war attempts by the western allies (Britain, France and the United States) to curtail civilian/non-combatant deaths were applied to their own populations not their opponents. After the Second World War, in the major wars for America, the problem of non-combat immunity again proved difficult.

In both the Korean War and the Vietnam War the United States fought on one side of a civil war. In these instances then the enemy could be difficult to determine since the supporters of either side were from one previously united country. The rapid and constant shifting of the front in Korea meant that civilians were easily caught up in the fighting. In Vietnam, although the war took part in South Vietnam for the most part, the presence of North Vietnamese sympathisers and insurgents made the identification of civilians who were loyal to the South Vietnamese government difficult. From this perspective, Americans fighting in Vietnam often failed to maintain the clear distinction between combatant and non-combatant. In addition, the bombing campaigns in both wars resembled those of the Second World War in the sense that the bombing was indiscriminate. That is not to say that there were not specific targets but rather that the use of bombing was no more precise than it had been in the 1940s. Also, in both wars the United States bombed areas within the country they were trying to help. All of this meant that during the Korean and Vietnam Wars the civilian casualty rate was high and indicated that non-combatants now made up somewhere between 85 and 95 per cent of all casualties.

In addition, while neither fire bombing nor obliteration of cities was part of America's air strategy during either of these wars, what few large cities there were, were indeed attacked and other air strategies emerged. For instance, the United States used napalm in both Korea and Vietnam, a petroleum-based component of incendiary bombs. Defoliants also played a part, especially in American strategy as a method of making jungle warfare in Vietnam more viable. Neither of these technologies could be restricted to enemy combatants and, as a result, there were more innocent victims of the fighting.

Another point sets these two wars apart from the two world wars and that is their limited nature. While the US decision to pursue the Korean War above the 38th parallel eventually drew in the Chinese as combatants, the war itself did not expand beyond the Korean Peninsula. The same is generally true for the Vietnam War, although America did expand the war at various times to Cambodia and Laos on a limited scale. Ultimately they were not world wars but rather they were fought on a limited basis.

One thing all four wars had in common in terms of the way they were fought, however, was the committing of acts of atrocity by American fighting men. In just war theory terms this could mean anything from deliberately killing enemy prisoners of war (POWs) to targeting women and children. Much of this has to do with the military demonising the enemy and the tendency to look upon the enemy, including combatants and non-combatants, as somehow inferior. Behaviour of this nature can range from the taking of body part 'trophies' off dead enemy soldiers to close combat killing of a group of civilians as happened at No Gun Ri in Korea and My Lai in Vietnam. The heat of battle or frustration over the course of war can explain these types of incidents but it cannot excuse them. Just war theory requires that anyone engaged in combat target only fellow combatants. But as the evidence suggests, the targeting or indiscriminate killing of non-combatants was a feature of the First World War, the Second World War , Korea and Vietnam, making it difficult if not impossible to suggest the United States fought these wars justly.

HOW THE WARS ENDED – JUSTICE AFTER THE WAR

Of equal importance to discussions of morality and warfare is the consideration that wars should end in a just way and in the post-war periods victors should strive to promote justice. When the fighting in the First World War ended in November 1918 the United States had earned a place at the peace negotiations. Woodrow Wilson, having announced his Fourteen Points in January 1918, very much wanted to instil a democratic order on the nations of the world. As a Progressive reformer, Wilson saw an opportunity to make a real change in the old world order. He called for free trade, freedom of the seas, open covenants, disarmament and, most especially, self-determination of nations. Wilson's vision of a world without war was going to be fulfilled, in his belief, by the establishment of a League of Nations to oversee future border and territorial disputes. But the United States was overruled in the Paris Peace Conference on several of these points and the other victorious nations insisted upon debilitating reparations from Germany and inserted a clause in the final version of the Treaty of Versailles that demanded Germany accept full responsibility for the war. Both reparations and the war guilt clause put the moral blame for the war with Germany as head of the Central Powers thus laying the foundations for future problems. This treaty was also a dictated treaty; Germany had no part in the negotiations.

Though Wilson recognised the treaty was a compromise document, he hoped to redress some of the problems through the offices of the League of Nations. Unfortunately for Wilson, when he returned to the United States from the negotiations he discovered that his hard work was set to be ignored by Congress. Despite his active campaigning for approval of the treaty, it was defeated in the Senate. Subsequently, the United States did not join the League of Nations, leaving this worldwide 'court' weakened and, ultimately, unable to act as a bulwark against future acts of aggression. While many new democracies were established in place of the old crumbling empires of Europe, they were then left on their own to survive. The United States abandoned its rhetoric of justice by withdrawing from the world stage. The ending of the First World War did not result in a fair and just peace.

When the United States finally became involved in the Second World War it was clear that it did not want to make the same mistakes at the end of the war. This time the United States would not only be heavily involved in final negotiations, it would work to control the peace process itself. The first step towards avoiding the post-war mistakes of the First World War was indicated when Roosevelt and Churchill announced the allied policy of unconditional surrender at the Casablanca conference in January 1943. Not only did it ensure that the member nations of the allied side would not negotiate separate treaties with the Germans or Japanese, it also meant that the war would not end prematurely. Ultimately unconditional surrender would lead to the occupation of Germany and Japan to guarantee the destruction of the elements within those societies that advocated aggression and conquest. It did not, as Roosevelt was quick to point out, mean the total destruction of Germany, Japan and Italy. Instead, Roosevelt wanted to provide the best possible atmosphere for the growth and development of true democracies. Critics of the Treaty of Versailles from the end of the First World War suggested that the allied nations had been too quick to accept surrender and stop the fighting. Critics of the policy of unconditional surrender, however, suggested that the adoption of this policy achieved negative results because it forced both the Germans and the Japanese to fight on much longer than necessary out of fear of what unconditional surrender would mean.

Another major difference in the US approach to the ending of the Second World War from that of the First was the decision of the American government not only to help establish and then join the United Nations (UN), a replacement for the ineffective League of Nations, but to dominate that organisation with monetary backing and by insisting its headquarters be in New York City. The United States did not retreat into isolationism this time. Instead, it planned to play a leading role in the post-war world in order to ensure that future aggression, and as a consequence future wars, would be dealt with rapidly and not allowed to evolve into the worldwide carnage of the last two great wars. Hopefully this would mean that American involvement in future wars would be just and those wars would end swiftly.

Equally important to the ending of the Second World War was the decision on the part of the allies to arrest, charge and prosecute those individuals responsible for the violation of the rules of war. A new charge of waging aggressive war entered the discussions about war crimes. Individuals from the German and Japanese governments and military were brought before courts charged with offences and acts that violated the established sense of proper wartime conduct and behaviour. It seemed only reasonable that, on the heels of learning the full story about German death camps and Japanese treatment of POWs, someone had to be held accountable. Stories outlining the full extent of the horrors of this war were beginning to emerge and newsreel footage captured the evidence for the world to see. Millions had died around the globe and many millions more were homeless refugees. With a righteous sense of justice the allied governments pursued those responsible. A simple war guilt clause in the final treaties was not going to be enough to compensate for the level of destruction that had occurred, this time levelled against the civilian population directly. A war guilt clause as well targeted a nation's whole population not the specific individuals responsible for unjust acts.

What the war crime trials did not do was administer justice evenly. No one on the allied side was brought to account for the war crimes they had committed. The fire bombings of Dresden and Tokyo, for example, went unpunished. Incidents of allied immoral behaviour in war were not discussed. And even the trials against the wartime enemies quickly lost the public's interest. The first Nuremburg Trials were packed with reporters and newsreel cameras from around the world, while subsequent trials often went unreported. However, the discussion of justice in war, and the pursuit of those responsible for wartime atrocities such as the Holocaust, went on for years after the Second World War and continues today. The other aim of unconditional surrender and occupation of former enemy nations was to help establish democracy in Japan and Germany. This did happen (in West Germany and Japan) and the process was later accelerated as the Cold War between the United States and the Soviet Union developed in the immediate post-war years.

Finding justice in the conclusion of both the Korean and Vietnam Wars is more complex. These wars differ on several levels from the First and Second World Wars and, hence, their conclusion is also quite different. Both wars were, in essence, civil wars, and both wars ended through negotiation and compromise rather than from a position of victory for the United States. In Korea, once the American government had decided to pursue a status quo ante settlement along the 38th parallel, there was little left to do but iron out a ceasefire/armistice and exchange of prisoners. In this case there was no decision to try to impose a more democratic vision onto the defeated enemy because the enemy was not defeated. The best the United States could hope for was that once the war ended North Korea could be kept from invading the South in the future. This was ultimately accomplished by the continued presence of the US military in South Korea long after the war had ended. In the Cold War atmosphere a just peace was one that kept the communists contained and, despite a brief attempt at eradication when the United States headed north over the 38th parallel, the communists were contained by war's end.

The end of the war in Vietnam had some similarities. It too had been a limited war and a civil war as well. It also ended at the negotiating table and not by an overwhelming victory for the United States against its enemy. In both Korea and Vietnam the American government and people lost the will to continue the fight; therefore, the only means of ending the war in a way that did not spell defeat for the United States was by talking to the enemy. In both cases as well, the negotiations went on for years while people continued to die – US soldiers, enemy soldiers, allied soldiers and the civilian populations of each country. These negotiated settlements, furthermore, took place between governments with little regard for the fate of the people. However, it could be argued that these wars ended more justly in the sense that the wars eventually reached a point of unsustainability resulting in the situation where both sides sat down across a table rather than a battlefield and discussed the future course of the war and an end to the killing. This happened while both sides were still undefeated and the governments were still intact. The ending then became a compromise rather than a dictated settlement or overwhelming defeat.

US HOME FRONT – JUSTICE AT HOME

The application of just war theory to the treatment of citizens at home by governments at war is appropriate. The US government, as we have seen, made a point of speaking about its involvement in the major wars of the twentieth century in moral terms. US participation in these four wars was explained to the American people by their presidents as being a case of America going to war for a just cause and therefore fighting a just war. However, while governments may indeed feel obligated to explain their decision to resort to deadly force in just war terms, they should then be certain that they do not sacrifice justice at home in the process. If they do, can they still be fighting a just war? As Arthur Marwick noted, war happens within and to a society, it is not separate from society.

On the home front in the First World War, Wilson and his government tried to rally support for the war through the Committee on Public Information (CPI) and at the same time led a concerted attack on the civil liberties of the American people. Justice on the home front was assaulted by a series of wartime acts passed by Congress outlawing the freedom of speech guaranteed under the Bill of Rights. This abuse of governmental power, notable in the Espionage Act, Sedition Act, Threats Against the President Act and others, was a direct assault on the rights of Americans to speak their mind and debate their government's actions.

Furthermore, the highest court in the branch of the government called upon to uphold the provisions of the Constitution, the Supreme Court, fell in with the government in this attack on civil liberties. By upholding the conviction of individuals charged under these acts the court made a judgement that while the government is conducting a war abroad it can curtail the rights of citizens at home. Under these circumstances there would be no need for governments to explain the disjunction between waging a just war against a foreign enemy while denying justice to its own citizens.

Ironically, while the US government was waging war against citizens' rights the war itself was working to improve the conditions of certain segments of American society. In a small scale compared to what we will see later, America's involvement in the First World War brought benefits to the people. Demand for labour increased the employment rate, for example, which included some groups previously struggling such as women and minorities. The participation of African Americans in the war effort generated some benefits in part due to the migration of many out of the South and into northern cities. Women were later given the right to vote, often linked at the time and later with their participation in the war effort. Yet these gains could be overshadowed by the increased pressure for conformity manifest in the campaign for 100 per cent

Americanism for instance. Vigilante attacks on all things German and the attacks on radicals suggest that American society itself struggled with a wartime sense of threat and paranoia. Ultimately the gains that some segments of society made during the war could often turn out to be temporary or for the duration.

The Second World War presented the US government with similar problems. The surprise attack on Pearl Harbor by the Japanese helped to unify the commitment of the American people to fighting and Roosevelt found it easy, under these circumstances, to argue that the United States was engaged in fighting a just war. However, as had been the case in the First World War, the rhetoric of justice did not always apply to American citizens. By establishing the Office of War Information (OWI) Roosevelt acknowledged a need to sell the war to the American people and to ensure that the information they received was supportive of the war effort.

While there was no Sedition Act or Threats Against the President Act during the Second World War, the Espionage Act was used and a new piece of legislation, the Smith Act, was introduced. The Smith Act, a direct assault on freedom of speech, outlawed advocating the overthrow of the government by speech or print and belonging to any organisation that advocated the overthrow of the government. As with the First World War, the Supreme Court upheld convictions under the Smith Act by suggesting that speech that had a 'bad tendency' could be restricted. The war then required that voices of dissent be suppressed and that the Bill of Rights be ignored. But a far more ominous attack on civil liberties occurred when the president signed Executive Order 9066, which sent American citizens into wartime internment camps. The second generation Japanese Americans caught up in this hysterical wartime act were American citizens by birth and therefore protected under the terms of the Constitution not least of which entailed the need for due process before being imprisoned. So a government waging a war in the name of ridding the world of totalitarian regimes and their use of arbitrary actions against innocent people perpetrated an arbitrary act against its own innocent civilians.

However, there were some areas of justice on the home front during the Second World War. Roosevelt issued Executive Order 8802, which called for equality in hiring in government jobs and among industries with government contracts. This attempt to address problems of discrimination faced by African Americans was a step towards government backing of civil rights for minorities. But, as with the First World War, the boom economy brought about by wartime production did more to help alleviate the economic problems of minorities than any piece of legislation. Moreover, the war did act to raise the consciousness of the wider African American community. The continued migration of blacks out of the rural South and into cities to work in industrial production, the launching of the 'Double V' campaign, their participation in the armed forces both at home and abroad and an incredible increase in membership in the National Association for the Advancement of Colored People (NAACP) meant that African Americans were poised to seize the initiative for change in the post-war era. Still there were setbacks. The government never did address the issue of civil rights directly and there were race riots such as the one in Detroit in 1943 as whites resisted any change in the status quo.

This desire to hold on to the status quo was felt by other segments of society as well. While the war brought new opportunities for women it also brought challenges. Women went into paid work at a much higher rate including married women and older women with children, but this change was seen as a necessity of the war and not a permanent shift in attitudes. The phrase 'for the duration' attested to the underlying belief that the war was a temporary event and once it was over the world in general, and America in particular, could return to the way things had been. So, as with the post-war period after the First World War, America after 1945 settled into a post-war conservatism that was brought forcefully to centre stage during the course of the next war.

There was little need to sell the Korean War to the American people. For one thing, the war was on a much smaller scale and did not require the mobilisation of the entire populace as the previous total wars had. More importantly, the war fought in Korea was about striking a blow against aggressive communism and America in 1950 was firmly in the throes of a domestic anti-communist agenda. The government did not need to convince Americans of the justness of the fight against North Korea; America was coming to the rescue of a small country, struggling to establish democracy, against an aggressive puppet regime linked to an ever-expanding communist block.

Still, during this war the government also failed to protect the rights of its citizens and, hence, did not fulfil its obligation to provide justice on the home front. In this case the attack on civil liberties did not entail the arrests or internment of a group on the basis of its ethnicity but rather focussed on concerns about people's political beliefs. In a country that publicly prides itself on being democratic, the right to choose your political party affiliation was denied. Government investigations by committees in both the Senate and House of Representatives looked for enemies within American society. The foreign policy concerns about the expansion of communism overseas had a domestic policy equivalent. The Smith Act was invoked to try to weed out members of the Communist Party of the United States of America (CPUSA) as did the McCarren Act. Spies were arrested and tried and, in the case of the Rosenbergs, executed. And the Supreme Court continued to uphold convictions under these acts until well into the late 1950s and early 1960s, long after the Korean War was over.

Because this war was short and limited in nature, there was less opportunity for the war to act as a major catalyst for democratic change. The early 1950s, instead, was a time of conformity and conservatism. While Truman had moved to desegregate the military in 1948, which was finally implemented during the Korean War, most African Americans saw little change in the nature of their position within American society. Further gains were problematic during the McCarthy era because African American civil rights groups were often tainted with the suspicion of being influenced or led by members of the Communist Party. Although challenges by African Americans to the status quo and decisions by the Supreme Court that began to address discrimination occurred during the early 1950s, it was not until after the war that the Civil Rights Movement began to make major strides in overturning decades of discrimination.

Equally, women and labour made some gains during the Korean War but mostly the fear of communism and the hunt for communist sympathisers overshadowed all aspects of American society. The government crack down on strikes, and attempts to control wages and prices worked against the rights of the labour force. In addition, the war was not large enough to transform the economy and manufacturing in such a way as dramatically to expand the size of the work force which meant that women did not have the opportunity to increase their level of employment at the same rate as in previous twentieth-century wars. However, more women did go into the work force in the 1950s and, slowly, began to expand their part in the development of the burgeoning consumer society. Yet it was not until the Korean War was over and the McCarthy era anti-communist hysteria had ceased that groups within the United States could begin to make significant progress in pursuit of equality. In part this was accomplished during the next war.

The US home front during the Vietnam War presents a far different narrative than the previous major wars of the twentieth century. In part this has to do with Lyndon Johnson's deliberate attempts to promote justice in the domestic arena rather than curtail civil liberties and civil rights. His war on poverty and Great Society campaigns, as well as his endorsement of the Civil Rights Act of 1964 and Voting Rights Act of 1965, attest to his earnest belief in the power of the government to provide its citizens with expanded rights and privileges. Equally important, Johnson did not suggest that once America was at war these rights and liberties needed to be curtailed. However, there were still problems in terms of the federal government and justice on the home front, not least in terms of the flow of information about the war to the public. Rather than establish an organisation to sell the war to the American people as had happened in the First World War and the Second World War , during the Vietnam era the government merely kept secret the facts of the war. This lack of openness was not new to this war but it was challenged to a much higher degree by the public, which put a new face on the impact of wars on the home front.

The New Left and student movement provide examples of the challenges Johnson faced. These movements not only wanted to increase civil rights for segments of American society, they also forcefully resisted attempts to curtail their vocal protests. The story of the Free Speech Movement at Berkeley illustrates the part played by grassroots groups in staving off governmental crackdowns on civil liberties. As Johnson escalated US involvement in Vietnam, and sent troops in 1965, numerous groups coalesced around the banner of an anti-war protest movement. Organised events such as the Stop the Draft Week, march on the Pentagon and attacks on Reserve Officer Training Corps (ROTC) offices on campuses illustrated a freedom to speak and act during a war that would have been unthinkable in previous wars. And, in direct contrast to the previous wars, the Supreme Court came out in support of these protests by safeguarding the freedom of speech element guaranteed within the Constitution. This movement allowed for a public discussion of the morality or justness of the war while the war was going on, rather than after the war ended as had been the case previously. Almost inevitably, as freedom of speech was exercised by more and more people, public support for the war decreased. This latter point perhaps illustrates clearly why governments often find it expedient to curtail freedom of speech during war.

Other groups also pushed for more and faster reforms while the war in Vietnam was raging. African Americans' demands for civil rights increased in the 1960s. From sit-ins to non-violent marches, the civil rights of African Americans were being expanded at a rapid rate. The combination of black activism and Johnson's belief in redressing past imbalances led to the passage of the Civil Rights Acts of 1964 and 1965. But the passage of these long overdue attacks on Jim Crow did not mean that African Americans finally had equality in America. Instead, problems persisted and protests turned violent with a series of race riots across America demonstrating the level of frustration within the African American community.

However, other groups were inspired by both the Civil Rights Movement and the student movement. The women's movement appeared in the 1960s and was just as vocal as its predecessors. Women wanted equal pay and equal recognition of their contributions to American society. Native Americans launched their own movement in an attempt to redress the consequence of decades of inequality. The Chicano movement also appeared in the 1960s. Each of these movements in their turn took to the streets with vocal demands for the government to recognise and address their concerns. All of this took place while the United States was still fighting the war in Vietnam and, almost predictably, a backlash developed.

Despite Johnson's initial belief in the power of government to do good for its own citizens, the proliferation of protests, riots and violence across the United States in the 1960s prompted the government, at local, state and federal level, to try to restore order. When Johnson signed the Omnibus Crime Act in 1968, making wiretaps easier, he was acting on a concern that some elements within society were getting out of control. Law and order elements including the Chicago police force during the 1968 Democratic convention and the National Guard at Kent State Ohio in 1970 hit back at these 'lawless' elements, sometimes with deadly consequences. US involvement in the war in Vietnam had stimulated a vocal protest against what many called an unjust war and the violence of the decade on the home front seemed to reflect the violent nature of the war. News broadcasts throughout the 1960s, and emergency bulletins that broke into regular scheduled programming, bombarded the American public with views of a society struggling to come to terms with its fate. America's involvement in a civil war abroad had generated a civil war at home. All four wars ultimately failed to sustain the rhetoric of just war on the home front. Civil liberties and civil rights, and the American people, became the victims of wartime injustice.

CONCLUSIONS

Clearly there is a need for governments to justify their participation in war. Throughout the twentieth century the United States has done just that, and in each instance has professed to be responding to attacks or acts of aggression making it clear that America's wars are just wars. In fact, in order to sustain the argument that America's wars are just wars, governmental and presidential addresses rely on the rhetoric of righteousness. Wilson, Roosevelt, Truman and Johnson all explained that they decided to go to war reluctantly but that in the circumstances war was necessary. The same is true of presidential rhetoric in previous wars and the wars since Vietnam.

Having gone to war for a just cause it is assumed that Americans will fight justly. This premise was relatively easy to uphold in the First World War but by the time of the Second, when civilian populations were being deliberately targeted by bomber aircraft, the high moral stand was difficult to sustain. But these deaths were often seen at the time, and certainly by those making strategic and tactical decisions, as justifiable. Civilian populations were active participants in the war effort in countries fighting a total war. Civilian populations were also at the heart of the next two wars, Korea and Vietnam, and bombing continued. Actions that elicited critical comment during these wars were acts against local populations by combat troops. While the incident at No Gun Ri in Korea came to light later, the My Lai 'massacre' was exposed during the ongoing Vietnam War. Justice was sought with the prosecution of Lieutenant Calley, although clearly there had been a cover up. Eventually only Calley was tried and the president then pardoned him.

Despite this lack of rigor in discovering and then prosecuting criminal behaviour in wartime, the rhetoric of fighting justly has not changed. Certainly technologically, with the development of guided missiles and smart bombs, it is possible now to bomb precisely. Yet there is often still 'collateral damage'. But this collateral damage is debated, discussed and condemned. Equally, American troops are held to account for violations of the code of conduct for war.

In addition, justice after war played a major role in the discussions of American policy makers' in each of these wars. The settlement reached at the end of World War I was not Wilson's ideal solution and, not only did the Senate refuse to participate by not ratifying the treaty, but the United States also withdrew from the international stage very rapidly. The fact that many people linked the end of the First World War with the start of the Second worked to justify a different approach to end the Second World War. Instead of a dictated or negotiated peace the allies moved in to occupy the defeated nations in the hope of making a sustainable peace. The countries were purged of their leaders and the allies made a long-term commitment to rebuilding the defeated nations. Korea and Vietnam ended differently, however. The enemy was not defeated and both wars ended with an uneasy truce. Subsequently, in Vietnam at least, the opposition eventually won while the reasons the United States had stayed in the country were defeated as well.

Since Vietnam the United States has struggled to find just ways to end wars. The example from the Second World War seems to suggest that occupation and investment are not only 'just' in the sense of helping the defeated nations return to the international community as equals but also fair since the people of the defeated nation are not held to account for the war itself. This policy, however, requires a great deal of commitment for it to work. US occupying forces remained in Germany and Japan for several years and American money helped to rebuild cities and economies shattered by the Americans themselves. After Vietnam the United States was reluctant to become 'mired' in a long-term commitment of American forces in war-ravaged countries. Also, the wars after 1945 did not always end with a defeated enemy.

Post-war justice has also required the hunt for those responsible for the war and those responsible for outrages committed during the war. The war guilt clause of the Treaty of Versailles laid the blame for the First World War on Germany. However satisfying this might have been for the victors, it did not deter the future resort to war of participant nations. The judicial war crimes trials at the end of the Second World War took a far more formal approach to the question of accountability. Charges were brought against individuals for the usual war crimes of waging aggressive war and violating battlefield codes of conduct but, added to this, were charges of crimes against humanity. People involved in the widespread murder and organised attempts to exterminate large segments of the civilian population needed to be called to account. That belief has sustained the war crimes trials that have taken place since the Second World War. The problem has been, however, that the war crimes trials continue to be, for the most part, victors' justice. In addition, the trials themselves are taking longer to complete. Slobodan Milosevic died in captivity before his trial ended and the trial of Saddam Hussein proved difficult. Despite the problems, however, prosecuting and punishing war criminals is clearly part of any just war settlement.

The maintenance and pursuit of justice on the home front, while the country is at war, seems to be key to any discussion of just war theory. How can it be possible for theorists and pundits to discuss the justice of going to war, the justice within the fighting of the war and the justice of the post-war settlement and then ignore the home front, especially in modern wars where the home front becomes as vital as the battle front? It is exceptionally important that countries fighting wars that they label as just, and who pronounce that they are fighting for justice, provide justice to their own people. Any sustained attack on citizens' civil liberties by a government at war calls into question the validity of that war. The most obvious example is when governments attempt to control freedom of speech and, hence, criticism of the government by the passage of legislation or executive orders that violate the Constitution of the United States. The debate about civil liberties received impetus from US participation in the First World War. As Oswald Garrison Villard noted in 1917, 'the right to criticize the government is never more vital than in wartime'. The stakes are too high for the populace to be silenced. The violations of citizens' rights perpetuated by the numerous pieces of legislation passed during the First World War, and upheld by the Supreme Court, eventually threw open the debate about civil liberties. In 1920 the American Civil Liberties Union was founded for the express purpose of defending the civil liberties and rights guaranteed to Americans by the Constitution of the United States. Still, the government in some subsequent wars was reluctant to allow dissent.

In the Second World War dissent was less of an issue because the catalyst for America's entry into the war, the attack on Pearl Harbor, helped to unite the majority of Americans behind the war effort. The character of the enemies during the war also generated a consensus view of the justness of the war. The evil of Nazi and Japanese expansion and aggression brought Americans together to fight what became known as 'the Good War'. Nevertheless, in this war, while freedom of speech may not have been as directly targeted by the government as had happened in the First World War, a segment of the population lost all their rights. With the internment of Japanese Americans, based on fear rather than due process, the president of the United States bowed to pressure and agreed to ride roughshod over the rights of law-abiding citizens. Once again, while fighting a just war the US government had acted unjustly at home, confirmed by the fact that 40 years later the American government issued an apology to the survivors of the internment episode.

During the Korean War voices of dissent were once again silenced by another consensus. As had been the case with Japanese Americans on the home front in the Second World War, the wartime consensus revolved around the identification of external enemies within the borders of the United States. The Cold War anti-communist atmosphere supported the governmental attempts to identify persons perceived as potential threats. Reinforced by high-profile hearings in the House and Senate and constantly reiterated by anti-communist spokesmen such as McCarthy, the Korean War era was one that did not allow ideologies or behaviours that deviated from mainstream American ideals. To speak out against the Korean War was to speak up for communism.

Not until the Vietnam War did freedom of speech and dissent finally prevail over the forces of a wartime government. Perhaps it was the gradual escalation of US involvement in Vietnam that helped to ensure the lack of legislation aimed at suppressing anti-war sentiments. There was no Zimmermann Telegram, Pearl Harbor or massive invasion across a zone of demarcation. The Tonkin Gulf incident, which eventually justified the use of troops by the US government, happened after there were already military advisors present and the American government was paying the majority of the costs of the southern resistance to the North. There was also a clear consensus that the United States should be involved in Vietnam, as evidenced by the near unanimous vote for the Resolution in the Senate and House. But no sooner had the Gulf of Tonkin Resolution been passed than the first anti-war protest occurred. The intervening years, between the end of the Korean War and the start of the Vietnam War (1953–1965) had witnessed a sea change in the push for civil rights and civil liberties on the American domestic front. The Civil Rights Movement and the student movement had emerged before the conflict in Vietnam became a war. So, dissident voices were already in place and quickly extended techniques of protest to the cause of stopping the war. Furthermore, the combination of lack of success on the battle front and increased protest on the home front worked to convince the American government to stop the war.

Voices left free to speak against government policy in war were able to have an impact. In the First World War, the Second World War and Korea these voices had been either gagged or muted. But, ultimately, the outcome of the Vietnam War and the character of the post-war period differed little from previous wars. These four wars undermined the reform spirit in America. They ended the Progressive Movement, the New Deal, the Fair Deal and the Great Society. These wars ushered in conservative elements in the post-war periods. The 1920s belonged to the Republican Party as did the 1950s and, with a slight delay due to

Watergate, the post-Vietnam period has been reclaimed by conservative forces. Furthermore, the government, during times of war, challenged citizens' rights and, while the war raged, was able to undermine constitutional authority.

After the Vietnam War the United States was once again, as it had been after the First World War, reluctant to engage in overseas wars. Congress passed the War Powers Act in 1973 in a deliberate attempt to make it more difficult for presidents to get America involved in overseas conflicts. Yet, since 1973, the United States has ventured into wars; first on a small scale, into interference with other countries' internal and foreign affairs, or in support of one side in national conflicts as, for example, against the Sandinistas in Nicaragua. These conflicts were limited in scope and carefully controlled in terms of news coverage, as was most obvious in Granada. And still these forays into armed conflict were discussed in just war terms by the ruling administrations. They had to be. It was even more important, post-Vietnam, that the American people were convinced that the war being proposed by the government, to be fought by American soldiers, was a war worth fighting against an enemy that had to be defeated.

When Iraq invaded Kuwait in 1990, the stage was set for a debate about just war. The Iraq leader, Saddam Hussein, sent in overwhelming troop numbers to quickly seize control of Kuwait and its large, productive oil fields. This aggressive act violated international law and threatened the uneasy peace within the region. Here was the same kind of naked aggression that had been appeased at the outbreak of the Second World War .Iraq was clearly the aggressor and the subsequent Persian Gulf War of 1991, like the First World War I, the Second World War II, Korea and Vietnam, was discussed as being a response to aggression. The invasion of a small country by a larger, bullying neighbour seemed to cry out for redress.

On 8 August US President George H.W. Bush called for immediate action to reverse the Iraqi invasion. In one sense reminiscent of Korea, the president worked to secure a large coalition of UN member states to oppose Saddam and liberate Kuwait. This coalition eventually comprised 30 nations including several leading Arab states and was empowered by UN resolutions authorising non-military measures and sanctions against Iraq. Bush sent US troops to neighbouring Saudi Arabia and, with congressional approval, issued an ultimatum that Iraq need to withdraw from Kuwait by 15 January 1991. On 17 January, when this had not happened, the United States began air strikes and on 23 February coalition forces attacked the Iraqi military. The fighting was over within days and resulted in 148 US soldiers killed and another 458 wounded. Bush declared 'we went halfway around the world to do what is moral, just and right'. Indeed, the just nature of the war, to counter aggression, was clear for most people to see, although there were voices of dissent suggesting that this action on the part of the United States had more to do with oil than with justice.

Still, the war was over and the United States had won. Many commentators suggested that the use of US troops in a precision action like this had laid to rest the ghost of Vietnam. The modern US military could, as it turns out, win. General Norman Schwarzkopf, himself a Vietnam veteran, was hailed as an excellent commander and, in the aftermath of the war, mentioned as having a potential future in politics. There was some concern about the nature of the attacks on a vehicle convoy fleeing the fighting, but for most observers the 'smart' bombs had spared civilian casualties and the just war had been fought justly. The American people back home had not been inconvenienced in the 42 days of war and the trademark operation designations of Desert Shield at first, and then Desert Storm once fighting began, boosted this sense of justice and patriotism. Some commentators suggested that had George H.W. Bush run for re-election in February 1991 his re-election would have been assured.

The only fly in the ointment, however, was how the war had ended. The Iraqi troops were out of Kuwait and a massive clear-up operation was underway to put out the oil fires ignited by retreating troops, but the coalition forces stopped at the border between Kuwait and Iraq. Saddam Hussein, whose aggressive ambitions had started the war, was able to and continued to persecute his own people and ethnic groups within the borders of Iraq. Perhaps the ghost of the Vietnam War had not been exorcised after all. The reluctance to expand the goals of the war from liberating Kuwait to toppling Saddam Hussein is understandable. Changing from liberation to aggression had not worked in Korea when the United States troops crossed the 38th parallel and there was little stomach for an aggressive policy that had the potential to pull the US military into a protracted fight. Besides, would this have been a just war? Liberating people from attack by a foreign army is one thing; liberating a people from their own government is another.

Instead, the United States and other governments in the coalition, backed by the UN, instituted a number of sanctions against Iraq in the hopes of getting the Iraqi leader to conform to western ideals of behaviour and, possibly, push the Iraqi people to liberate themselves. Trade embargos, no-fly zones, sanctions and constant monitoring and inspections of military sites were meant to curtail Iraqi aggression but also had the effect of increasing United States presence in the Middle East, which did not please everyone in the region. All the while Saddam Hussein maintained his grip on his people.

Nevertheless, the American people supported President George H.W. Bush in the fight in Kuwait. Public opinion was behind the war and its brief nature (17 January to 28 February 1991) did not allow much time for dissent. Equally important, the government, having learned a lesson from the Vietnam War, tightly controlled media access to the battle front. The Gulf War was hailed as a victory and, as the last war of the twentieth century; this war seemed to suggest that the United States had learned a valuable lesson about how future wars could be fought to win. But what exact lesson had the United States learned? Perhaps that wars needed to be clearly justifiable, as in the case of naked aggression, and short, in order to sustain civilian support. Clearly the future wars to avoid were those reminiscent of Vietnam; wars that could easily turn into protracted wars in countries full of irreconcilable factions, fought on a limited basis without overwhelming use of force and with only minority support for the United States from within the country. The war would still need to be seen as just, but importantly, it would need to be short. In addition, at the end of the twentieth century, the concept of war itself remained that of one nation against another or one coalition of nations against another, much like it had been at the start of the century.

Epilogue

Shortly after the twenty-first century began, on 11 September 2001, the face of battle changed. The scope of the tragedy and number of victims of the 9/11 attacks made the rhetoric of 'just' war ring true from an early stage of the United States response. The terrorist attacks in New York City and Washington DC, like the attack on Pearl Harbor, meant that America was at war. But this time the enemy was elusive, not confined to a single nation or coalition of forces, not restricted to one geographic locality and not fighting in any traditional sense of combat. The combined fatalities of the attacks on the World Trade Center, Pentagon and the failed attack and subsequent plane crash in Pennsylvania claimed the lives of over 3200 civilians from over 80 countries. Commandeering commercial aircraft, full of innocent civilians, and turning them into deadly missiles took the Second World War concept of kamikaze attacks to unexpected new levels of warfare and paled in comparison to the attack on Pearl Harbor. The sea change witnessed in this attack as opposed to the four major wars of the twentieth century was that it *deliberately* targeted civilians. This was not a war like other wars for the United States.

Equally important, the attack was not launched by a sovereign nation but rather by a dissident group. It did not utilise conventional weapons, instead turning everyday objects into weapons. The men who carried out the attacks were not recognizable as soldiers from a foreign nation attacking on the field of battle. Instead they used the openness of American society to infiltrate the United States and plan their attack. They belonged to the growing number of combatants known as suicide bombers, which the American people had experience of only on a limited basis. The 1993 car bomb attack on the World Trade Center and the truck bomb attacks on US Army barracks in Saudi Arabia in 1996 and American embassies in Africa in 1998 had not prepared the United States for the attacks on their home front on 11 September. Although the international terrorist network al-Qaeda had declared war on the United States as early as 1998, America did not consider itself 'at war'.

Within hours of the attack the American people reacted in a superpatriotic way. The American flag was everywhere and seemed to indicate a united America determined to rebound from these events. The makeshift memorials and crowning of fire fighters and police in New York with superhero status underpinned a nearly unanimous belief that the United States needed to respond. Seeming eerily like the Vietnam era Gulf of Tonkin Resolution, on 14 September, just three days after the attacks, a unanimous Senate and a House majority of 420 to 1 voted to authorise the use of force against those found to be responsible. The President reinforced these sentiments. Despite his failure to respond immediately on the day of the attacks, as the days progressed he found the words to reflect his sense of justice. On 20 September George W. Bush addressed a joint session of Congress and the American people and proclaimed 'whether we bring our enemies to justice, or bring justice to our enemies, justice will be done'.

Bush's announcement of a war on terror made in that same speech put the United States on the path to a twenty-first century war. He demanded that the Taliban regime of Afghanistan hand over Osama bin Laden, already identified as the mastermind behind the 11 September attacks. At the same time, he appointed a Director of Homeland Security to oversee and monitor the level of threat of terrorist attack within the United States. Bush's rhetoric knew few bounds as he proclaimed that the 'war on terror ... will not end until every terrorist group of global reach has been found, stopped and defeated'. The war aim had quickly gone from securing the capture of those responsible for specific attacks to tracking down every terrorist group on the planet. He told America they could be 'assured of the rightness of our course, and confident of the victories to come'. Sounding like twentieth-century wartime presidents before him, Bush assured the American people that the United States would defeat this new enemy, as it had defeated its enemies in the past. Apparently he too had forgotten about the Vietnam War.

After this Bush began to put together a coalition, as his father had done, but this time to invade Afghanistan. Several states joined with America including some states of the former Soviet Union and Pakistan, which bordered Afghanistan. The United Nations' Security Council passed resolutions to implement measures to combat terrorism. On 4 October, British Prime Minister Tony Blair released information to the waiting press that verified bin Laden's role in the training, equipping and directing of terrorists in Afghanistan. Three days later the United States launched its attack on the Taliban regime with air strikes, closely followed by ground forces. The operation name was originally Infinite Justice but wiser heads prevailed after Muslim complaints and it became known as Operation Enduring Freedom. By late November the Taliban was on the run and had fled Kabul and eventually Kandahar. By January 2002 the United States and coalition forces had virtually defeated the Taliban. The war in Afghanistan lasted just over three months and seemed to reinforce Bush's claims that the United States would track down the forces of terror. Unfortunately, the ultimate objective of the war, the capture of Osama bin Laden, was not achieved.

Without the capture of bin Laden and with Taliban leaders still on the loose, the US military remained in Afghanistan as part of a peacekeeping force. This post-war situation turned American troops into occupation forces of a sort. The goal was to institute democratic rule in Afghanistan and to that effect the people of Afghanistan voted for and approved a national constitution in 2004 and in October 2006 the North Atlantic Treaty Organization (NATO) took over official leadership of the peace-keeping forces. It would seem then that the war had been a just one and had ended in a just manner, but what of the fighting itself and the war's impact on the American home front?

The biggest controversy of the Afghan war was the capture of enemy combatants and their subsequent detention in a high security US facility at Guantánamo Bay, Cuba. The US government carried out the trans-portation to and retention of these prisoners in great secrecy at first. However, as news reports began appearing and the photos showing prisoners forced to kneel with hoods over their heads surfaced, some people began to question the legality and morality of the treatment these prisoners were receiving. If, as most people believed, these were prison-ers of war (POWs), then there were internationally agreed rules in place to govern their treatment. The Bush forces, however, denied this status and instead proclaimed that these were unlawful combatants, which avoided the protocols of the Geneva Conventions.

The approximately 600 detainees, some US citizens, were not charged and were held without reference to the length of their incar-ceration. Over the years since the camp was established in January 2002 some prisoners have been returned to their country of origin. There have been recent charges of abuse of detainees as well as hunger strikes, attempted suicides and successful suicides. In an effort to defend their handling of the prisoners of Guantánamo the Bush admin-istration has consistently claimed that these men pose a direct threat to world security.

The people at home in America seemed to agree as, despite some repeated attempts at challenging these detentions in the US court system, the courts have been reluctant to go against the executive's authority although there have been dissenting opinions within the court cases. Equally, on the home front, there was little protest against the passage of the Patriot Act in October 2001, within weeks of the 9/11 attacks. This act was initiated with the intention of pursuing potential terrorists before they had a chance to act. In this view, the suspect may not have committed a crime, but rather had the potential or intention to commit a crime. This was reminiscent of the argument used by authorities in the Second World War as a justification for the internment of Japanese American citizens. Congressional approval for the Patriot Act gave the Attorney General powers to eavesdrop, which in turn gave authorities more latitude in the gathering of intelligence information. It allowed indefinite imprisonment of non-citizen suspects without trial and, if tried, suspects could be tried in military tribunals rather than open court. It was passed overwhelmingly in both the Senate and the House while polls showed that Americans supported the government's efforts to protect them from future terrorist attacks.

Not everyone was behind this action, however. The American Civil Liberties Union (ACLU) came out to condemn the act as unconstitutional and there have been repeated attempts to challenge the act ever since. To date, these challenges have been unsuccessful and, as will be shown later, the Patriot Act has even been strengthened and extended. When President Bush proposed the Patriot Act he stated that it 'broke down barriers that prevented law enforcement and intelligence agencies from sharing vital information on terrorist threats' despite the fact that these 'barriers' may have been in place to safeguard the civil liberties of American citizens. Whether 'emergency ethics' allows for unethical conduct, as Walzer says, remains to be judged in this case. The problem is, of course, the perpetual state of the emergency that an open-ended war on terror implies. In *Time* magazine in October 2006 Shimon Peres noted that 'fighting terror is rather like fighting crime, not like fighting another army'. Peres' point was that regardless of a state's actions it cannot eradicate crime and the same may be true of terrorism.

Not to be deterred from his preferred course of action, however, President Bush launched another prong of his attack on terrorism in 2002 when he announced the Bush Doctrine. In words very much reminiscent of the anti-communist era, Bush proceeded to lay the foundations of what he hoped would be both a policy and a strategy to lead the United

States into the twenty-first century by suggesting that 'we are in a conflict between good and evil'. Declaring that 'the war on terror will not be
won on the defensive', Bush suggested the necessity of a pre-emptive
doctrine that would allow the United States, and its allies, to attack
regimes before those regimes had attacked another country. The notion
of a pre-emptive strike or even a pre-emptive war is not new to just war
theory. It is considered a reasonable course of action if a country knows
that an attack is imminent; if they are about to be attacked themselves.
However, this part of just war theory is seen to be severely restricted by
the understanding of the term imminent and the evidence of a threatened
attack. To re-enforce the sense of necessity for such a doctrine Bush spoke
often of the most obvious potential enemy nations in his January 2002
State of the Union address when he declared Iraq, Iran and North Korea
as consisting of an axis of evil. He later added Cuba, Libya and Syria to
his enemies list. In an almost complete reversal of America's previous
strategic beliefs, the Bush Doctrine noted that 'we must take the battle to
the enemy, disrupt his plans, and confront the worst threats before they
emerge.' The obvious question is how is it possible to know what the
worst threats are if they have yet to emerge? Walzer notes that there is
almost always room for deliberation before pre-emptive war. Bush then
went on to suggest that 'America needs partners' but also let it be known
that the United States would act unilaterally if necessary.

It did not take long for the Bush administration to identify their next
enemy nation in the ongoing war on terror and to initiate the Bush
Doctrine. Towards the end of 2002 the Bush administration increased the
tone and frequency of its rhetorical attacks on the evil nature of Saddam
Hussein and his regime in Iraq. The message suggested that his regime
and his actions directly threatened the rest of the world in general and
America in particular. Reports of weapons of mass destruction, accumulation of chemical weapons and continued progress on the attempt to
obtain nuclear capacity filled the pages of newspapers and were discussed
on the nightly news. Bush attempted to form a coalition in opposition to
Saddam while Saddam openly allowed UN weapons inspectors back into
his country. In addition, France and Germany continued to oppose any
rulings on future actions against Iraq being discussed in the UN at that
time. Refusing to be dissuaded, Bush continued to proclaim links
between Saddam Hussein and al-Qaeda and other terrorists. He also
made some progress in establishing a coalition of sorts with the strong
backing of Great Britain and the often token backing of 17 other nations.
By February 2003 anti-war protests were occurring in various nations

around the world with the largest demonstrations taking place in London and New York.

Despite the opposition, the United States launched a war on Iraq on 19 March 2003 with a series of air strikes on Baghdad. The next day coalition forces attacked and Operation Iraqi Freedom began on the ground. As with the war in Afghanistan, things moved quickly and battlefield victories unfolded. The United States had mustered a total of 150,000 troops, both American and allied, and tended to rely, as with the first Gulf War, on high-tech weapons. By early April American troops were moving into Baghdad and on 9 April the world was beamed pictures of the symbolic destruction of the Iraqi regime when images were shown of US forces and Iraqi civilians working together to topple a statue of Saddam Hussein. On 1 May, approximately six weeks after it all started, the US government announced that major combat had ended.

The US government then turned its attentions to establishing a democracy in Iraq and seeking out those members of the Iraqi regime, including the dictator Saddam Hussein, who had eluded capture. American plans called for repair of damage to Iraq's electricity and water supplies as well as hospitals and schools. The United States would oversee the establishment of a democratic government and, many hoped, quickly turn over the day-to-day running of the country and its defence to Iraqis themselves. Acknowledging that this might take some months, Bush had declared that 'we fight as we always fight for a just peace' and his administration went on to help establish a coalition government, get voting systems in place and appointed a US ambassador to Iraq. Unfortunately, the post-war situation in Iraq quickly deteriorated. No sooner had the victory celebrations finished then the factions within Iraq began asserting themselves. What became known as a terrorist insurgency commenced and attacks on United States and allied military and civilian staff were combined with attacks by Iraqis on Iraqis. United States and coalition forces had to stay on to attempt to restore order and peace, although as kidnappings and threats increased, various allied nations began to withdraw their segments of the coalition forces.

Even the capture of Saddam Hussein in late 2003 did little to alleviate the factionalism. Attacks continued and increased in frequency and deadliness throughout 2004, 2005 and 2006. A war launched as an attack on terror had resulted in the breeding and proliferation of terrorism. While Bush military advisors may have been able to claim 'just' victory in the war they had definitely lost the peace. This war did not end justly; in fact it has yet to end. And despite even the public trial of a captured Saddam

Hussein, his execution on 30 December 2006 ended with accusations of dishonourable behaviour on the part of his executioners. In his last minutes, Saddam was taunted and photographed resulting in a rather seedy conclusion to what might have been a testament to bringing a dignified end to a murderous tyrant.

The problems of fighting a just war in a just way were further complicated as stories began to emerge about the treatment of POWs and civilian detainees at the United States controlled Abu Graib prison. Amazingly, US military personnel put in charge of guarding Iraqi prisoners took photographs and videos of their illegal actions and shared them with their friends and colleagues. As these pictures inevitably came to light the world was shocked and outraged. Systematic torture was not only alleged, it was documented. This, coupled with the continual accusations about treatment of POWs at Guantánamo Bay and the revelations that the United States and other allied governments had participated in a system of extraordinary rendition (the secret Central Intelligence Agency transportation of prisoners to countries that condoned torture), will make it nearly impossible for the US government to argue convincingly that it fought the war on terror in a just way.

If the United States had not learned about just war on the battle front by the twenty-first century, it could at least be hoped that it had learned its lessons from the past with regard to government policies on the home front during wartime. Unfortunately, this was not the case. As noted earlier, the US Patriot Act, together with the establishment of the Office (later Department) of Homeland Security in the immediate aftermath of 9/11 have threatened the civil liberties of US citizens on a variety of levels. Although the original House Resolution on the Patriot Act noted that 'the civil rights and civil liberties of all Americans ... must be protected', this has not stopped the US government from increasing the powers of authorities to institute warrantless wiretaps, invading privacy by collecting personal data on US citizens and allowing government agencies to spy on innocent Americans. In what must surely be likened by future historians to the McCarthy era, the Bush era will be known for attempting to address the unprecedented challenges to national security posed by the 9/11 attacks in such a way as to run roughshod over not only American ideals and basic principles, but also the lessons of the past.

But in other ways, as Bob Woodward noted, 'it is almost a war without a home front.' Despite longer lines and more complex check-in procedures at airports, the profiling of passengers, occasional sensational arrests and scares, and the obvious real fear and grieving of soldiers' families, the American people go about their lives as normal. There is no draft to resist. In fact the all volunteer military explains why the military is so small and so overly stretched in this ever-expanding war on terror. Yet the estimated cost of $9 billion per month according to the Congressional Budget Office and the steadily rising federal deficit may yet make the war on terror significant enough to Americans on the home front to enlarge the anti-war forces.

The continuing occupation of Afghanistan is witnessing the resurgence of the Taliban, the Guantánamo prisoners remain under lock and key without having experienced due process of law despite challenges within the legal system and the situation in Iraq is growing deadlier while the Democratic Congress calls for a date for the withdrawal of troops. In March 2005 the president's commission on Iraq concluded the pre-war intelligence about weapons of mass destruction was faulty and the Iraq Study Group Report of 2006 suggested that the US government speak directly with Iran and Syria, two of Bush's evil regimes, to attempt to bring the Iraq situation under control. More and more people are making analogues between Iraq and Vietnam. Bush's response was to propose a 'surge' in US forces, which occurred in 2007, the results of which are not yet clear. Perhaps in the case of the war in Afghanistan, the cause and the fighting seemed just and the enemy represented ultimate evil. Making the world safe from terrorist attack seemed to be a sentiment, on the surface, that was noble. However, like Wilson's proclamation in the First World War that the United States went to war to make the world safe for democracy, it would turn out to be a sentiment that was not only impossible to achieve but would ultimately lead to greater conflict and far more difficult circumstances. The Iraq conflict merely extended those once lofty ambitions into a less clearly justifiable war. It is hard to understand how Bush could declare, in 2006, that in the case of Afghanistan and Iraq 'America is safer and the world is secure because these two countries are now democracies'.

The question of how to end a war justly has not disappeared and in 2007 the United States struggles with the aftermath of victory in the recently 'liberated' Iraq. The results of the idealised war on terror and the real war in Afghanistan and Iraq have yet to play out. The debates about and ramifications of the 9/11 attacks and the US response will exercise historians and commentators, as well as just war theorists, for many years to come.

Annotated Bibliography and Further Reading

Listed below are major works on the general issues and topics raised in the body of this book arranged by each of the major wars. This is a selected bibliography and is meant to point the reader in the direction of works that expand upon the major themes detailed earlier. Not all aspects of all the topics covered in this volume have a corresponding bibliographic reference and some of the books that are listed overlap from one war or era to another. For example, many books on the experiences of American women or the civil rights movement cover time periods such as the post-Second World War era, which includes both the Korean and Vietnam Wars.

GENERAL

The body of this text provides an introduction to the idea of just war theory through a discussion of America's major wars of the twentieth century. The starting place for information about just war theory in a historical context, I would suggest, is the general text authored by Michael Walzer, *Just and Unjust Wars: A Moral Argument with Historical Illustrations* (Basic Books, 2000), now in its third edition. Walzer lays out the general tenets of just war theory using examples from history in such a way as to make it accessible to non-specialists. He is seen by many as one of, if not the, leading just war theorist of this age. There are even books about Walzer himself such as the one by Brian Orend, *Michael Walzer on War and Justice* (University of Wales Press, 2000). Orend, along with Jean Bethke Elshtain, (editor) *Just War Theory* (Basel Blackwell, 1990), have written on just war theory and continue to do so in relation to post-9/11 US wars. For general texts on military history, other than those listed under specific war headings below, the reader may want to have at hand books such as John Whiteclay Chambers II (ed.) *The Oxford Companion to American Military History* (Oxford University Press, 1999), Franklin D. Margiotta (ed.) *Brassey's Encyclopedia of Military History and Biography* (Brassey's, 2000) or the three volume work of Peter Karsten (ed.) *Encyclopedia of War and American Society* (Sage Publications, 2005).

There is a wide range of books on general US military history including very general texts such as Robert Leckie *The Wars of America Volume II: From 1900 to 1992* (Harper Perennial, 1992) and Maurice Matloff (ed.) *American Military History Volume 2: 1902–1996* (Combined Books, 1996). A useful publication for general information as well as suggested further reading is Jerry K. Sweeney (ed.) *A Handbook of American Military History from the Revolutionary War to the Present* (Westview Press, 1996). A general text which covers US wars through Vietnam is

Peter Karsten (ed.) *The Military in American: From the Colonial Era to the Present*, revised edition (The Free Press, 1986). More recent books that take a cultural but still chronological look at US warfare are Adrian R. Lewis *The American Culture of War: The History of U.S. Military Force from World War II to Operation Iraqi Freedom* (Routledge, 2007) and M. Paul Holsinger (ed.) *War and American Popular Culture* (Greenwood Press, 1999). Specific works on how wars begin include Gary R. Hess *Presidential Decisions for War: Korea, Vietnam, and the Persian Gulf* (Johns Hopkins University Press, 2001), John G. Stoessinger *Why Nations Go to War* (St. Martin's Press, 1990) and Arthur M. Schlesinger, Jr's contribution to the debate on war in *War and the American Presidency* (W.W. Norton and Co., 2005).

There are also books available on the issue of United States military conduct such as Peter S. Kindsvatter *American Soldiers: Ground Combat in the World Wars, Korea, and Vietnam* (University of Kansas Press, 2003). Finally, a book that explores war in the twentieth century by looking at post-war ramifications is Donovan Webster *Aftermath: The Remnants of War* (Constable, 1997) while Joanna Bourke *An Intimate History of Killing: Face-to-Face Killing in Twentieth Century Warfare* (Granta Books, 1999) challenges the near universal belief that killing in wartime is done reluctantly. Statistical information can be found in works such as the U.S. Department of Commerce, Bureau of the Census *Historical Statistics of the United States, Colonial Times to 1970* (Government Printing Office, 1975).

CHAPTER 2 – THE FIRST WORLD WAR

General texts on the history of the Second World War abound. A few examples are as follows: Keith Robbins *The First World War* (Oxford University Press, 1993), J. H. Johnson *Stalemate! The Great Trench Warfare Battles of 1915–1917* (Arms and Armour Press, 1995) and, probably one of the most detailed accounts, Martin Gilbert *First World War* (Weidenfeld and Nicolson, 1994). All of these have sections on warfare including the use of gas. A classic work on the impact of the war is Arthur Marwick *The Deluge: British Society and the First World War*, second edition (Macmillan, 1991) and a recent look at the more global aspects of the war is John H. Morrow Jr. *The Great War: An Imperial History* (Routledge, 2004). Books about the experience of the United States in the First World War are also numerous. These include recent works such as Thomas Fleming *The Illusion of Victory: America in World War I* (Basic Books, 2003), Robert H. Zieger *America's Great War: World War I and the American Experience* (Little, Brown and Company, 2000) and standards such as Edward Coffman *The War to End All Wars: The American Military Experience of World War I* (University of Wisconsin Press, 1986). For the combat experience of Americans in the First World War the reader may want to first consult Mark Meigs *Optimism at Armageddon: Voices of American Participants in the First World War* (Macmillan, 1997) while Jennifer D. Keene *Doughboys, the Great War, and the Remaking of America* (Johns Hopkins University Press, 2001) explores the issue of conscription and its post-war impact as well as the wartime experiences of the soldiers.

For general texts on the American home front in the First World War the reader should start with classic works by David M. Kennedy *Over Here: The First World War and American Society* (Oxford University Press, 1980) and Ellis Hawley *The Great War and the Search for a Modern Order: A History of the American People and Their Institutions, 1917—1933*, second edition (St. Martin's Press, 1992). A starting place for discussion of civil liberties in wartime is Paul L. Murphy *World War I and the Origin of Civil Liberties in the United States* (W.W. Norton and Co., 1979) while Diana Preston *Wilful Murder: The Sinking of the Lusitania* (Corgi Books, 2003) provides an excellent insight into the wartime controversy of the use of unrestricted submarine warfare.

Work about the experience of women in the war include Lettie Gavin *American Women in World War I: They Also Served* (University Press of Colorado 1997), Susan Zeiger *In Uncle Sam's Service: Women Workers with the American Expeditionary Force, 1917–1919* (Cornell University Press, 1999), Kathleen Kennedy *Disloyal Mothers and Scurrilous Citizens: Women and Subversion During World War I* (Indiana University Press, 1999), Dorothy and Carl Schneider *Into the Breach: American Women Overseas in World War I* (Viking, 1991), Kimberley Jensen 'Women, Citizenship, and Civic Sacrifice: Engendering Patriotism in the First World War' in John Bodner (ed.) *Bonds of Affection: Americans Define Their Patriotism* (Princeton University Press, 1996), and Harriet Hyman Alonson 'Gender and Peace Politics in the First World War United States: The People's Council of America' *The International History Review* 19 (February 1997) 83–102 as well as Maurine Weiner Greenwald *Women, War, and Work: The Impact of World War I on Women Workers in the United States* (Greenwood Press, 1980).

More is being written on the experience of African Americans in World War I; some of the best works in the past were Bernard Nalty *Strength for the Fight: A History of Black Americans in the Military* (Free Press, 1986) and Arthur E. Barbeau and Florette Henri *The Unknown Soldiers: Black American Troops in World War I* (Temple University Press, 1974). Mark Ellis in 'Federal Surveillance of Black Americans during the First World War' *Immigrants and Minorities* 12 (March 1993) 1–20 examines the attitude of the federal government towards African Americans while William Jordan in '"The Damnable Dilemma": African-American Accommodation and Protest During World War I' *Journal of American History* (March 1995) 1562–1590 explores the difficulty for African Americans in supporting the war in light of the discrimination they faced at home.

The institution of the draft during the war generated a great deal of concern and many historians have sought to illuminate the underlying issues such as Jeanette Keith in 'The Politics of Southern Draft Resistance, 1917–1918: Class, Race, and Conscription in the Rural South' *Journal of American History* 87 (March 2001) 1335–1361; Harry Marmion 'Historical Background of Selective Service in the United States' in Roger Little (ed.) *Selective Service and American Society* (Russell Sage Foundation, 1969); James Mennell in 'African-Americans and the Selective Service Act of 1917,' *The Journal of Negro History* 84 (Summer 1999) 275–287; and John O'Sullivan and Alan Meckler (eds) *The Draft and Its Enemies: A Documentary History* (University of Illinois Press, 1974). Other issues of civil liberties and home front repression have also drawn the attention of historians, including David Rabban *Free Speech in Its Forgotten Years* (Cambridge University Press) 1997; E. A. Schwartz 'The Lynching of Robert Prager: The United Mine Workers, and the Problems of Patriotism in 1918' *Journal of Illinois State Historical Society* (Winter 2003) and Christopher Capozzola 'The Only Badge Needed is Your Patriotic Fervor: Vigilance,

Coercion, and the Law in World War I America' *Journal of American History* 88 (March 2002) 1354–1382. If the reader wishes a specific volume on the peace process they may want to start with Thomas A. Bailey *Woodrow Wilson and the Lost Peace* (Franklin Watts, 1978).

CHAPTER 3 – THE SECOND WORLD WAR

The general texts on the Second World War fill many shelves in most libraries. A recent run of books has appeared as the Second World War generation disappears; however, a good place to start for interested readers might be with some of the classic works. Martin Gilbert *Second World War* (Fontana, 1990) gives a month-by-month account of the events of the war while the two volume work of Peter Calvocoressi, Guy Wint and John Pritchard, *Total War: The Causes and Courses of the Second World War, Volume 1: The Western Hemisphere, Volume II: The Greater East Asia and Pacific Conflict* (Penguin, 1989) offers the reader another detailed account of the events of the war on both fronts. More recent work, however, has added to the list of accounts of the war, especially Williamson Murray and Allan R. Millett *A War to Be Won: Fighting the Second World War* (Harvard University Press, 2000), which analyses the military operations of the war. While there are hundreds of recent synopses of the war, one of the recent concise publications, part of the Twentieth-Century Wars Series, is Spencer C. Tucker *The Second World War* (Palgrave Macmillan, 2004). Books on almost every aspect of the war exist including classics such as the examination of racism during war produced by John W. Dower *War Without Mercy: Race and Power in the Pacific War* (Pantheon Books, 1986) and, of course, a whole range of recent work on the Holocaust.

To understand the Second World War experience from the American perspective, readers may want to start with William A. O'Neil *A Democracy at War: America's Fight at Home and Abroad* (Harvard University Press, 1993) or David Kennedy *Freedom From Fear: The American People in Depression and War, 1929–1945* (Oxford University Press, 1999). A concise volume suitable for students just beginning to learn about the Second World War would be Martin Folly *The United States and World War II: The Awakening Giant* (Edinburgh University Press, 2002). Two of the earliest works dealing with the United States home front are Richard Lingeman *Don't You Know There's a War On?': The American Home Front 1941–45* (GP Putman's Sons, 1976) and John Morton Blum *V Was for Victory: Politics and American Culture During World War II* (Harcourt Brace Jovanovich, 1976). The American combat experience has attracted a great deal of recent attention by historians and continues to do so as major anniversaries of specific battles occur. For example, Stephen Ambrose's work on *D-Day, June 6, 1944: The Battle for Normandy Beaches* (Pocket Books, 2002) and *Band of Brothers* (Pocket Books, 2001) as well as *Citizen Soldiers: The US Army from the Normandy Beaches to the Bulge to the Surrender of Germany* (Touchstone, 1997) illustrates the continued interest of historians in the topic of America's participation in the Second World War. Equally important are works by Gerald Linderman *The World Within War: America's Combat Experience in World War II* (The Free Press, 1997), Paul Fussell *The Boys' Crusade: American G.I.s in Europe: Chaos and Fear in World War Two* (Random House, 2003) and the highly critical Michael C. C. Adams *The Best War Ever: America and World War II* (Johns Hopkins University Press, 1994). Thousands of articles could be added to the list as well including Benjamin L. Alpers 'This Is the Army: Imagining a Democratic Military in World War II' *Journal of American History* (June 1998) 129—163, which examines issues arising in the formation of a military by a democracy.

The starting place for anyone interested in the wartime experience of American women are the classic works by Karen Anderson *Wartime Women: Sex Roles, Family Relations, and the Status of Women During World War II* (Greenwood Press, 1981) or D'Ann Cambell *Women at War with America: Private Lives in a Patriotic Era* (Harvard University Press, 1984), while Alice Kessler-Harris *Out to Work: A History of Wage-Earning Women in the United States* (Oxford University Press, 1982) puts much of this in a broader context. Joshua Goldstein's *War and Gender: How Gender Shapes the War System and Vice Versa* (Cambridge University Press, 2003) looks at gender politics during wartime. Other, more specific titles involving the role of women in wartime include: Rachel Waltner Goossen *Women Against the Good War: Conscientious Objection and Gender on the American Home Front, 1941–1947* (University of North Carolina Press, 1997); Leisa D. Meyer *Creating GI Jane: Sexuality and Power in the Women's Army Corps During World War II* (Columbia University Press, 1996); Judy Barrett Litoff 'Southern Women in a World at War' in Neil R. McMillen (ed.) *Remaking Dixie: The Impact of World War II on the American South* (University Press of Mississippi, 1997); Robert B. Westbrook '"I Want a Girl, Just Like the Girl That Married Harry James": American Women and the Problem of Political Obligation in World War II' *American Quarterly* 42 (December 1990) 587–614; Deborah Hirshfield 'Gender, Generation, and Race in American Shipyards in the Second World War' *International History Review* 19 (February 1997) 131–145; and in a broader context Mark H. Leff 'The Politics of Sacrifice on the American Home Front in World War II' *Journal of American History* (March 1991) 1296–1318 to name just a few. Other work has been done on the issue of gender and race as well.

The issue of African Americans during the Second World War has generated a great number of books; one of the first books on this topic was Neil A. Wynn *The Afro American and the Second World War* (Elek Books Ltd, 1976), and a more recent addition is Maggi M. Morehouse *Fighting in a Jim Crow Army: Black Men and Women Remember World War II* (Rowman and Littlefield, 2000). Many other works, on a variety of topics associated with African Americans, have appeared including: Daniel Kryder *Divided Arsenal: Race and the American State During World War II* (Cambridge University Press, 2000); the general text on African Americans in wartime, Bernard Nalty *Strength for the Fight: A History of Black Americans in the Military* (Macmillan, 1986); Lawrence Samuel 'Dreaming in Black and White: African-American Patriotism and World War II Bonds' in John Bodnar (ed.) *Bonds of Affection: Americans Define Their Patriotism* (Princeton University Press, 1996); Clayton R. Koppes and Gregory D. Black 'Blacks, Loyalty, and Motion-Picture Propaganda in World War II' *Journal of American History* 73 (September 1986) 383–406; and Beth Bailey and David Farber 'The "Double-V" Campaign in World War II Hawaii: African Americans, Racial Ideology, and Federal Power' *Journal of Social History* (Summer 1993) 817–843 to name just a few. The above list shows the variety of themes to be explored on the issue of race including work on the experience of African American women during the Second World War by authors like Brenda L. Moore *To Serve My Country, To Serve My Race: The Story of the Only African*

American WACs Stationed Overseas during World War II (New York University Press, 1996).

Equally, works on specific issues on the home front, related to civil liberties abound. For a look at the issue of free speech in the Second World War the place to start is Richard W. Steele *Free Speech in the Good War* (Macmillan Press Ltd., 1999), while the issue of censorship has generated books, such as George H. Roeder, Jr *The Censored War: American Visual Experience During World War Two* (Yale University Press, 1993) and Michael S. Sweeney *Secrets of Victory: The Office of Censorship and the American Press and Radio in World War II* (University of North Carolina Press, 2001). The government's use of propaganda has also been explored in works like Nicholas John Cull *Selling War: The British Propaganda Campaign Against American 'Neutrality' in World War II* (Oxford University Press, 1995) and Gerd Horton *Radio Goes to War: The Cultural Politics of Propaganda during World War II* (University of California Press, 2002). The history of the internment of Japanese Americans has generated numerous volumes from an early piece by Michi Weglyn *Years of Infamy: The Untold Story of America's Concentration Camps* (Morrow Quill Paperbacks, 1976) to more recent work such as Greg Robinson *By Order of the President: FDR and the Internment of Japanese Americans* (Harvard University Press, 2001) and Eric Muller *Free to Die for Their Country: The Story of the Japanese American Draft Resisters in World War II* (University of Chicago Press, 2001).

The reader may also want to pursue topics on the ethics of the Second World War by looking at books about the Holocaust, bombing campaigns and the war crimes trials. A good place to start would be Martin Gilbert *The Holocaust: The Jewish Tragedy* (Collins, 1986), which gives a thorough account of the facts, and books such as David S. Wyman *The Abandonment of the Jews: America and the Holocaust, 1941–1945* (Pantheon Books, 1985) which highlights the shortcomings of the United States government in dealing with the crisis. Numerous books and articles deal with the issue of the bombing of civilians including the work by Mark Grimsley and Clifford J. Rogers (eds) *Civilians in the Path of War* (University of Nebraska Press, 2002) which looks at wars since the Athenian empire and, most recently, A. C. Grayling *Among the Dead Cities: The History and Moral Legacy of the World War II Bombing of Civilians in Germany and Japan* (Walker and Company, 2006). Equally numerous are those works that deal with the use of the atomic bomb against the Japanese cities of Hiroshima and Nagasaki. Two of the most controversial and revisionist works are Gar Alperovitz *The Decision to Use the Atomic Bomb* (Vintage Books, 1996) and Ronald Takaki *Hiroshima: Why America Dropped the Atomic Bomb* (Little, Brown and Co., 1996). More conservative accounts of the use of the atomic bomb can be found in most of the general works on the Second World War noted above. Stephen L. McFarland *America's Pursuit of Precision Bombing, 1910–1945* (Smithsonian Institute, 1995) gives the conservative view of the use of bombing by the United States. Finally, the trial and execution of axis war criminals at the end of the Second World War has been examined by numerous historians with a good overview provided by Ann Tusa and John Tusa in *The Nuremberg Trial* (McGraw-Hill, 1983) and brought up to date by more critical work such as Donald Bloxham *Genocide on Trial: War Crimes Trials and the Formation of Holocaust History and Memory* (Oxford University Press, 2001). The Japanese war crime trials have been covered by writers such as Yuki Tanaka *Hidden Horrors: Japanese War Crimes in World War II* (Westview Press, 1996), while the book by Antonio Cassese *The Tokyo Trial and*

Beyond (Polity Press, 1993) is formatted around an interview with one of the judges, B.V.A. Röling.

CHAPTER 4 – THE KOREAN WAR

There are various books that give a general overview of the Korean War including concise volumes by Max Hastings *The Korean War* (Pan Books, 2000) and Steven Hugh Lee *The Korean War* (Pearson Education Ltd., 2001) and multivolume works such as Bruce Cumings *The Origins of the Korean War: Volume II, the Roaring of the Cataract, 1947–1950* (Princeton University Press, 1990). Some works have taken a particular viewpoint such as Rosemary Foot *The Wrong War: American Policy and the Dimensions of the Korean Conflict, 1950–1953* (Cornell University Press, 1985); Joseph C. Goulden *Korea: The Untold Story of the War* (Times Books, 1982); Clayton D. James *Refighting the Last War: Command and Crisis in Korea, 1950–1953* (Free Press, 1993); Steven Hugh Lee *Outposts of Empire: Korea, Vietnam and the Origins of the Cold War in Asia, 1949–1954* (Liverpool University Press, 1995); Callum A. MacDonald *Korea: The War Before Vietnam* (Macmillan, 1986); William Stueck *The Korean War: An International History* (Princeton University Press, 1995) and David Rees *Korea: The Limited War* (Macmillan, 1964). Numerous books look at the role of President Truman as well as the conflict with MacArthur such as Paul G. Pierpaoli Jr *Truman and Korea: The Political Culture of the Early Cold War* (University of Missouri Press, 1999) and John W. Spanier *The Truman–MacArthur Controversy and the Korean War* (W.W. Norton, 1965). Historians have been slower to address the issue of the military in Korea although there are several books that deal with some aspect of the fight including Conrad Crane *American Airpower Strategy in Korea* (University of Kansas Press, 2000) and Kindsvatter *American Soldiers* noted earlier.

As there are no books that focus solely on the United States home front during the three years of the Korean War, readers interested in getting an overview of the 1950s and the context of the Korean War on the home front would do well to start with David Halberstam and his epic volume *The Fifties* (Fawcett Columbine, 1993), although there is no shortage of other works on the era including discussions of politics in Alonzo L. Hamby *Beyond the New Deal: Harry S. Truman and American Liberalism* (Columbia University Press, 1973) and Lary May (ed.) *Recasting America: Culture and Politics in the Age of Cold War* (University of Chicago Press, 1989). Other general texts include Michael S. Sherry *In the Shadow of War: The United States Since the 1930s* (Yale University Press, 1995), J. Ronald Oakley *God's Country: America in the Fifties* (Dembner Books, 1990) and William L. O'Neill *American High: The Years of Confidence, 1945–1960* (Free Press, 1986) as well as Stephen J. Whitfield *The Culture of the Cold War*, second edition (Johns Hopkins University, 1996).

There are many good books on the anti-communist and McCarthy era with two of the classic works being David Caute *The Great Fear: The Anti-Communist Purge Under Truman and Eisenhower* (Simon and Schuster, 1978) and Ellen Schrecker *Many Are the Crimes: McCarthyism in America* (Princeton University Press, 1998). More recent work includes Thomas Doherty *Cold War, Cool Medium: Television, McCarthyism, and American Culture* (Columbia University Press, 2003) and Ted Morgan *Reds: McCarthyism in Twentieth-Century America* (Random House, 2004).

To begin to explore the issue of domestic spying, a good place to start is Majorie Garber and Rebecca L. Walkowitz (eds) *Secret Agents: The Rosenberg Case, McCarthyism, and Fifties America* (Routledge, 1995).

As with the topic of communism, work on the African American experience during the brief years of the Korean War is often contained in larger works on the 1950s or the civil rights movement in general. One exception to this is Sherie Mershon and Steven Schlossman *Foxholes and Color Lines: Desegregating the U.S. Armed Forces* (Johns Hopkins University Press, 1998). General texts on the civil rights movement include works such as Robert Cook *Sweet Land of Liberty? The African-American Struggle for Civil Rights in the Twentieth Century* (Pearson Education Limited, 1998) and Adam Fairclough *Better Day Coming: Blacks and Equality, 1890–2000* (Penguin Books, 2001). Wilson Record in *Race and Radicalism: The NAACP and the Communist Party in Conflict* (Cornell University Press, 1964) and Jeff Woods *Black Struggle, Red Scare: Segregation and Anti-Communism in the South, 1948–1968* (Louisiana State University Press, 2004) look at the confluence of the civil rights movement and McCarthyism. Other helpful volumes include Jeanne F. Theoharis and Komozi Woodard (eds) *Freedom North: Black Freedom Struggles Outside the South, 1940–1980* (Palgrave, 2003) and Mark V. Tushnet *Making Civil Rights Law: Thurgood Marshall and the Supreme Court, 1936–1961* (Oxford University Press, 1994). Recent research also includes Mary L. Dudziak *Cold War Civil Rights: Race and the Image of American Democracy* (Princeton University Press, 2000).

As with the topic of civil rights, the issue of the war's impact on women can be found within works on the broader post-Second World War period such as Elaine Tyler May *Homeward Bound: American Families in the Cold War Era* (Basic Books, 1988); Leila J. Rupp and Verta Taylor *Survival in the Doldrums: The American Women's Rights Movement, 1945 to the 1960s* (Oxford University Press, 1987); Joanne Meyerowitz (ed.) *Not June Cleaver: Women and Gender in Postwar America, 1945–1960* (Temple University Press, 1994); William Chafe *The American Woman: Her Changing Social, Economic and Political Roles, 1920–70* (Galaxy Books, 1974); and William Chafe *Women and Equality: Changing Patterns in American Culture* (Galaxy Books, 1978). A different take on the issue of women's sphere can be found in Laura McEnaney *Civil Defense Begins at Home: Militarization Meets Everyday Life in the Fifties* (Princeton University Press, 2000). Finally, Tom Engelhardt *The End of Victory Culture: Cold War America and the Disillusioning of a Generation* (Basic Books, 1995) looks at American society in the aftermath of the uncertain conclusions of the wars in Korea and Vietnam.

CHAPTER 5 – THE VIETNAM WAR

There are hundreds of volumes written about the war in Vietnam. One of the earliest was George C. Herring *America's Longest War: The United States and Vietnam, 1950–1975* (Alfred A. Knopf, 1979) followed by Paul M. Kattenburg *The Vietnam Trauma in American Foreign Policy, 1945–75* (Transaction Books, 1986). Others include James S. Olson and Randy Roberts *Where the Domino Fell: America and Vietnam, 1945 to 1990* (St Martin's Press, 1991) and those books looking at specific administrations such as Larry Berman *Lyndon Johnson's War* (W. W. Norton, 1989) and the recent work by David Kaiser *American Tragedy: Kennedy, Johnson, and the Origins of the Vietnam War* (Belknap Press, 2000) which includes a chapter on the Eisenhower administration although he is not mentioned in the title. Daniel C. Hallin looks at the issue of censorship and Vietnam in *The 'Uncensored War': The Media and Vietnam* (Oxford University Press, 1986), while Mark Taylor *The Vietnam War in History, Literature and Film* (University of Alabama Press, 2003) gives a good, concise reading of the Vietnam War in other media. A very useful volume, as is the case with most of the works in the Blackwell companion series, is Marilyn B. Young and Robert Buzzanco (eds) *A Companion to the Vietnam War* (Blackwell, 2006) which has essays on a wide range of topics from strategy and tactics through minorities in the military to the impact on the home front and the anti-war protests. Equally, Guenter Lewy *America in Vietnam* (Oxford University Press, 1978) is a rich volume with an excellent chapter on military tactics and the law of war.

As with books on the war, books about the United States during the 1960s are appearing all the time. Classic earlier works include Todd Gitlin *The Sixties: Years of Hope, Days of Rage* (Bantam Books, 1987) and Allen Matusow *The Unraveling of America: A History of Liberalism in the 1960s* (Harper and Row, 1984). Both of these books look at the history of the 1960s which includes the emerging student movement, civil rights, the women's movement and anti-war protests. One of the first books to look at the sixties through the words of those who lived through the period is Milton Viorst *Fire in the Streets: America in the 1960s* (Touchstone, 1979). For students unfamiliar with the history of the decade these are good volumes to use as a starting point. More recent works include Dominick Cavallo *A Fiction of the Past: The Sixties in American History* (Palgrave, 1999), Jon Margolis *The Last Innocent Year: America in 1964, The Beginning of the 'Sixties'* (HarperCollins, 1999) and Edward J. Rielly *The 1960s* (Greenwood Press, 2003).

As for the experience of the soldiers in Vietnam, there are numerous volumes here as well and often these take the form of oral histories. Early works include Mark Baker *Nam: The Vietnam War in the Words of the Men and Women Who Fought There* (Quill, 1982), Heather Brandon *Casualties: Death in Vietnam; Anguish and Survival in America* (St. Martin's Press, 1984), Myra MacPherson *Long Time Passing: Vietnam and the Haunted Generation* (Doubleday, 1984), and the classics Bernard Edelman (ed.) *Dear America: Letters Home from Vietnam* (Pocket Books, 1985) and Peter Goldman, Tony Fuller, Richard Manning, Stryker McGuire, Wally McNamee and Vern E. Smith *Charlie Company: What Vietnam Did to Us* (Ballantine Books, 1983).

The experience of minority soldiers is also contained in works such as Herman Graham III *The Brothers' Vietnam War: Black Power, Manhood, and the Military Experience* (University Press of Florida, 2003), James E. Westheider *Fighting on Two Fronts: African Americans and the Vietnam War* (New York University Press, 1997) and the classic Terry Wallace *Bloods: An Oral History of the Vietnam War by Black Veterans* (Presidio Press, 1985). Recent work has expanded to include other groups and can be found in books such as Walter Capps (ed.) *The Vietnam Reader* (Routledge, 1991) and George Mariscal (ed.) *Aztlán and Viet Nam: Chicano and Chicana Experiences of the War* (University of California Press, 1999). Stuart Kallen has produced a work about *Women of the 1960s* (Lucent Books, 2003) which looks at their contributions to the events and movements of the era.

The turbulent home front of 1960s is contained in many of the works previously cited and can be further understood by looking at Kenneth J. Heineman *Put Your Bodies Upon the Wheel: Student Revolt in the 1960s* (Ivan R. Dee, 2001) and Michael S. Foley *Confronting the War Machine: Draft Resistance During the Vietnam War* (University of North Carolina Press, 2003). As noted earlier, the list of books on the 1960s continues to grow and it would be impossible to include a list of all the relevant work here, but a recent addition to the list is Mark Hamilton Lytle *America's Uncivil Wars: The Sixties Era from Elvis to the Fall of Richard Nixon* (Oxford University Press, 2006).

EPILOGUE

The number of books that have appeared addressing the issue of Americans at war in the post-9/11 context are also already too numerous to list. Their contents run the gambit of terrorism, civil liberties, torture and all topics in between. As a starting place, and following on from the main theme of this book the reader would do best to look at Michael Walzer *Arguing About War* (Yale University Press, 2004) which, in a collection of essays, continues his main arguments on just war theory by looking at terrorism, the Gulf War, Kosovo and 9/11. Walzer, of course, is not the only theorist to address these issues. Alex J. Bellamy in *Just Wars From Cicero to Iraq* (Polity Press, 2006) traces the development of just war theory and then expands on the revisionist view of war. Jean Bethke Elshtain *Just War Against Terror: The Burden of American Power in a Violent World* (Basic Books, 2003) takes a careful look at the impact of 9/11 on America's international position and United States action. While Dominic McGoldrick *From '9–11' to the 'Iraq War 2003': International Law in an Age of Complexity* (Hart Publishing, 2004) offers a look at the legal ramifications of war in the twenty-first century, Phil Scraton (ed.) in *Beyond September 11: An Anthology of Dissent* (Pluto Press, 2002) edits a volume of essays by authors opposed to US intervention abroad. Scholarly journals also overflow with articles on the events of 9/11 and beyond with the single topic volume of the *Journal of American History* on History and September 11: A Special Issue, 89 (September 2002) as a good case in point. No investigation into 9/11 would be complete without consulting *The 9/11 Commission Report: Final Report of the National Commission on Terrorist Attacks Upon the United States* (W. W. Norton and Co.).

As the war on terror broadened into the actual wars in Afghanistan and Iraq, various volumes emerged. The most ambitious is the three-volume work of Bob Woodward *Bush at War* (Pocket Books, 2003), *Plan of Attack* (Pocket Books, 2004) and *State of Denial: Bush at War Part III* (Simon and Schuster, 2006). Obviously other views and volumes exist including a collection of essays edited by Rick Fawn and Raymond Hinnebusch *The Iraq War: Causes and Consequences* (Lynne Rienner Publishers, 2006). As with the events of 9/11, no consideration of the war in Iraq would be complete without consulting the bipartisan report by James A. Baker III and Lee H. Hamilton (co-chairs), Lawrence S. Eagleburger, Vernon E. Jordon, JR., Edwin Meese III, Sandra Day O'Connor. Leon E. Paretta, William J. Perry, Charles S. Robb and Alan K. Simpson *The Iraq Study Group Report: The Way Forward – A New Approach* (Vintage, 2006). The aftermath of the initial 'victory' in Iraq has also been examined most especially in works looking at the uncovering of torture committed by United States troops. Mark Danner *Torture and Truth: America, Abu Ghraib, and the War On Terror* (New York Review Books, 2004) includes documentary evidence as well as reproductions of the damning photographs and is a good place to start any investigation on the subject. Paul Robinson *Military Honour and the Conduct of War: From Ancient Greece to Iraq* (Routledge, 2006) has good sections on Vietnam and touches on Iraq.

The issues of civil liberties and the consequences of war on the home front have also attracted many authors. Richard Ashby Wilson (ed.) *Human Rights in the 'War on Terror'* (Cambridge University Press, 2005) includes a series of essays by prominent writers covering arguments on both sides of the divide with regard to the issue of human rights during wartime. Likewise, Mark Tushnet (ed.) has collected a series of scholarly essays on the theme of *The Constitution in Wartime: Beyond Alarmism and Complacency* (Duke University Press, 2005) with an especially interesting article by Mark A. Graber on 'Counter-Stories: Maintaining and Expanding Civil Liberties in Wartime'. Placing many of these issues in their historical perspective and from a constitutional viewpoint, John Yoo in *The Powers of War and Peace: The Constitution and Foreign Affairs after 9/11* (University of Chicago Press, 2005) adds to the debate by defending some actions of various Commanders in Chief. But critics of the Bush administration's home front policies abound and a collection of essays by Cynthia Brown (ed.) *Lost Liberties: Ashcroft and the Assault on Personal Freedom* (New Press, 2003) and Frances Fox Piven *The War at Home: Domestic Costs of Bush's Militarism* (New Press, 2004) make for sober reading. A balanced account, appearing in the Opposing Viewpoints Series produced by Thomson Gale, is Louise I. Gerdes (ed.) *The Patriot Act* (2005).

All of the works listed above provide the basis for an investigation into America and the wars of the twentieth and twenty-first centuries.

Index

Communism, 4, 6, 31, 39, 42, 45, 80, 82,
83, 85, 87, 93, 97, 102, 104, 109, 111,
114, 117, 118, 120, 128, 151, 152,
165, 166, 172
See also anti-communist
Communist Control Act, 95
Communist Party of the United States, see
American communist party
concentration camps, 47
conformity, 28, 79, 94, 97, 163, 166
Congress of Racial Equality
(CORE), 66, 104, 131, 137, 139,
140, 141
conscientious objection, 35, 92,
136, 142
conscription, see draft
Constitution, 9, 29, 33, 37, 97, 142, 143,
163, 164, 167, 171
constitutionality, 33, 74, 97, 106, 136,
143, 173, 179
consumerism, 99, 142
containment, 82, 109, 111, 112, 114,
151, 152
credibility gap, 124, 126, 135, 149
Creel, George, 28
Cuba, 8, 111, 178, 180
Cuban Missile Crisis, 111
Bay of Pigs, 111
Czechoslovakia, 40, 41, 48

Dardanelles, 22, 39
D-Day, 57, 60
Debs v. the United States (1919),
33, 34
Debs, Eugene, 33, 35
Defoliants, 120, 124, 158
Democratic Republic of Vietnam, 112,
114, 115
Democratic People's Republic of Korea
(NK), 82
Democratic Party, 43, 66, 82, 91, 97, 102,
109, 117, 129, 130, 132, 144, 145,
146, 148, 149, 168, 183
Dennis et al. v. United States (1951),
72, 94
depression (Great Depression), 43, 44, 51,
63, 70, 75, 78, 98, 131, 151
Department of Labor, 36, 37

Desegregation, 66, 81, 100, 105, 136,
145, 148
Destroyers for Bases, 4, 52
Détente, 127
Detroit, 66, 69, 138, 139, 165
Dien Bien Phu, 114, 115, 152
Diem, Ngo Dinh, 115, 116, 118,
120, 121
Dies Committee, 72
disarmament, 159
discrimination, 9, 36, 65, 70, 75, 100, 101,
102, 104, 138, 143, 164, 166
dissent, 6, 29, 31, 32, 34, 35, 42, 74, 118,
136, 164, 171, 172, 174, 175, 179
divorce, 71, 98, 142, 145
Domino Theory, 114, 117
Double V Campaign, 65, 165
draft, 24, 26, 32, 33, 35–6, 41, 52, 53, 55,
63, 81, 92, 107, 126, 133, 135, 141–2,
167, 183
Dresden 60, 156, 157, 161
Du Bois, WEB, 102–3

Eastern Front
World War I, 20, 23
World War II, 59
Eisenhower, Dwight, 57, 60, 91, 96,
97, 104, 106, 107, 108, 109, 111,
114, 119
El Alamein, 56, 57
Espionage Act, 32, 33, 35, 72, 96,
163, 164
Estonia, 41, 54
Ethiopia, 46, 49, 50
Executive Orders
8802, 65, 164
9066, 73, 164
9835, 94
9981, 81, 100
10450, 97
extraordinary rendition, 182

Fair Deal, 81, 130, 172
Fair Employment Practice Committee
(FEPC), 65, 105
Fascism, 6, 45, 46, 48, 94
Federal Bureau of Investigation (FBI), 30,
33, 72, 96